Professor Fiona Sampso[n] [obscured] [obscured]t
published in thirty-eig[ht] [obscured] [obscured]e
Down, was awarded th[e] [obscured] [obscured]n
Frashëri Laureateship, [obscured] [obscured]r.
A Romanticist, literary biographer and critic, [obscured] *of
Mary Shelley* was internationally acclaimed, and *Two-Way Mirror:
The Life of Elizabeth Barrett Browning* (2021) was a *New York Times*
Editors' Choice and *Washington Post* Book of the Year, a *Sunday
Times* Paperback of the Year, and finalist for the Plutarch Prize
and the PEN Jacqueline Bograd Weld Award for Biography.

Praise for *Starlight Wood: Walking back to the Romantic Countryside*

'Although rigorous scholarship and extensive
biographical knowledge underpin Sampson's text, for the
reader it is like watching her throw a subject into the air
to see what appears in its reflective surface, then following
its bounces along the path, beach, or woodland floor . . .
entertaining and illuminating . . . erudite . . . arresting . . .
Among the pleasures of the book is Sampson's subtle
attentiveness to place and atmosphere'
TLS

'Constantly stimulating . . . Sampson's own
personal connections regularly push through her literary
ruminations [and] it's by such interweaving that the great
Romantics remain our contemporaries'
London Magazine

'Fine evocations of place and season'
Literary Review

'For Shelley, Byron and Wordsworth and their multitudinous imitators, walking was a serious business. Walks in nature inspired, provoked and transformed them. And, Sampson lays out with a leavening of memoir, it transforms nature too: how we see it and how we feel about it, and how we behave when we leave the settled confines of the city and walk into Shelley's "clear universe of things around"'
The Tablet

'An eloquent, evocative meditation'
Saga

'Like Shelley, Sampson has an eye for catching reality and experience that are not processed, but in process. This hybrid book [. . .] enlists Romanticism from many fields and domains: poetry of course, music, painting, architecture and landscaping, philosophy and science, politics and criticism, [. . .] to release the freshness of the past as much as that of her present.[. . .] Debunking the fetishes of Romanticism. [. . .] Sampson is most Romantic in the way her discourse lives up to the freshness of live experience and thinking, [. . .] there is also the sheer aesthetic pleasure of reading the sensuous prose, that of a poet [. . .] Sampson's work of (very creative) nonfiction [. . .] might be seen to be more like a fiction than a rite'
English Studies review

Praise for Fiona Sampson:
For *In Search of Mary Shelley: The Girl Who Wrote Frankenstein*

'Even for those of us who thought we knew everything about the young author of "Frankenstein," Fiona Sampson's brilliant new biography, "In Search of Mary Shelley," has many surprises in store' *Washington Post*

'If we get another literary biography in 2018 as astute and feelingful as this one, we shall be lucky'
Sunday Times

'Sampson is as adept as Frankenstein himself, giving life to a figure who convincingly aches and bleeds. The landscapes and interiors within which Sampson's subject moves are as crisply rendered as Frankenstein's own plane of Arctic ice'
Guardian

'Fiona Sampson is a sleuth of a biographer. Rarely has my jaw dropped on so many occasions while reading a biography'
Daily Mail

'Astonishing scenes are laid before the reader in the manner of vivid tableaux. Fascinating and ambitious'
Irish Times

'It is a passionate demonstration of the elements that have kept her story vibrant for 200 years. It is moving, it is alive, it is a success'
Spectator

For *Two-Way Mirror: The Life of Elizabeth Barrett Browning*

'Poet Fiona Sampson's brilliant, heart-stopping biography, *Two-Way Mirror: The Life of Elizabeth Barrett Browning*, reads like a thriller, a memoir and a provocative piece of literary fiction all at the same time. [. . .] *Two-Way Mirror* reads as a vividly drawn exchange between a living poet and a dead one . . . throughout this magical and compelling book, Sampson shows us that we, too, can speak to the dead, or, at the very least, we can listen to their words'
Washington Post

'Pushes back against the neglect, bordering on amnesia, that has descended on a poet once widely celebrated . . . battling polite silence more than the mistakes or omissions of earlier critics and biographers, Sampson wants readers to see Barrett Browning afresh'
New York Times

'Fiona Sampson spins an intriguingly complex account of her subject . . . a refreshing, contemporary take on a poet who, no matter her bodily constraints, ranged freely over subject area, form and feeling'
Wall Street Journal

'Fiona Sampson's vivid new biography gives us Elizabeth Barrett Browning as busy and ambitious rather than a swooning sleeping beauty . . . Sampson paints a lively picture . . . biography, she suggests, is itself a mirror that both reveals and distorts its subject . . . Beautifully told'
Mail on Sunday

'This new biography . . . is an empathetic – and much-needed – reassessment which tells a fascinating story'
Telegraph

'In this fine biography . . . the content . . . is spot-on. Sampson is particularly interested in Barrett Browning's personal and political entanglement with empire and race . . . Sampson is . . . judicious . . . but she understands enough about the pleasures of transgression to leave . . . possibility in play'
Guardian

'Fiona Sampson's passionate and exacting biography
[is] a bristling lyric sandwich of philosophy and action.
It is also a page-turner . . . It feels as if the stakes couldn't
be higher for Sampson, and this gives an enormous
charge to a vividly personal account'
Irish Times

'The award-winning poet Fiona Sampson . . . in her
intriguing biography of and meditation on EBB, making the
convincing claim that she was the first female lyric poet . . .
as a poet she puts the work before the life, and that
surely is the right way round'
Sunday Times

'It takes a biographer of Fiona Sampson's lateral brilliance
to re-argue EBB's importance. She does by very carefully
framing not just the life, which is far more vivid and complex
than usually supposed . . . Sampson is superb on how much
EBB's work is . . . "written on the body"'
Herald

'Sampson explores . . . with compassion and scepticism . . .
an astute, thoughtful and wide-ranging guide'
The Times

'The first biography of Barrett Browning in more than 30 years is
a nuanced and insightful account. Fiona Sampson, a poet herself
as well as a biographer of Mary Shelley, argues that central to
Barrett Browning's story is the construction of identity – both in
her life and the myth-making that surrounds it'
New Statesman

'Aims for breadth and depth – and achieves both . . .
An acute and insightful study of the life and work of
a pathbreaking 19th-century poet'
Kirkus Reviews

Also by Fiona Sampson

Poetry:

Come Down
The Catch
Coleshill
Night Fugue: New and selected poems
Rough Music
Common Prayer
The Distance Between Us
Travel Diary
Folding the Real
Picasso's Men

Non-fiction:

Two-Way Mirror: The Life of Elizabeth Barrett Browning
In Search of Mary Shelley
Limestone Country
Lyric Cousins
Beyond the Lyric
Percy Bysshe Shelley
Music Lessons
A Century of Poetry Review
Poetry Writing
On Listening
Writing: Self and Reflexivity (with Celia Hunt)
Creative Writing in Health and Social Care
A Fine Line (with Jean Boase-Beier & Alexandra Buchler)
The Healing Word
The Self on the Page (with Celia Hunt)
Two-Way Mirror: The Life of Elizabeth Barrett Browning

Translator:

Evening Brings Everything Back by Jaan Kaplinski
Selected Poems by Jaan Kaplinski (co-translator)
Day by Amir Or

Fiona Sampson

STARLIGHT WOOD

Walking Back to the Romantic Countryside

corsair

CORSAIR

First published in the United Kingdom in 2022 by Corsair
This paperback edition published in 2023

1 3 5 7 9 10 8 6 4 2

A CIP catalogue record for this book
is available from the British Library.

ISBN: 978-1-4721-5603-7

Printed and bound in Great Britain by
Clays Ltd, Elcograf S.p.A.

Papers used by Corsair are from well-managed forests
and other responsible sources.

Corsair
An imprint of
Little, Brown Book Group
Carmelite House
50 Victoria Embankment
London EC4Y 0DZ

An Hachette UK Company
www.hachette.co.uk

www.littlebrown.co.uk

for
Aylwin Arthur Sampson
1926–2021

A Note About The Pictures

In the late 1940s my father, Aylwin Sampson, enrolled at what was then the Central College of Art in Nottingham, and is now the Nottingham School of Art & Design. It was a time of poverty and euphoria. The war was over. By the time he'd finished his studies a new young queen, born in the same year as him, would be on the throne: I think of my dad as the consummate New Elizabethan. I also think of him as someone who by 1949 had survived service in the RAF, and was more than ready to live. On his last birthday he asked me to look after his archives when he died. And it's since his death that I've had the chance to see his early work for the first time, and in doing so to glimpse the young man who made it. The notebooks dated between 1949 and 1952 are particularly full of playfulness and delight, as he gets to study his surroundings at college and at home (however dimmed by post-war austerity), to travel in continental Europe with student friends, and to draw and draw and draw. All the pictures in this book come from that period at the very midpoint of the last century: from that turn towards optimism and engagement.

Contents

INTRODUCTION: The Extollagers
Duns Tew, Oxfordshire   1

FIRST WALK: Walking
Wye Valley, Herefordshire   23

SECOND WALK: Framing
Elan Valley and Nanteos, Ceredigion   53

THIRD WALK: Surveying
Romney Marsh, Kent   91

FOURTH WALK: Eating
The Quantocks, Somerset   117

FIFTH WALK: Accelarating
Coniston Water, Cumbria   151

SIXTH WALK: Securing
Tennyson Down, Isle of Wight   183

SEVENTH WALK: (Not) Belonging
Aldeburgh, Suffolk   211

EIGHTH WALK: Feeling
Dedham Vale, Essex   239

NINTH WALK: Transforming
Skipness, Kintyre Peninsula   269

TENTH WALK: Paying Attention
Lugg Valle, Herefordshire   299

Acknowledgements   333

Notes   335

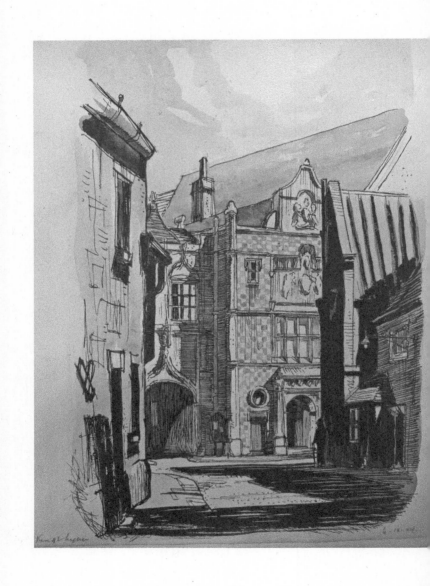

Introduction

The Extollagers

> . . . I sought for ghosts, and sped
> Through many a listening chamber, cave, and ruin,
> And starlight wood, with fearful steps pursuing
> Hopes of high talk with the departed dead.

PERCY BYSSHE SHELLEY,
'Hymn to Intellectual Beauty'

E very story starts somewhere. From the backseat of the family car, stuck behind tractors and caravans on meandering B roads, I glimpsed a countryside I didn't know. Did I want to? I'm not sure. I was a kid daydreaming out the window, and the trees and hedges appearing and disappearing beyond its smudged glass seemed no more than process shots I might have dreamt up.

If my dad did pull in, it was only to let us scuffle behind a hedge to pee, or for my mum to find the thermos. Passing lorries shook the car, and the cold tea in our plastic cups. Yet those lost laybys had a note of their own. Dust on elder leaves, cigarette butts and clover in drain covers, the smell of petrol. Occasionally a five-bar layby gate swung open not onto nettles and rutted ground but into a wide view that took your breath away. Then my father would pull a joking face and exclaim, 'Nature's annual miracle!' or, 'A winter wonderland!' Even as a small child, though, I understood that such jokes masked a warning. To be moved by beauty must be to admit a kind of fallibility. So I screwed my eyes tight, and tried not to see the soft groupings of trees all the way to the horizon, or the small roofs set among them like stories.

Every story starts somewhere. At the centre of the visionary landscapes Samuel Palmer painted and sketched at Shoreham in Kent in the decade from 1824, a wicket gate stands ajar, a stile punctuates a fence, a path leads under the trees and through standing corn. Blossom overwhelms the painted orchards and fills the sky; inky outlines strain at the conventions of picture surface, as if mere looking will no longer do. 'Start here . . . ' these images say, pressing the viewer to follow their visual logic. They draw the eye on, into a transformational experience where the usual, hard-worked farmland becomes an unfamiliar paradise garden, and flowers are like stars, and stars like lamps.

Romanticism isn't a cultural artefact: it's a way for thought to move. Palmer's gates open not only into Kentish orchards but onto the wider Romantic landscape. Charged with emotional energy, his oils and watercolours challenge us to see things anew. In following their glowing paths we seem to bypass cliché and witness the freshness of the actual encounter between a Romantic sensibility and its rural surroundings:

it looks like transcendent, personal revelation. In fact it's a record of shared vision and carefully elaborated ideals. In 1826–27 Edward Calvert and George Richmond, themselves also emerging artists and disciples like Palmer of William Blake, paid regular visits to their friend in Shoreham. The trio took to calling themselves 'the Ancients', and 'walked much in the deep twilight and into the night', earning themselves the suspicion of neighbours who – shrugging off the luminous symbolism they accrue in the young men's pictures – nicknamed them 'the Astrologers'. I like the way this sceptical countrymen's humour must have passed around the village, from field gate to cottage porch. And it turns out to be one of those sweetly accidental truths language stumbles upon, since it came out in local dialect as 'the Extollagers' – a coinage brilliantly apt for the Romantic tendency to leave no insight un-propounded, or choice un-advocated.

I see now that my dad, who had been born just five miles from Samuel Palmer's Shoreham, *was* moved by the view beyond the layby gate. But the very culture it made him nostalgic for afforded no way to express this. He rarely spoke about the summers of his boyhood in the impoverished east of England, where draft horses continued to bring home the harvest even as, elsewhere, the countryside welcomed motorcars and TV sets. When he did reminisce, his memories had a halo of feeling about them. ''Tis Distance lends enchantment to the view,' he would conclude, turning away and shaking the dregs from his thermos cup.

Not that I or probably he knew, but this was a thoroughly Romantic line. It's a quotation from Thomas Campbell's 1799 poem *The Pleasures of Hope*, a book-length riposte – and homage – to Samuel Roger's *The Pleasures of Memory, a Poem*, which had been published seven years earlier. While Rogers faced back to where 'spirits of the dead [. . .] hold sweet converse on the dusky green', Campbell faces forward to *prospects* of various kinds:

> At summer eve, when Heav'n's ethereal bow
> Spans with bright arch the glittering hills below,
> Why to yon mountain turns the musing eye,
> Whose sunbright summit mingles with the sky?
> Why do those cliffs of shadowy tint appear
> More sweet than all the landscape smiling near?—
> 'Tis Distance lends enchantment to the view,
> And robes the mountain in its azure hue.

This opening stanza deftly combines several key elements of the Romantic encounter with the countryside: distance and the movement of time; the picturesque framing device of that 'bright arch' of sky; above all, the 'musing eye' that isn't a passive lens but instead knows itself to be engaged in a reflective business of observation. Yet possibly such deftness is a barrier. The muted lyricism and formal iambic pentameter make it hard today to hear the radicalism in this; to remember that Romantics like Campbell were among our first western moderns.

Hard, too, to think of them as *working out* the attitudes to the countryside that we take for granted. International Romanticism lasted arguably twice as long as the four decades that constituted its British heyday; stretching from 1770, the year Ludwig van Beethoven, G. W. F. Hegel, Friedrich Hölderlin and William Wordsworth were all born, to around

1850 when, within the space of twenty-six months, Honoré de Balzac, Emily Brontë, Frédéric Chopin, Maria Edgeworth, Edgar Allen Poe, Mary Shelley and the long-lived Wordsworth died. Simply to list such profoundly differentiated protagonists is to acknowledge the movement's remarkable variety and extent. Yet certain beliefs united it, and across decades, disciplines and countries it viewed 'nature' as a capacious resource that could teach both awe and atheism, scientific exploration and human meaning. And if there was a tendency to conflate *nature* with the *countryside* where it becomes most evident: that oversight remains not unusual among thinkers, and crucially policy makers, even today.

Figures in a landscape. The individual who in that era enjoyed and was moved by the natural world might – if they had the means – engage eagerly with the new practices of experimental science, perhaps attending public scientific lectures and demonstrations or investing in the powerful milled-glass lenses of the new microscopes and telescopes. But his or her own embodiment remained somewhat exempt from examination; a relative *terra incognita* in a time when – for example – medicine still relied on mediaeval 'cupping' for the release of 'humours'. It was as if the human occupied a central, yet detached, position within the natural world; almost as if self-hood were a panopticon, that social and architectural surveillance structure Jeremy Bentham first fully articulated in 1791. Yet how material we in fact are; how continuous with the natural world in matters of microbes and minerals, in wateriness and entropy. Today, sitting at an open door onto an Oxfordshire village garden, I let the zebra lines of apple tree twigs – each fiercely delineated with shine and dark – form a moiré dazzle in – it must be – my aqueous humour. The new spring air seems to be both a draught and an odour, cool with the smells of new-cut grass and thawed earth, and I am so clearly here, it tells me, in both mind and body.

Whenever I visit the Romantics' countryside, I find myself circling this distinction between self and context, the human and the rural environment: their remarkable cosmogony. There are other ways in, of course. The country also held an immediate, practical appeal for late eighteenth- and early nineteenth-century radicals. Apart from anything, it was cheap. In July 1797 Samuel Taylor Coleridge could boast – with exclamatory underlinings – about Alfoxton Park, a grave Queen Anne mansion near his own village home in the Quantocks:

> a gentleman's seat, with a park & woods, elegantly & completely <u>furnished</u> – with 9 <u>lodging rooms,</u> three parlours and a Hall – in a most beautiful & romantic situation by the sea side – 4 miles from Stowey – this we have got for Wordsworth at the rent of <u>£23 a year, taxes included!!</u>

Such relative affordability meant space to share with like minds; and time to work. What J. W. von Goethe in his 1809 novel of that title called 'elective affinities', *die Wahlverwandtschaften,* could become an organising principle of life. Sometimes like-minded communities formed for the duration of a short visit: later in the same letter, Coleridge invited its addressee, Robert Southey, to stay at Nether Stowey. Or, in fantasy at least, they might last a lifetime, like the 'Pantisocracy' the two had planned five years earlier.

At that time they'd proposed to locate an ideal community in Susquehanna, Pennsylvania, near the home of a famous Romantic exile – Coleridge's 'patriot, and saint, and sage' – the British research chemist Joseph Priestley. The friends had planned that their Pantisocracy would follow strictly egalitarian principles, with all property held in common. Subsistence could be assured by just two or three hours of manual labour a day, they believed, and the rest of the time spent in reading and writing, intellectual discussion, and home educating children. The idea was to live according to one's own nature, not tradition – though the resemblance to the monastic day is noticeable. At any rate, this was country life as more than simple economic expedient; it allowed Romantic protagonists to experiment with ways of living – including substituting for social convention a new informality and even sometimes taboo-busting sexual behaviour.

In Britain, this first radical generation was already familiar with ideas about the innate goodness of *human* 'nature' – later oversimplified into the compound figure of the 'noble savage' – that Jean-Jacques Rousseau had been propounding since 1762's *Du Contrat Social; ou Principes du droit politique* and *Émile, ou De l'éducation.* Coleridge, and Mary Wollstonecraft, notably adopted a child-centred Rousseauian approach to parenting and teaching. 'Natural' interpersonal mores could be discomforting, however. While Coleridge was settling William and Dorothy Wordsworth into their Somerset 'gentleman's seat' in 1797, he got into the habit of taking long walks with the siblings which, to his wife's distress, included rambling alone after dark with an unchaperoned Dorothy.

These expeditions were chaste: but that would not always be

the case in Romantic communities. In 1814, when the dashing advocate of free love Percy Bysshe Shelley carried off a sixteen-year-old Mary Godwin to the Swiss Alps, he also asked along both her stepsister, who took up the invitation to live in a new kind of community, and the wife he'd just abandoned – who did not. Two decades earlier, in the highly influential *An Enquiry Concerning Political Justice* (1793), Mary's own father, the anarchist philosopher William Godwin, had advocated doing away with marriage as one of the traditional institutions, along with the monarchy and the Church, that kept British society locked in injustice and social inequality. But by painful irony he had rowed back from arguing for this kind of direct action by the time his daughter and former disciple embraced it.

I'm brought up short by Godwin. With his long intelligent nose and thinning hair, he had none of his future son-in-law's handsome bounder looks. And, while it's easy to joke at Shelley's expense about the convenience of making a virtue of freely available sex, Godwin's earlier promulgation of the idea is a reminder that these protagonists did feel the stakes to be purely, even austerely, political. The ideal Romantic rural community was more even than a secular, creative cloister: in this way it differed from the superficially similar atelier communities of the Arts and Crafts movement, led by William Morris, Eric Gill and others, that would follow a century later. It was a radical political statement about remaking society itself. Until the Terror of 1793–4, most early Romantics supported the French Revolution. (Many continued to do so afterwards – a curious parallel with some twentieth-century French intellectual support of Stalinsim and Maoism in the face of mounting evidence of atrocities.) For them, revolution meant self-determination in the doubled sense of democracy and national self-rule. And support entailed action. It was in this spirit that Lord Byron set out in 1823 to fight in the Greek War of Independence from Ottoman rule and that, later, both Mary Shelley and Elizabeth Barrett Browning actively supported the Italian Risorgimento.

The tension between local self-determination and dangerous 'ethnic' nationalism is one Romantic legacy still being played out today, for example in the Balkans. At the turn of the nineteenth century, however, the movement appeared to threaten the British state from within. Napoleonic empire-building made France a volatile and dangerous neighbour, and pro-Revolutionary, 'Jacobin' sentiments appeared – and not just to the political establishment – dangerous to the point of treason. For Britain was not entirely the settled society of roast beef and marriage games that Jane Austen's contemporaneous novels might have us believe. These were years of foment. Politically dissenting writers and editors could be tried and found guilty of sedition, as Thomas Paine was in 1792 for writing and publishing *The Rights of Man*. Two years later, the first of a series of Acts suspending Habeas Corpus – the right to be present to defend oneself: in effect, to fair trial – was enacted. In 1794, the sequence of Treason Trials which had opened with the conviction of Paine's publisher culminated in mass arrests; the Prime Minister, William Pitt the Younger, ordered that three radical campaigners, Thomas Hardy, John Horne Tooke, and John Thelwall, be tried for high treason. Though all three were eventually acquitted, if found guilty they would have been executed by the hideous method of hanging, drawing and quartering.

A threatening pattern was being established. In 1804, when it was William Blake's turn to be tried for sedition, he too was acquitted. But in 1813 Leigh Hunt was felt to have got off relatively lightly with two years' imprisonment for publishing, as editor of *The Examiner*, radical material that included an attack on the Prince Regent. A further Habeas Corpus Suspension Act in 1817 precipitated the flight of the Shelley household into European exile the following spring.

In this context the countryside, even in Britain, offered a place to live somewhat under the radar; although it wasn't only in Shoreham that uncomprehending neighbours could pose difficulties for 'Extollagers'. In 1797, as the Wordsworths were settling in at Alfoxton, a local decided they must be French spies and alerted the Home Office, which sent an agent of its own, called James Walsh, to report on them.

It must have been hard to ignore such paranoiac white noise. Two decades later, Mary Shelley's *Frankenstein* – which she completed in the months before her own flight to Europe – features political radicals who are indeed rural 'cottage-dwellers', being spied upon by a concealed witness. This spy, though, is Frankenstein's creature; he inverts radical anxieties by being both beneficent towards, and the beneficiary of, those he observes. He utters an ethical *cri de coeur* –

> For a long time I could not conceive how one man could go forth to murder his fellow, or even why there were laws and governments; but when I heard details of vice and bloodshed, my wonder ceased, and I turned away with disgust and loathing.

Which more than hints that the Romantic countryside might also be a place to wash one's hands of the contemporary world.

But rural life was and is also simply pleasurable. There's nothing to beat the piercing focus of the way a field smells in late March. Earth has been loosened by moles all along the upper ground, and there's a nutty odour of clay. The willows near the river have turned an orange that looks as though it couldn't possibly be natural; on the hedges are white splashes of thorn blossom and a yellow haze so barely-there, and yet so sharp, it almost sets your teeth on edge. Carrying the last of the haylage up to the sheep, you find yourself embracing an armful of sweetness. The sheep can't wait: they come at a gallop, tugging mouthfuls from under your elbow. You walk with them to the creep feeder. Then, maybe, you come down to the house and coffee percolating on the stove under the beams in the old kitchen.

Mary Shelley's third novel, *The Last Man*, paints a seductive portrait of life at Bishopsgate in Windsor Great Park, where she and Percy Bysshe had spent nine months in 1815–16. As she sets the scene:

Ruins of majestic oaks which had grown, flourished and decayed during the progress of centuries, marked where the limits of the forest once reached. [. . .] Behind, the cottage was shadowed by the venerable fathers of the forest, under which the deer came to graze, and which for the most part hollow and decayed, formed fantastic groups that contrasted with the regular beauty of the younger trees. [. . .]

A light railing surrounded the garden of the cottage, which, low-roofed, seemed to submit to the majesty of nature [. . .]. Flowers [. . .] adorned her garden and case-ments; in the midst of lowliness there was an air of elegance which spoke the graceful taste of the inmate.

Her correspondence reveals how much she longed for this. 'A house with a lawn a river or lake – noble trees & divine mountains that should be our little mousehole to retire to –,' she wrote to Percy Bysshe, in the uncertain years after their elopement and before marriage. 'Shall we neglect taking a house – a dear home? – No my love I would not for worlds give up that –.'

Thought and energy went into perfecting such ideal domestic arrangements: choosing *where* to live was part of reinventing *how* to do so. Small wonder if some writers were tempted to identify the countryside with their per-sonal creative strengths: the country view as *ars poetica*. In Wordsworth's Preface to the 1802 edition of *Lyrical Ballads*, country life distils moral clarity:

Low and rustic life was generally chosen, because in that condition, the essential passions of the heart find a better soil in which they can attain their maturity, are less under restraint, and speak a plainer and more emphatic language; because in that condition of life our elementary feelings co-exist in a state of greater simplicity, and, consequently, may be more accurately contemplated, and more forcibly communicated; because the manners of rural life germinate from those elementary feelings; and, from the necessary character of rural occupations, are more easily compre-hended, and are more durable; and lastly, because in that condition the passions of men are incorporated with the beautiful and permanent forms of nature.

Fourteen years later, in Percy Bysshe Shelley's 'Mont Blanc', it does almost the complete opposite. His Alpine landscape inspires speculative, imaginative thought, and a writing style that's anything but 'plainer':

> and when I gaze on thee
> I seem as in a trance sublime and strange
> To muse on my own separate fantasy,
> My own, my human mind, which passively
> Now renders and receives fast influencings,
> Holding an unremitting interchange
> With the clear universe of things around;
> One legion of wild thoughts, whose
>   wandering wings
> Now float above thy darkness, and now rest
> Where that or thou art no unbidden guest,
> In the still cave of the witch Poesy[.]

Romantic visual artists, too, found the countryside newly continuous with creative practice. In the second half of the eighteenth century, the landscape finally developed artistic and social status as a subject, thanks in no small part to that precursor, Thomas Smith of Derby (1715–67). Indeed it would become the key visual genre in a century which had previously held that non-narrative, unpeopled images were – as French critics would later write of John Constable – mere 'Paintings without subjects [. . .] like music.'

In 1855, when Robert Browning put a final full stop to Romantic verse with the modernising *in persona* storytelling of *Men and Women*, one of that book's definitive poems would be 'Two in the Campagna'. What happens, it asks, when lovers visit beautiful countryside together and yet the anticipated romantic, even ecstatic, experience doesn't materialise? It's perfectly possible to read 'Two in the Campagna' as part of the perhaps unconscious struggle within Browning's own marriage to Elizabeth Barrett, that older, more successful *female* poet. But the poem also wrestles Romanticism itself to the ground, for the Roman countryside, adopted from the itineraries of the old Grand Tour, had become one of the movement's touchstones, repeatedly painted by British, European and American artists.

It wasn't necessary to travel, however, to find landscapes which spoke to the era's sensibility. Those preeminent artists J. M. W. Turner and John Constable, close contemporaries born respectively in 1775 and 1776, developed new, though widely divergent, visual vocabularies for the varieties of natural light peculiar to Britain. Samuel Palmer, who would discover his own way to illuminate Shoreham landscapes in paint and etching, was born three decades later, in 1805. The artists of the influential Norwich School of Painters, including John Crome (1768–1821) and John Sell Cotman (1782–1842), and – country-wide – numerous other artists both gifted and jobbing, searched out and recorded landscapes to satisfy the new Romantic appetite for emotional experience or awe-inspiring drama, and the paintings they produced transformed the visual vocabulary of their clients: in other words, of prosperous society at large.

Of course, there were exceptions. William Blake's impoverished urban settings or visionary, post-Biblical landscapes represent the by-and-large indoor, highly internal, life of an uneducated London craftsman living and working among books and engraving plates, dissenting pulpits and printers' workshops. Yet in 1800 even he moved to the village of Felpham in Sussex for four years to work on illustrating a local poet, William Hayley. Another outlier remains John Clare, who between 1820 and 1835 wrote poems of enormous feeling about his native Northamptonshire countryside, but whose great tragedy was that he *was* native, and had been an agricultural labourer since childhood. His mental collapse by the age of forty-four was hastened by extreme poverty, not just of income but of creative opportunity.

Today, images of the Romantic countryside are pressed into double service by mainstream culture, supplying the collective imaginary both with a gallery of famous Britons (Byronic Lord Byron, tragic John Keats) and with representations of the British landscape as essential and unchanging. Alas this is a piece of doubly bad faith. There's nothing intrinsically British about Romanticism, that upheaval in Western culture which started on the continent of Europe and reached as far as North America, Scandinavia and the Caucasus. More: it's at precisely this time that the British countryside was being radically transformed by the rupture of the Agricultural Revolution. And when the twenty-first century embraces the clearly period genres in which Romantic representations of rural life are couched – nineteenth-century poetics, the classical sonata, oil paint – an odour of the disingenuous, sharp as white spirit, rises from canvas and page. Too often, they're being co-opted to the conservative wish to turn back (a thoroughly anti-Romantic resistance to progress) to a story which swerves the atrocious history of British industrialisation to face instead towards an 'essential' national identity of thatched cottages, milkmaids and ploughing teams.

Of course, as human animals we share a nostalgia for the natural world of which we're part. The pastoral, that millennia-old literary tradition, has since the Classical Greek of Hesiod's *Works and Days* (written in roughly the seventh century BCE), or Virgil's first-century BCE *Eclogues*, associated the countryside with a desire to reach back across time to some lost good life. The impulse is pre-Romantic, in other words, by a couple of millennia. Lit by a sensuous Proustian light, the pastoral arcadia is surely a dream of childhood, '*Longtemps . . .*', when we lived more intensely, free from the tedium of adult life. White tassels of grass in a blue sky. The pattern of sycamore leaves interlocked against the light.

Every day of their married life my grandparents, products of urban poverty who had no rural idyll to look back on themselves, laid their table with placemats on which John Constable's paintings of carts, mills and fords were murkily reproduced – and so freighted these images for me with nostalgia for my own childhood. For my parents' generation, J. M. W. Turner succeeded Constable as the ubiquitous visual cliché: steam trains replaced horse-drawn carts, and misty meteorology the rippling precision of Constable's foliage on china mugs and address-book covers. But today we take both artists' personal visions as read. Like Percy Bysshe Shelley's 'Ode to the West Wind', or the 'Wee, sleekit, cowrin, tim'rous beastie' of Robbie Burns's 'To a Mouse, on Turning Her Up in Her

Nest With the Plough', they've become part of the cultural commons, seemingly so obvious as to be hardly worth noting.

The Romantic idea of a human-centred countryside keeps on re-emerging in the stories Britain tells itself, from the suited and booted mammals of Kenneth Grahame's Edwardian *The Wind in the Willows* (1908) to *The Archers*, that 'everyday story of country folk' invented in the mid-twentieth century. Yet even ideas a society has internalised are still ideas. Those open gates and receding paths in Samuel Palmer's Shoreham paintings ask us always to step out past them into the natural environment itself, which he called the 'valley of vision'.

In the unfinished, posthumously published *Reveries of the Solitary Walker*, which he wrote in 1776–8, Jean-Jacques Rousseau goes walking in an attempt to put himself together after a descent into social exile. Occasionally botanising, often reminiscing, he circles his preoccupation with this descent, usually not getting anywhere very much at all. It's in homage to this kind of divagatory exposition that I've taken the *Reveries'* ten chapter 'walks' as the structure for my book. Although my own are rarely solitary. The countryside I live in is no mysterious realm apart, but an inhabited territory; when I walk, it's nearly always with P and our dogs. More widely, and perhaps loosely, I often catch myself reflecting that Romantic literary prose resembles less an argument on the march from *a* to *b* than a meander with excursions and I wonder how much this was encouraged through payment by the word. Thomas de Quincey's notoriously non-linear style, for example, might owe as much to publishers' invoices as to morphine addiction. All the same, this bagginess seems surprisingly apt for writing about place. Country miles are famously winding – something more than full measure, like a baker's dozen – for the country-side, after all, is itself discursive. It intervenes in the process of getting from here to there, adding contours and thickets, colouring in unfordable rivers and shading unscalable scarps.

To walk is to trace the way that terrain resists intention; how landscape is more than something to look at. Rousseau's walks, however, had become a way of staying put. His *Reveries* resist the dialectical progress walking so often makes in Western philosophy. One step leads to another in Plato's fourth-century BCE *Dialogues* or, more than two millennia later, in Martin Heidegger's walking paths. But in its lingering refusal to just move along, Rousseau's last book most resembles a work of mourning. Which is a process – as Philippe Arìes points out in *Man Faced with Death*, a work which was a cultural sensation of the 1970s – that modern culture since Romanticism pretty much refuses to countenance. Mourning is inconvenient. Though moving in deep shadows, it too is a kind of reverie, and like reverie it refuses to tidy things away.

Reverie circles around and returns to whatever it comes across. In this it resembles the labyrinth. That familiar Bronze Age roundel is surely the early apotheosis of the Western metaphor, from Dante's *Divine Comedy* to John Bunyan's *Pilgrim's Progress*, of life as a walk of gathering complexity. Strolling across a Suffolk common looking for a place to picnic one hot June day, my companion P and I stumbled on the Saffron Walden labyrinth. There was a sweetly municipal smell of baking grass. Families and young couples dotted the shade beneath an avenue of horse chestnuts; the labyrinth, on the other hand, was deserted.

We strode up onto the structure's embanked rim, with its

four corner loops or 'bellows', and saw a close-packed brick path folded in parallels: a hallucinatorily redoubled form which is called a Super-Chartres after the one in the marble floor of that northern French cathedral. Every time I blinked, the pale lines appeared dizzyingly to jump, like the slats of an old-fashioned blind in sunlight. But it felt ok to sit on the bank to eat; and so we did. We tore apart the sourdough, unwrapped a cheese that was emptying itself out of itself, and helped ourselves from the paper-bag of tomatoes with their dusty geranium smell. As we ate, I squinted and tried to follow the labyrinth path with my eye. But it is, astonishingly, nearly a mile long; the eye trips, jumps and loses its place.

Saffron Walden's turf labyrinth was already old in 1699, when its first recorded restoration took place: it must have been cut with the same swung string and stick technology as 1980s crop circles. But unlike those fake-alien performances, a labyrinth isn't a trick: unlike a maze, it has no dead ends to trap the unwary. Instead – like mourning, like reverie – it circles as if to nudge things towards pattern. A walk, too, is a kind of fitting things together; a wandering line through a landscape. When I set out to walk it's with a sense of entering into, rather than just passing through, something. The doorway I step out of, the field gate I open, are at the threshold of possibility. Now I see the trees and far fields just the opposite way from how they were when I was that kid in the car, watching the back of my dad's neck.

As Sigmund Freud famously pointed out in *Mourning and Melancholia* (1918), mourning is a work of reparation. Rousseau wanted nothing more than to mend his own reputation. My own walks have become a work of mourning for my father, who died as I was writing this book. It may – just – be premature to grieve the biosphere. But in mourning what's already been lost – in circling and ruminating – perhaps we do repair. After all, mourning doesn't have to be melancholic. It can also mean unpacking the tea-chests and lifting treasured, half-forgotten things up to the light to admire them. I open the first of the boxes containing my dad's pictures and I'm straight back in the lanes and laybys of his prime. Long-gone elms lean towards each other across a gate, and I'm with him under the bushy canopies that thresh lightly in a summer breeze – though elms had disappeared by the time I was a kid. The round-backed old cars park beside a churchyard wall, and I smell the oil and hot metal of their bonnets, although these are models I've seen only in films. Someone I could never have met hoes his vegetable garden, while beyond him rises the slope where I know the late summer light is laying down its streaks of gold. Inside the labyrinth, the journey surrounds you.

As it flows around difficulty and towards things it doesn't yet know, reverie – daydream – replaces resistance with pleasure. Its process of unforced discovery is, I think, not unlike the kind of attentive land management that starts from the ground up, instead of forcing a landscape in ways that are, literally, against its nature. Limiting intensive agriculture; ploughing along a gradient to preserve the topsoil; clearing ditches so streams don't suffocate: if this makes the countryside, as it starts to regenerate, look more like the lost landscape of past childhoods, so much the better.

The Romantics are imperfect guides to the British countryside: but guides – and extollagers – they are all the same. Whether well-known or obscure, as they walked, observed, settled, travelled and retreated, engineered and ate, colonised and mapped and tried to define the rural environment, these protagonists encountered it not as a well-thumbed gazetteer of the places they might make famous, but with revelatory freshness. And so with these ten walks I want to retrieve Shelley's lovely, lilting phrase, 'Hopes of high talk with the departed dead,' from its sceptical context in 'Hymn to Intellectual Beauty'.

I'm walking as if to catch up with the Romantics: if not for 'high talk', at least for some of the gossip of witness. Way-finders, they go ahead of me through my familiar landscapes – railway embankments, woodland walks, parks at dusk – like stars glimpsed through the branches of a wood.

Manor House Farm, Duns Tew,
Oxfordshire OS Grid ref SP455283.

Walking

And *this*, the naked countenance of earth,
On which I gaze, even these primeval mountains
Teach the adverting mind.

PERCY BYSSHE SHELLEY, 'Mont Blanc'

A lozenge of river gleams between the viaduct piers and, somewhere out of sight, a mallard kvetches. I swing my arms, smelling damp, riverine things. The dogs and I are walking in the valley of the middle Wye, a pastureland so fertile it's almost stuffy. It's July. Cattle graze in a halo of horseflies. When I heave open a field gate, outsize nettle and willowherb sway above my head.

I'm exercising the dogs; but I also want to think about what the countryside must have been like for the Romantics. I have this image of a wicket gate standing ajar, and a sunlit pasture beyond it, like a mnemonic for entering into the eighteenth- and nineteenth-century landscape. Of course I can never step through that pictured gate. The countryside has changed profoundly in the intervening two centuries; and while my mind may be a jumble of pentameter, mayflies and rookeries just as it could have been then, it's also busy with anachronisms – social media memes, or the jet slicing silently overhead.

All the same, I do grapple with the idea of authentic encounter. In his 1816 meditation on how we witness the natural world, 'Mont Blanc: Lines written in the Vale of Chamouni', Percy Bysshe Shelley writes that 'the naked countenance of earth,/ On which I gaze, even these primeval mountains/Teach the adverting mind.' 'Adverting' makes intuitive sense. It seems obvious nowadays that paying attention to our environment is important. But I stumble over the high stakes of the word 'naked', which denotes the bare Alpine rockface but also suggests a perhaps shocking unveiling. The 'countenance' that looks back at us may not, after all, be a friendly 'Mother Nature'.

A summer breeze shivers the water by the old railway embankment like a frisson. 'Nakedness' charges Shelley's line, evoking those sexual proprieties the poet could also have expected to outrage. Who, exactly, is out walking in the countryside? For whatever reason – lousy infrastructure, digital access, time famine – in the twenty-first century only an emergency, like poverty or a pandemic, can persuade us go somewhere on foot. By the end of the eighteenth century, too, it was customary to get about on horseback or in some kind of carriage, even if just a public stagecoach or (one of the era's new colloquialisms) a trap. Walking cross-country had become unusual among those who could afford an alternative: the very people with the economic breathing room actually to *be* Romantic. To become a pedestrian – the term is itself an eighteenth-century coinage – was an intentional, even wilful, act that transgressed against the common sense of taking a safer, faster way through the rural muck.

In the 1820s, for example, the radical pamphleteer and farmer William Cobbett, then in his sixties, spent years criss-crossing the British countryside to record his 'actual observation of rural conditions' of the suffering that resulted from the Corn Laws. As his famous title, *Rural Rides*, underlines, this pressing task had no time to waste on the whimsies of pedestrianism. Published twenty years later in 1851, but also set in the 1820s, George Borrow's *Lavengro* – that delightful hybrid of travel writing with a memoir of youthful adventure, of fact, embroidery and fiction – reminds us how even early nineteenth-century traveller communities, tinkers and Roma alike, owned horses and carts. Only vagrants, the homeless destitute, crossed the country on foot as they were shunted from parish to parish by a patchwork of local Poor Laws mediaeval in origin.

Of course, within every landscape that Cobbett rode and Borrow adventured through, there were locals walking about their business. Viewed from horseback, these muddied figures at ground level, who quite possibly stank of the beasts and muck they worked with, must almost have seemed to *wear* their surroundings – like camouflage. Here for example is Mary Shelley's famous sans-culotte, Frankenstein's creature, crossing glaciers, snow and rocks to challenge his maker. He arrives like an emanation of the landscape of exile itself:

He bounded over the crevices in the ice, among which I had walked with caution; his stature, also, as he approached seemed to exceed that of a man [. . .] I perceived, as the shape came nearer (sight tremendous and abhorred!) that it was the wretch whom I had created.

Bounding towards us out of the heart of the novel, the creature is less genius loci than Brocken spectre – that Romantic trick of the mountain light first identified in 1780 by the Lutheran pastor and amateur scientist Johann Silberschlag. But at the time of *Frankenstein*'s first publication, in 1818, all British agricultural labourers walked between their homes and the fields where they worked, and then walked as part *of* that work: behind the plough, with the sheep. This walking, even when it continued for hours a day, remained local; indeed, walking was part of *being* local, a literal daily revisiting of the known that could function, within an individual life, like the beating of a personal parish boundary. Driving livestock long distances to market, for example from Wales to London, and often behaving riotously as they did so, drover gangs were carnivalesque exceptions that proved this socially cohesive rule.

Yet many Romantics did walk cross-country. When Percy Bysshe and the future Mary Shelley first arrived in the Alps in 1814, they had hiked much of the way there, across a Europe half-destroyed by Napoleonic wars. Admittedly, this was mostly accidental. That July, the poet had run away with sixteen-year-old Mary Godwin and her stepsister Jane. The trio planned to establish an ideal community in the Swiss Alpine canton of Uri, a place they imagined as both socially enlightened and aesthetically inspiring and which was also, importantly for the runaways, outside British jurisdiction. However, poor decision-making and financial mismanagement quickly reduced their expedition to footslogging farce. They bought an ass that was too worn out to carry riders, were cheated by the postilion they'd hired to drive them, and had so little money by the time they finally reached Lake Lucerne that they were forced ignominiously to return to Britain as quickly and cheaply as possible, by river-barge.

Two years later, Shelley composed his meditation on 'Mont Blanc' during the summer that this same group (with the addition of the infant William Shelley) famously spent on Lake Geneva alongside Lord Byron, who had taken the commanding Villa Diodati, and Byron's doctor-travelling companion John William Polidori. The Shelleys rented on the lake foreshore below, and it was from here that (leaving baby behind) they made an outing in July to the Mont Blanc massif. It proved hard going. 1816 was the Year Without a Summer; the global climate was undergoing temporary transformation after a massive eruption in what was then the Dutch East Indies. Volcanic debris crammed the atmosphere, crowding out sunlight and creating wintry, starvation conditions across Europe. The Alps were no exception. At Saint-Martin, around 20 km short of Mont Blanc, the trio became 'fatigued to death' while making their way along the valley of the River Arve, even though this time they had planned ahead, and taken the precaution of hiring mules. The closer they got to their destination, the tougher the progress. Mary's *Journal* records how, about three quarters of the way from Chamonix to the source of the river near Col des Montets, they were forced to dismount,

and continued our route on foot, over loose stones, many of which were of an enormous size. [. . .] An immense glacier was on our left, which continually rolled stones to its foot. It is very dangerous to go directly under this.

The next day, descending Montenvers in torrential rain after a failed attempt to view the Mer de Glace, the famous glacier on the north face of the Mont Blanc massif,

Shelley went before, and, tripping up, fell upon his knee. This added to the weakness occasioned by a blow on the ascent; he fainted, and was for some minutes incapacitated from continuing his route.

A human body whose weakness has been exposed by the landscape in this way seems suddenly naked. Scale and contrast have re-established the environment's primacy and power. The incident reminds me again of that central scene in *Frankenstein*, which Mary wrote a few months after this trip, and which contrasts her inventor's human frailty with his creature's super-human ability to cope with this very environment. In emerging from the Mer de Glace like some primaeval wild man, the creature becomes both a Romantic ideal, for whom the new shorthand will be the 'noble savage', and the bearer of a much older and deeper social anxiety about the limits of human civilisation. This concern manifested across mediaeval Europe in the uncanny figure of the Green Man, and in carnival customs whose participants dressed as beasts, vegetation, monsters: Croatia's bellringing *dondolaši*, Bulgarian *babugeri* in bearskins, and goat-skinned Sardinian folk devils. In Britain, only traces – the Abbots Bromley horn dance, the Burryman of Queensferry – have survived the Agricultural Revolution's dispersal of the peasantry and its beliefs into the cities. *Frankenstein* gained its almost instant renown within popular culture at the very time this dispersal was taking place, almost as if to continue the tradition by other means.

In 1908, a narrow-gauge railway replaced the laborious 7-kilometre-long, 1,800-metre-high ascent to view the Mer de Glace, which Percy Bysshe, Mary and a pregnant Claire Clairmont ended up making twice in three days. From the geranium-lined terrace of the Refuge de Montenvers, built for this purpose in 1880, twentieth-century trippers could gaze out over a thickly filled ice valley, the longest glacier in France; today's visitors must descend hundreds of stairs to reach the thin, greyish tongue of remaining ice, whose environmental message speaks for itself.

On this mild Herefordshire afternoon the dogs track ahead of me between bleached waterside hummocks and willow stumps. Zed, who was born in a Thessaloniki kafenio, is eager, chestnut brown, almost a pointer; Dee is a shaggy and saturnine collie—lurcher cross from Bala in North Wales. I envy them the diligence with which they read off our encoded surroundings. Not their literacy in fox piss or otter spraint — even my human nose can spot these — but their commitment to what is both here and not here.

I'm finding it increasingly hard to walk the British countryside without feeling that its 'noble savagery' has drained away; that we're witnessing only the afterburn of immanence in a used-up environment. Yet walking does still *take* you somewhere — and perhaps that sense of *being taken*, if only tangentially to do with rapture and ravishment, is one reason twenty-first-century walking lets itself be weighed down by gear. As if map sleeves and water bottles and zip-off trousers cast some veil, a kind of nylon decency, over the nakedness of the desire to set out.

It feels almost subversive to return to Shelley and find him refusing to check any such baggage in either 'Mont Blanc' or what is in many ways its companion piece, written the same summer, 'Hymn to Intellectual Beauty'. On the contrary: 'Hymn' is a song of regret about how little control we have over our experience of the natural world, as of life itself. However much it may be longed for, the poem says, the actual encounter with this 'Spirit of Beauty' is by nature spontaneous:

> [. . .] at that sweet time when winds are wooing
> All vital things that wake to bring
> News of buds and blossoming, –
> Sudden, thy shadow fell on me;
> I shrieked, and clasped my hands in ecstasy!

The natural world may let us glimpse, through its displays of beauty, how meaning slips into human experience:

> The awful shadow of some unseen Power
> Floats through unseen among us,— visiting
> This various world with as inconstant wing
> As summer winds that creep from flower
> to flower,—
> Like moonbeams that behind some piny
> mountain shower,

But it also shows how it can slip away again,

[. . .] and leave our state,
This dim vast vale of tears, vacant and desolate[.]
Ask why the sunlight not for ever
Weaves rainbows o'er yon mountain-river,

So that our task is to cast the 'frail spells' of poetry and insight,
even though they may not 'avail to sever [. . .]/Doubt, chance
and mutability.'

This afternoon, as 'summer winds [. . .] creep' across my
bare forearms and lift a sour note of chicken shit from this
'mountain-river', I think again how beautiful the Wye looks,
even so contaminated with phosphates that it can scarcely
breathe. With or without 'rainbows', it remains a mnemonic
of the great fishing river it was until some half-dozen years ago.
All the same, I wish I could walk here without leaving a mark,
pure as an avatar crossing a screen. Landscape architects know
all about desire lines: the wear and tear, so visible in the landscaped turf of city parks and verges, that reveals how people got
where they were going. In these water-meadows, because we
have no legal right to roam more widely, the footpath I'm following is like a desire line worn, in enormously slow motion,
through centuries of landscape use. Landownership tells a
compound story about how our relationship to the countryside
is partial and mediated; but walking such public rights of way
retraces maps of access (and against possession) on the ground.

This part of the Wye valley was designated an Area of
Outstanding Natural Beauty in 1971, and hidden among hedges
and between 'real' farming activities are campsites, holiday
cottages, pop-up coffee vans. On summer evenings in the
lower lane, lightly clad stragglers fold their arms and tug down

bottom-skimming shorts against a sudden drop in temperature at dusk. Their voices are spurts of sound in the quiet. They believe in the innocent directness of their relationship with the river and its valley – this beautiful illusion – even while we locals can't help but parse its economic nature: which pub they ate at; where they're staying.

It's as if it were always just too late to step out into the countryside with no money and nothing but the desire to explore: that peripatetic, personal pastoral. In 1969's *As I Walked Out One Midsummer Morning*, Laurie Lee maintained that his Spanish peregrination of 1935–36 could not be repeated. Published eight years later, *A Time of Gifts* is Patrick Leigh Fermor's exequy for any possibility of a great walk down the Danube, such as he undertook in 1933–4. Both journeys were eventually overtaken by fascism: our intuitive sense that walking is essentially costless is most challenged when the countryside is under stress. I remember 2001, when foot-and-mouth disease emerged in British livestock and six million animals were slaughtered as a preventive measure. I remember the officials in hazmat suits, the smoking pyres of corpses; I also remember how closing some rights of way to stop contagion being walked onto farms led journalists in distant cities to declare 'The Countryside Is Closed.'

Still, here's the river flowing with equanimity between pink and orange banks; 'rolling [. . .] / With a soft inland murmur' as it did over two centuries ago, when William Wordsworth described it in his scrupulously-titled 'Lines Composed a Few Miles above Tintern Abbey, On Revisiting the Banks of the Wye during a Tour. July 13, 1798'. Here at the shingle beach of Lower Biblets, the old river crossing reappears every summer. Come autumn, when cows saunter down these banks to drink, the shallow water will barely cover their hooves, and they will seem to stand not in but on the river, a peaceful bovine miracle.

This July afternoon a little egret, *Egretta garzetta*, mooches in duplicate below the far bank. In 1798, Wordsworth saw cliffs 'connect/The landscape with the quiet of the sky'; at Biblets today it's trees that connect water, fields and sky to 'impress/ Thoughts of a more deep seclusion.' The 'sylvan Wye' is everywhere a 'Wanderer thro' the woods,' and here it has created a voluptuous rather than a dramatic terrain. Low hills roll down to meet ambling water. Slope after slope, what Wordsworth called the 'sportive wood', deciduous woodland maintained for timber and shooting, shelters its course, a local litany: West Wood, Fownhope Park, Kidley Hill Wood, Ballingham Wood, Capler Wood, Carey Wood, Aramstone Wood, Castlemeadow Wood, Bayton's Grove, How Caple Wood, Lyndor Wood, little Monk's Grove.

From Hereford downstream to Tintern is roughly thirty miles as the crow flies, but sixty as the river meanders. Lavish oxbows snake across pastureland, or churn through four-hundred-foot gorges below Yat Rock. Yet I'm turning left, to gaze west, for in 1870, the Revd Francis Kilvert recorded in his *Diary* that Wordsworth – who was his literary hero – actually preferred the Wye in the opposite direction from Tintern, forty-five winding miles upstream from here:

We fell into conversation about Wordsworth and the following are some of Mr George Venables' recollections of him. '[. . .] He used to say that the Wye above Hay was the finest piece of scenery in South Britain, i.e. everything south of himself.'

This would be a satisfyingly surprising volte-face if true, though I suspect the laureate was simply being polite. Still, it suggests the possibility of reading his famous poem not as a static postcard but a compound homage to the river, and so to its essential unity. Even though it's never the same river twice, it *is* always the same river, and almost anywhere along its course – almost anywhere, that is, except ironically IN Tintern itself, then home to one of the country's first blast furnaces or the cliffs and gorges immediately upstream from there – Wordsworth could have observed:

> These plots of cottage-ground, these orchard-tufts
> Which at this season, with their unripe fruits,
> Are clad in one green hue, and lose themselves
> 'Mid groves and copses [. . .] these pastoral farms,
> Green to the very door; and wreaths of smoke
> Sent up, in silence, from among the trees!

'Green,' his poem iterates. 'One green hue . . . Green to the very door.' Then an almost-tautology, 'green earth' and, *crescendo*, 'this green pastoral landscape'. The repetition is an artful intensifier; it overwhelms my inner eye with its blizzard green, this colour for which we haven't enough names, just as the Wye valley itself can feel overwhelmed by its thickly shadowed, almost menacingly abundant woods, hedges and fields.

This afternoon, a patchwork of white and grey clouds the sky. The light is silvery. It rained in the night; dampness lingers in the grooved bark of the willows and bog oaks dotting the meadow. But the dogs trot ahead with tails high, that canine equivalent of a smile. They know, I think, how much setting out to walk matters. But why does it, exactly? Is it the walking rhythm? Or perhaps the way that walking pace seems to be a measure of the self, foot to gait to intention all fitting without resistance — so it feels possible simply to keep on walking forever, across fields and streets, up fells and through streams and buildings and under railway bridges.

I'm reminded how feats of walking on this kind of hallucinatory scale appealed to two of the twentieth century's most polymathic neo-Romantics: pianist-composer and inventor Percy Grainger, racing the train between stops on his Australian concert tours, and the poet and composer Ivor Gurney, who habitually walked the hundred-odd miles between London and his native Gloucester. Such freedom to plunge into the countryside became so much a Romantic convention that by 1886, in *Beyond Good and Evil*, Friedrich Nietzsche could transform it into a metaphor with which to mock the movement itself:

> Then came the honeymoon of German philosophy. All the young [. . .] went off right away into the bushes – all looking for 'faculties'. And what didn't they find – in that innocent, rich, still-youthful time of the German spirit, in which Romanticism, that malicious fairy, played her pipes and sang, a time when people did not yet know how to distinguish between 'finding' and 'inventing'! Above all, a faculty for the 'super-sensory'. Schelling christened this[.]

Nietzsche's birth in 1844, one year after William Wordsworth became the British poet laureate, and two before the Brownings married, situates him firmly as *post*-Romantic, and in what I think of as a classically Oedipal cultural opposition to philosophers close to Friedrich Wilhelm Joseph von Schelling, his target here. Schelling (1775–1854), one of the German Idealists who along with Johann Gottlieb Fichte and Georg Wilhelm Friedrich Hegel built most successfully on the work of Immanuel Kant, was an early architect of Romantic *Naturphilosophie*. Between the ages of twenty-two and twenty-five he published four books on the subject: *Ideas for a Philosophy of Nature as Introduction to the Study of this Science* (1797), *On the World Soul* (1798), *First Plan of a System of the Philosophy of Nature* (1799) and *System of Transcendental Idealism* (1800).

In *Naturphilosophie*, '*Natur*' is both the material given – ourselves and the world we live in – and at the same time, more narrowly and exemplarily, wildlife and countryside. Experience is the encounter with the natural world, partly because that's where we tend to be most 'nakedly' aware of actually *having* experience – outdoors, on an expedition to the countryside, for example – and partly because the natural world is fundamentally *what there is*. Manmade objects modify this world: but at the time is Schelling writing there's no such thing as a completely built environment. When I try to think about eighteenth-century townscapes, I find my mind running along the edges of dressed stone – porticos, embrasures, street corners – or past wrought iron railings. In that world dressed with iron, ceramic and glass the natural origins of even man-made objects have not yet been obscured. They remain palpable forms of the mineral given; often roughcast, or faintly globular in ways that betray a molten past. By the time Shelley composed his 'Hymn to Intellectual Beauty' in 1816, a couple of decades after Schelling published *Ideas for a Philosophy of Nature*, readers in the poet's circle would have understood this newly

double sense of 'nature', and could imagine how 'the truth/
Of nature on my passive youth/Descended.' Besides, those
who, like the poet, had benefitted from a classical education
already had a sense of the givenness of nature, for the idea that
the 'nature' of the material world is inherent, and discrete
from human intervention or understanding, had been part
of Western philosophy since Aristotle's *Physics* in the fourth
century BCE.

When Leigh Hunt published Shelley's 'Hymn' in *The Examiner*
the following January, readers would also have understood
that a 'passive youth' referred to something more than those
Sundays 'devoted to Love in idleness' which Mary Shelley's
early *Journal* records. At the heart of Romantic understanding of understanding itself is a notion of spontaneous, naked
intuition as an alternative to 'passive' rote-learning. In her best-
known novel Captain Walton's description of Frankenstein,
whom he has just rescued, evokes these kinds of traits in order
to elicit the reader's intuitive sympathy rather than our logical
judgement, which might have its suspicions about the stranger:

> Sometimes I have endeavoured to discover what quality it is
> which he possesses, that elevates him so immeasurably above
> any other person I ever knew. I believe it to be an intuitive
> discernment; a quick but never-failing power of judgement;
> a penetration into the causes of things unequalled for clear-
> ness and precision; add to this a facility of expression, and
> a voice whose varied intonations are soul-subduing music.

I've always found this passage uncomfortable. Why should
a charming voice indicate intelligence – leave alone integrity?

The *action* of the novel offers absolutely no indication that Frankenstein possesses a 'never-failing power of judgement': quite the contrary. But this idea of intuitive wisdom is not purely Romantic. The movement's home culture, Christianity, is a revealed religion, not reasoned out but 'revealed' to believers as a special sign that they are elect. The opening of Percy Bysshe's 'Mont Blanc' evokes the almost naked receptiveness of just such a state of mind:

> The everlasting universe of things
> Flows through the mind, and rolls its rapid waves,
> Now dark—now glittering—now
>   reflecting gloom—
> Now lending splendour, where from secret springs
> The source of human thought its tribute brings
> Of waters,—

The river in this metaphor is the Arve, whose 'dark, deep Ravine' on the northern side of the Mont Blanc massif remains full of glacier melt today. In the poem it represents not only 'nature' but the stream of human consciousness – though William James wouldn't coin that phrase itself for another three quarters of a century, in *Principles of Psychology* (1890). As he does this, Shelley catches hold of something that rivers, walking and thinking have in common: the paradox of an active motion that rests on the cusp of passivity.

After rising from the Mer de Glace, the Arve flows for roughly sixty miles towards Geneva where, just south of the famous lake, it swerves to join the Rhône instead. The Wye has a similar near miss. Rising on Pumlumon, as do the Severn and the Rheidol, and just seventeen miles from the sea, it heads inland instead, on the 155-mile detour that makes it Britain's fourth longest river. Today, near its midpoint, I've reached the footbridge where a thick-trunked willow narrows the Carey tributary, creating a shady pool where the dogs love to swim. The water's brown all year round and the steep sides are furred with leaf mould. But today a pair of damsel flies flicker between willow fronds, bright against foliage, dark against daylight. The dogs work the pool to and fro; Dee swims, Zed paddles.

I lean on the wooden handrail and let a horse fly buzz me. Under my forearms the rail's warm wood gives off the sandy, savoury odour of pencil shavings. Down the next field a wood pigeon winds itself up: *ooh, ooh, oooooooh*. These modest details seem to make the experience shift into 3-D, like those animal cards that used to come with petrol when I was a kid. The single twig in the foreground was enough to make the tiger appear to move towards you.

I'm learning to mistrust generalisation, when it replaces such detail. So it's a subversive joy to find Mary Shelley writing in the first volume of her *Rambles in Germany and Italy* (1844) about a disappointingly cool July afternoon just like this one, on Lake Como, 'Strange to say, there is discontent among us. The weather is dreary, the lake tempest-tossed; and, stranger still, we are tired of mountains.' She has just acknowledged the power of quotidian detail:

To me, indeed, there was something even thrilling and affecting in the aspects of the commonest objects around. Every traveller can tell you how each country bears a distinctive mark in the mere setting out of the room of an inn

[. . .]. Window-curtains, the very wash-hand stands, they were all such as had been familiar to me long, long ago. [. . .] Strange and indescribable emotions invaded me; recollections, long forgotten, arose fresh and strong[.]

'Stranger still, we are tired of mountains.' The *Rambles*, which Mary undertook between 1840 and 1843 with her son and friends, record both her inner world and a collegiate experience of 'rambling' which was characteristically Romantic. A quarter century earlier, Percy Bysshe's Mont Blanc poems had explored the inner world of his thoughts and feelings during an experience which was also neither private nor solitary. Mary and Claire made the Alpine trip with him but the poem ignores them. Its 'mind' is *singular*.

Still, because it moves simultaneously like this through our inner and outer worlds, walking affords opportunities for thoughtful conversation. In 1797, the year Schelling published his first work of *Naturphilosophie*, William and Dorothy Wordsworth settled within three miles of Samuel Taylor Coleridge's home at Nether Stowey, in the lee of the Quantock Hills. The Wordsworth siblings had been living near the south Dorset coast, at the foot of Pilsdon Pen, for a little under two years when, that summer, they walked thirty-four miles north across the neck of the West Country peninsula to visit Coleridge and his family. The Quantocks are pretty, hilly landscape. As Dorothy herself wrote to Mary Hutchinson, her school friend and future sister-in-law:

There is everything here; sea, woods wild as fancy ever painted, brooks clear and pebbly as Cumberland, villages so romantic; and William and I, in a wander by ourselves, found out a sequestered waterfall in a dell[.]

But it wasn't just the scenery that made them abruptly decide to settle. 'Our principal inducement was Coleridge's society,' Dorothy told Mary six weeks later. At the age of seventy-three, William Wordsworth recalled for his nephew Christopher's *Memoirs* some of the walking conversations of Somerset days:

In the Spring of the year 1798, [Coleridge], my sister, & myself started from Alfoxden, pretty late in the afternoon, with a view to visit Linton & the Valley of Stones near it, and as our united funds were very small we agreed to defray the expence [*sic*] of the tour by writing a Poem to be sent to the New Monthly Magazine [. . .] Accordingly we set off and proceeded along the Quantock Hills, towards Watchet, and in the course of this walk was planned the Poem of The Ancient Mariner, founded on a dream, as Mr Coleridge said, of his friend Mr Cruickshank. Much of the greatest part of the story was Mr Coleridge's invention; but certain parts I myself suggested, for example, some crime was to be committed which should bring upon the Old Navigator [. . .] spectral persecution [. . .] I had been reading in Shelvocke's Voyages a day or two before that while doubling Cape Horn they frequently saw albatrosses [. . .] "Suppose," said I, "you represent him as having killed one of these birds on entering the South Sea, and that the tutelary Spirits of these regions take upon them to avenge the crime." [. . .] I also suggested the navigation of the ship by the dead men [. . .] We began the composition together on that to me memorable evening.

Walking facilitates monologue, too. Jean-Jacques Rousseau's late work of self-analytic memoir, *Reveries of the Solitary Walker* – the French is *Les rêveries du Promeneur Solitaire* – deploys the definite article of its title with intent. 'The solitary walker' is singular in every sense. Many of the happiest times of the Genevan-born philosopher's life had been spent living on various country estates: as the guest of patrons or, in early adulthood, of his aristocratic lover Françoise-Louise de Warens. His final months would be spent in a cottage on René-Louis de Girardin's estate at Ermenonville in the Oise, surrounded by de Girardin's experimental landscape garden, one of the first on the continent to adopt the English picturesque style. But the *Reveries*' ten essays, published posthumously in 1782, dramatise walks he took on the outskirts of Paris during his last two years. In the Second Walk, for example:

> taking the paths across the vineyards and meadows, I crossed the charming stretch of countryside that separates Ménilmontant from Charonne; having reached this village I made a detour [. . .] feeling the same pleasure and interest that agreeable landscapes have always aroused in me, and stopping now and then to examine plants by the wayside.

Among these 'wayside' plants, he records *Picris hieracioides*, or hawkweed oxtongue, a crinkle-leafed member of the daisy family – though it looks like a small dandelion – which grows in gravel and shallow soil. In our Wye valley yard it springs up between the cobbles as a series of exclamation points. On the same walk he notes *Bupleurum falcatum*, or sickle-leaf hare's ear, whose umbelliferous starbursts of yellow pollenous flowers

I associate with the margins of Cotswold fields. And he's delighted to spot what we call water chickweed, 'even rarer, especially on high ground, the *Cerastium aquaticum*, which [. . .] I later found in a book I had been carrying and transferred to my collection.'

What can I pick out from the Wye riverbank to offer in return? Purples and whites, the imperial colours. On the water, common water-crowfoot, *Ranunculus aquatilis*, whose long mermaid strands make carpets on which the white flowers float like crumpled paper. Along the bank, clumps of woolly thistle, *Cirsium eriophorum*, the upcombed purple petals of their florets crammed above white-fluffed bracts, which stand slightly apart, while blackberry suckers swarm down and dirty through the ungrazed grass. The pinky-purple bramble flowers are over, but the first blue-black fruit are already ripe. They hang with an air of dark importance in the shelter of thorny leaves. Although today the water crowfoot is missing, suffocated by phosphate dump from the chicken farming all the way up the river catchment.

White and yellow, Rousseau's own lost flowers dot what have since become the 11th and 20th arrondissements of Paris, districts that stretch east and a little north from the Place de la Bastille and embrace the one hundred and ten acres of Père Lachaise. Few notable wildflowers have survived that famous cemetery's landscaping, not to mention the more than one million interments since its opening in 1804, although trees still line the site. As his Walk passes through this palimpsest, lost countryside, Rousseau characteristically fills it with a Romantic sense of human meaning:

I gradually passed from these detailed observations to the equally agreeable but more affecting impressions made on me by the complete picture. The wine harvest had been completed a few days earlier, the city dwellers no longer came out this way, and the peasants too were leaving the fields until it was time for their winter work. The country was still green and pleasant, but it was deserted and many of the leaves had fallen; everything gave an impression of solitude and impending winter. This picture evoked mixed feelings of gentle sadness which were too closely akin to me in age and experience for me not to make the comparison.

In this translation *picture* does duty for both *ensemble* and for *impression*, but Rousseau twice uses *l'aspect*, meaning *appearance* in the sense of the visible surface of things, rather than of how they strike us. (For the latter French offers, among several alternatives, *apparaître*, *avoir l'air de* or *l'aspect de*, *paraître*, *ressembler*, or *sembler:* make an appearance, have an air of, resemble, seem.) It's not exactly the picturesque, but the compositional hand is explicitly at work.

Indeed the entire excursion turns out to be a mere back projection. For 'at about six in the evening' on 'Thursday, 24 October 1776', as Rousseau was coming back into town, he was run over. The accident would have been humiliatingly public: it occurred near the famous Galant Jardinier *guinguette*, a wine-garden with dance floor which by the mid-nineteenth century was *the* local summer meeting place, serving up to six hundred covers at a time. It was also a serious, life-changing trauma which may have led Rousseau to develop epilepsy, and perhaps contributed to his death less than two years later from a bleed to the brain. So the passage that precedes this accident becomes, in retrospect, more decorative floral frame than a genuine botanising. Though plant science was undergoing rapid expansion in the 1770s, thanks to the new era of experimental citizen science, the great Swedish botanist Carl Linnaeus's new taxonomies were not yet common knowledge. Rousseau cheekily gives us oxtongue, hare's ear and chickweed all flowering together in late October, though actually only the first of these would have been in bloom then: something the author, who was devouring books on his old hobby of botany at the time, must have known.

Rousseau is a problematic companion in other ways too. The *Reveries* can disappear into a maze of circular thinking and self-pity; reading them as if they were the work of a career thinker from the twenty-first century can be exasperating, if often also touching and funny. And yet such clumsiness is one corollary of doing something new: this is a writer who is attempting a pioneering form of internal self-examination, a whole century before Sigmund Freud identified the unconscious. As he framed it a decade earlier, in *The Confessions:*

I have entered upon a performance which is without example, whose accomplishment will have no imitator. I mean to present my fellow-mortals with a man in all the integrity of nature; and this man shall be myself.

I know my heart, and have studied mankind; I am not made like any one I have been acquainted with, perhaps like no one in existence; if not better, I at least claim originality, and whether Nature did wisely in breaking the mould with

which she formed me, can only be determined after having
read this work.

'Without example': in 1776 reflexivity wasn't even an idea,
and the folded, opaque and multiple nature of human consciousness was not yet a truism. Rousseau is more than simply a
gregarious, albeit literary, 'me-talker'. The stylistic differences
between the pioneering *Confessions*, completed in 1769, and
the two works that followed, the *Dialogues*, written between
1772 and 76, and the *Reveries* (1776—78), don't indicate a simple
loss of technical control or a developing paranoia. These are
late, artful works. Rousseau may have known how to hold a
grudge but, unlike Nietzsche, he didn't disappear into hallucinatory psychosis. The *Dialogues,* which stage three arguments
between 'Rousseau' and 'a Frenchman' about the scandalous
character of one 'Jean-Jacques', adopt the well-established
form of philosophical dialogue and are reflexive enough for any
twenty-first-century theorist. Both continuation and rejoinder,
the *Reveries* followed with a turn inward to memory, motive and
emotion. The solitude they lead us into is not only the newly
underpopulated nineteenth-century French countryside: 'cities
are the devourers of the rural,' as Rousseau had remarked in
Émile (1762). They explore the essential loneliness of finding
oneself — as we all must — *inside* oneself, where no one, not
even the most avid reader, can follow:

Lonely meditation, the study of nature and the contemplation of the universe lead the solitary to aspire continually to
the maker of all things and to seek with a pleasing disquiet
for the purpose of all he sees and the cause of all he feels.

Rousseau's Fifth Walk, recalling two months on 'the Island of Saint-Pierre in the middle of the Lake of Bienne,' oscillates between pegging contemplation as serious intellectual work – 'I decided to devote my walk of the following day to a self-examination on the subject of falsehood', and suggesting something spontaneous, closer to daydream:

Emerging from a long and happy reverie, seeing myself surrounded by greenery, flowers and birds, and letting my eyes wander [. . .] I fused my imaginings with these charming sights, and finding myself in the end gradually brought back to myself and my surroundings, I could not draw a line between fiction and reality; so much did everything conspire equally to make me love the contemplative and solitary life I led in that beautiful place.

Rêverie is the French word for *daydream*, at least as much as it is for *reflection* or for *sleeping dream*. But perhaps this blurred line is immaterial since, whether they're acknowledged or not, imagination, fantasy and desire all form part of the self: 'I could not draw a line between fiction and reality.' Besides, Rousseau's unreliability as a narrator has long been accepted by readers. (Alongside the sexual boasting, for example, is his even less palatable claim that he had a number of children by his partner Thérèse Le Vasseur, and placed them all in a foundling hospital.)

As I turn at the dressed stone pillars of Ballingham viaduct, I reflect how to walk *out* is to walk *into* one's own company – something that's true even of city strolls. I look back, and see the whole shallow valley stage a perspective. Walking down the thought – walking the thought down – as I have this afternoon is progressive. Rousseau's *Reveries* may be messy, but they retain a sense of linearity; of the line of thought.

The idea of progress has linked walking with thinking since Plato's time. After the death of his teacher Plato recorded the Socratic method of dialogue in reconstructions which place the character of 'Socrates' in dialogue with one or more disciples, who act as fall guys to personify the resistances, FAQs, false assumptions and intellectual dead ends against which one of Plato's, or 'Socrates's', ideas proves itself. The *Dialogues* 'by' Plato, which would have been so well known to the (male) Romantics, are therefore themselves in dialogue with his late, great master. There's a well-known illustration by Matthew Paris (1217–59) for a thirteenth-century anthology of fortune-telling which exemplifies this. In the picture on the old Bodleian Library postcard – which was to become notorious as the starting point of Jacques Derrida's *Carte Postale* (1980), little Plato whispers in the ear of a larger, seated Socrates who is busy writing, apparently at his dictation. The successor Plato has become the author as puppet master, enlarging the figure of Socrates by giving him all the best lines.

Learning through debate is a model that every radical generation appropriates. In teach-ins and manifestos, the *soixante-huitards* of Derrida's generation embraced it as eagerly as Socrates's disciples had. The Romantics were no exception. Mary Shelley's Introduction to her 1831 edition of *Frankenstein* lets us eavesdrop on an example which she credits as the partial origin of her novel. In summer 1816, five weeks before they set off to climb Mont Blanc, the Shelleys were with Byron at his villa on Lake Geneva, a location chosen in part because Rousseau was a Genevan:

Many and long were the conversations between Lord Byron and Shelley, to which I was a devout but nearly silent listener. During one of these, various philosophical doctrines were discussed, and among others the nature of the principle of life, and whether there was any probability of its ever being discovered and communicated.

I wonder, as I break my stride to untangle a dog lead, whether walking is conducive to debate because of the way it conducts thought onward – limitlessly, it seems. For two German poets whose work bookends the Romantic period, the Romantic Friedrich Hölderlin (1770–1843) and the post-Romantic Rainer Maria Rilke (1875–1926), the path of creative thought, in particular, is almost angelic. In Hölderlin's 'Homecoming' #3, 'Whatever poets think/Or sing, it's addressed mostly to [God] and the angels.' The famous opening of the first of Rilke's *Duino Elegies* reaches towards angelic understanding: 'Who, if I cried out, would hear me among the Angelic/Orders?'

We reach the middle stile. First one dog jumps it, and then the other. In Hölderlin's quatrain 'Conviction', insightful understanding becomes almost mystical, even transforms our human status:

> The way day shines brightly around people
> And with the light rising from the heights
> Brings together dawning perceptions
> So is knowledge deeply won by spirituality.

In the aftermath of their experiences in Switzerland in 1816 both the Shelleys' work reprises this idea of *shining people*. The leaping intelligence which Mary ascribes to Frankenstein is mirrored by 'the wise, the great, and good', in Percy Bysshe's 'Mont Blanc', who 'Interpret, or make felt, or deeply feel' the 'mysterious tongue' of 'The wilderness', 'not understood/By all.'

However, they inherited this faith in a certain kind of thinking which viewed itself as vaulting over pedestrian logic more directly from older British Romantics. Coleridge had introduced elements of German idealism, including a version of Schelling's *Naturphilosophie*, to Britain, and in the *Memoirs* Wordsworth would describe how when they in turn were young, his friend's intellectual brilliance resembled:

a majestic river [. . .] which was sometimes concealed by forests, sometimes lost in sand, then came flashing out broad and distinct, then again took a turn which your eye could not follow, yet you knew and felt that it was the same river: so there was always a train, a stream, in Coleridge's discourse.

If the waters of the middle Wye represent thought of any kind I fear it's no such radical ideas. The river seems to hang motionless. Only occasional direct daylight catches the surface, making it 'flash out broad and distinct' between the wooded hills or below a fisherman's line. Just ahead some twenty swans, maybe more, float on the black water. Some upend as they feed. Others raise wings to preen: new adults, gleaming white. Perhaps the Wye can at least, as Hölderlin wrote of the River Main in 1799, 'teach quietly gliding songs, and to live in silence.'

The dogs trot peacefully ahead, tired out by exercise. Like Rousseau on one of his dreamy walks, we've made a long loop and need to head home. The lane climbs slowly away from the late afternoon calls of coots and wood pigeons; and suddenly, on Hancock's Meadow, all the pigments of the tired summer turf seem briefly to lift, as if lit from within by 'The way day shines brightly around people/And [. . .]/Brings together dawning perceptions.'

Walk 1: Biblets to Ballingham Wood, from Biblets layby, Lower Lane, Hoarwithy, Herefordshire OS Grid ref 5536530123.

Second Walk

Framing

How best to bid the verdant Landscape rise,
To please the fancy, and delight the eyes;
Its various parts in harmony to join
With art clandestine, and conceal'd design;
T'adorn, arrange; - to sep'rate, and select
With secret skill, and counterfeit neglect . . .

RICHARD PAYNE KNIGHT, *The Landscape*

Playing 'cameras' as a child, I made a square of my forefingers and thumbs and squinted to see what fell within the frame. I quickly discovered how to compose and recompose the picture by moving my hands around. I'd jam this finger-frame against the car window and try to capture the scenery streaming past.

What's the link between this desire to capture experience, on the one hand, and the movement and transformations of travel on the other? On 13 September 1848, Edward Lear

set out west from a cholera-ridden Thessaloniki, then called
Salonica, on a painting tour of the southern Balkans:

> The broad, sandy road [. . .] soon grew tiresome [. . .] a
> colourless, desert *pianura* – such seemed my day's task to
> overcome. Nevertheless, although the picture was a failure
> as a whole, its details kept me awake and pleased, varieties
> of zoology attracting attention on all sides. [At the River
> Vardar] I sketch the bridge, and watch the infinite novelty
> of the moving parts of the scene, which make this wild,
> simple picture alive with interest, for the bridge and a few
> willows are foreground and middle distance: remote view
> there is none.

'Foreground and middle distance': it's such framing that com-
poses the picture. In *Journals of a Landscape Painter in Greece and
Albania,* which Lear published three years after making this
trip, framed views flicker repeatedly in and out of focus within
his text, the way filmstock flickers, though with indescribable
celerity, through what is really a series of composed stills.
Possibly without his even realising it, the *Journals* reveal the
topographical artist's mind at work.

Or perhaps he realised it full well. The extravagantly
gifted Lear had been a self-taught prodigy, employed by the
Zoological Society as an ornithological draughtsman when he
was still in his teens. By the time he published the *Journals*, in
his late thirties, he can hardly have been unaware how useful
such a book could be for his profile. Indeed, he went on to
publish accounts of journeys in Calabria (the following year)
and Corsica (in 1868). An epileptic who kept his condition

secret – and, it's now generally accepted, a closeted gay man too – Lear had had plenty of practice in self-invention. Besides, he needed sales: he had grown up compelled to earn his living, since his father had been bankrupted when he was an infant. Despite such pressures, what makes the *Journals* such a good read is their apparent straightforwardness. They're free of the purple passages that clot so much nineteenth-century prose. Possibly this is because Lear isn't trying to *describe* what he sees: he has his pictures to do that: 'How I wished all these things could be pourtrayed satisfactorily, and how I looked forward to increasing beauty of costume and scenery.' Like a good craftsman, he simply records the *context* of this 'art'.

Lear's paintings, particularly the pen and wash drawings he made on the spot, are markedly unclotted too. Limpid and easy to read, they have the characteristically open texture of much Romantic watercolour art. The clarity of his prose feels related to – perhaps even learnt from – them. When he goes on to list 'all these things' that he wishes 'could be pourtrayed satisfactorily', for example, everything is lucid, not muffled by sentiment:

> Herds of slow, bare-hided buffalo, each with a white spot on the forehead, and with eyes of bright white – surrounded by juvenile buffalini, only less awkward than themselves; flocks of milk-white sheep, drinking in the river; here and there a passing Mohammedan on horseback, one of whom, I observed, carried a hooded falcon, with bells on his turban.

Lear is writing fewer than twenty years after Greece achieved independence from the Ottoman Empire, in the war famous to his British readers for Lord Byron's death at Missolonghi; and 'Mohammedan', a neutral term in 1848, is making a necessary distinction in this religiously and culturally mixed region, while avoiding the then-politically freighted 'Turkish' or 'Ottoman'. It's also a visual note: shorthand for the differentiated costumes and headgear which he only partially puts into words.

Just how particularly the artist is creating a diary of *looking* becomes obvious when we compare his description with, say, William Martin Leake's topographical account of this very spot in *Travels in Northern Greece* (1835):

> From Saloníki to Aláklisi in five hours and fifty minutes [. . .] deducting halts. The road lies all the way through the plain. After three and a half hours we came to a bridge over the *Axius*, now called Vardhári, by which name it was known before the twelfth century, as appears from Anna Comena. [. . .] The bridge of the Vardhári is about 1800 feet long, and crosses an island lying in the middle of the river, which occupies about a third of the whole breadth between the banks.

With his measurements and citations Leake, a retired military man, looks at the same site in a conspicuously different way from Lear. Yet both these inveterate explorers had been formed by Romanticism.

Nearly four decades separated them, however. Leake, born in 1777, came from the same generation as Samuel Taylor Coleridge and William Wordsworth and, among painters, John Constable and John Sell Cotman. By the time Lear was born in

1812, five days after Robert Browning, Lord Byron had already swum the Hellespont and given his maiden speech in the House of Lords. Indeed, it was only thanks to Lear's precocity that he emerged as an artist while British Romanticism was still in full swing. Like Leake, though, he owed his methods of observation to the movement's new interest in scientific observation. Poor sight encouraged him to move on from his training, but as a zoological draughtsman Lear had been part of his era's revolution in taxonomy. Leake, whose major legacy is his pioneering 1821 *Topography of Athens*, had developed expertise in innovative measuring techniques during a British military and diplomatic career spent supporting the Ottoman Empire against Napoleonic France.

Edward Lear's approach was avowedly aesthetic. In 1848, he anticipated 'increasing beauty of costume and scenery when among the wilder parts of the country' as he travelled north through what are today Greece, North Macedonia and Albania. Two decades later, 'fascinated by Corsica', he would 'discover that it is far fuller of landscape beauty that I had thought; those long vistas of valley and mountain must needs contain stores of interest and novelty', while in 1847 he could already enthuse:

Calabria! – No sooner is the word uttered than a new world arises before the mind's eye, – torrents, fastnesses, all the prodigality of mountain scenery – caves, brigands, and pointed hats [. . .] costumes and character – horrors and magnificence without end [. . .] Yet this land of pictorial and poetical interest has had but few explorers; fewer still have published their experiences.

But framing up a view does reduce it to a picture. And at its worst this can be a distancing device, dehumanising or even voyeuristic: 'caves, brigands, and pointed hats [. . .] costumes and character – horrors and magnificence.' Lear, who responded similarly when he travelled in the Middle East, has rightly been accused of Orientalism. Westerners who find cultures different from their own to be picturesque are, however enthusiastic they feel, being reductive: fetishising difference, and assuming their own cultural viewpoint is somehow neutral – or universal. Does it make it better or worse that Lear did the same thing not only in Europe but as he travelled the British archipelago? His pictures of the Lake District and Ireland are full of picturesque drama – ruined abbeys, cliffs, lakes and mountains, shaggy copses and cataracts – but empty of the quotidian, familiar to a boy brought up in similar poverty, being carried on among them: lambing and potato-picking, doing the laundry or making bread.

One of the landscapes I'd try dreamily to frame up as a kid was the pass we regularly took through the Cambrian mountains. Between Llangurig and Eisteddfa Gurig the A44 loops extravagantly around the southern slopes of the 2,500-foot peak of Pumlumon Fawr, as it has since a toll road opened here in 1812. In my early memories we are always heading west, and ahead of us the road describes its roughly level route around slopes that billow and retract, billow and retract out of sight almost to the Atlantic. Wet weather draws the brilliant white of waterfalls down between spurs, but the surrounding summits have an unremitting quality. The enormous scale of geological time feels pressingly close.

Below the road the small, stony Gwy, or Wye, straggles

in the opposite direction. At Sweet Lamb Motorsport — no longer the farm I remember with the gatepost sign, 'Mountain lambs are sweeter', that made a local landmark — it closes on us, passes through a rhododendron thicket, threads under the road, and disappears uphill. Its place among scree and ruined mine buildings is taken by the Tarennig tributary, which the little Castell replaces at Eisteddfa Gurig. Running alongside too, gently rattling chains of misquotation and historical inaccuracy, are those imagined 'sweet lambs'. They're Romantic ghosts from 'The War-Song of Dinas Fawr', composed in 1829 by the satirical novelist Thomas Love Peacock for *The Misfortunes of Elphin,* a mediaevalist novel he set here in Dyfed:

> The mountain sheep are sweeter,
> But the valley sheep are fatter;
> We therefore deemed it meeter
> To carry off the latter.

Fatter/latter, sweeter/meeter (meat-er): these feminine endings clink almost as irritatingly as the wrong register of the neologism 'meeter'. No one could seriously mistake such jingle-jangle verse for the work of those mediaeval princes' poets, the *Beirdd y Tywysogion,* which it seeks to pastiche. Yet, technically speaking, this almost *is* the seven-syllable line of the mediaeval Welsh *cywydd* form, and there are traces too of its *cynghanedd* technique — the 'sounding together' pattern of strict assonance across the four half-lines of a couplet — in the assonance that marries 'valley' to 'fatter', and 'deemed it' to 'meeter'.

Nor is the Dyffryn Gwy by any stretch the 'Dyfed's richest valley' of Peacock's poem. Only the A44 lends it importance as *the* route through these mountains. To live on the seaward side of the Cambrians is to know its litany of landmarks, like the coastal stations of the Shipping Forecast, or lines in a film watched so often you have almost the whole script by heart: title, *Homecoming*. Rising from the left, the Forestry Wales pines of aptly named Hirgoed-ddu (Black Long Wood) obscure the first long downhill. The Elvis rock at Eisteddfa Gurig now bears the anagrammatical conspiracy legend *Elvis Lives*. It used simply to exclaim *Elvis*, and before that *Elis*, for the writer Islyn Ffowc Elis when he stood as Plaid Cymru (Party of Wales) candidate here in 1962. That was the era of roadside graffiti. The *Cofiwch Dryweryn*, 'Remember Tryweryn' – the north Welsh valley drowned to supply Liverpool with water – on the Aberystwyth to Aberaeron coast road dates from the same era. The original painters of *Elis*, on this rock so close to Eisteddfa Gurig farm they could surely not have executed it in secret, have long since proudly claimed their handiwork. Every time I pass it, I think of that generation of long-haired activists, with their tight sweaters and flared jeans, whose motorbikes and tractors were chariots of war and who led the language revolution in this country.

After the turn to Devil's Bridge come Ponterwyd and the George Borrow Hotel, named after that Romantic traveller and philologist, who stayed here on his 1854 trip through *Wild Wales*. Then the desolate tract past the ruined silver mines, Nant yr Arian (Silver Stream), and first sight of the sea some dozen miles ahead and below. The Druid Inn at Goginan. The low-lying water meadows at Lovesgrove where, once, the National Eisteddfod came to town. And finally, like coming in to land, Aberystwyth.

When I was a child, such homecomings were often in the dark. Half asleep under a blanket on the backseat of the Mini Clubman, I'd hear the hum of my parents' voices, see my mum's headscarf silhouetted in the dim back-glow of the head-lights. The car was a small travelling world. Darkness pressed against the windows, the mountains fitting themselves to the windowpanes. But setting out was different. I'd be half-asleep as my parents locked up the house. We walked to the car in a dawn still tentative with damp. But by the time we'd left the sea behind and risen up through grim Llywernog, where the Kites Nest caff still faces a poisoned-looking marsh, I'd be awake; and it was now, as the mountains slid past, that I'd start to frame them up, squinting between the fingers I pressed to the window glass. What I wanted, I think, was something to fit inside the frame of what was manageable. Patches of near hillside appeared simply indistinguishable, and I struggled to pay them much attention. At least waterfalls, viewed across the valley, were small enough to frame. I'd scoot across the backseat to look out of the right-hand window – which always made my dad tell me off.

My parents were not Welsh. Their main response to this landscape, into which my dad's new job had thrown them, was resistance. They turned away with an English shudder from what poet-priest R. S. Thomas, who had only recently left the nearby parish of Eglwys Fach, saw in 'The Welsh Landscape':

There is no present in Wales,
[. . .]
There is only the past,
Brittle with relics,

> Wind-bitten towers and castles
> With sham ghosts;
> Mouldering quarries and mines;

Combining the gothic, awe, and lyrical nationalism this poem, published in Thomas's *An Acre of Ground* in 1952, could scarcely be more post-Romantic. Its pulpit rhetoric demands declamation. But my parents were Romantic, too, in their own way. The mild landscapes of south-east England had formed them, and as they looked at the 500-million-year-old Cambrian slate mountains they tried hard to locate the picturesque in them.

Primroses and violets for my mum, vernacular buildings for my dad. The picturesque starts with the eye converting landscape into picture. In eighteenth-century France, landscape gardening, hitherto renowned for its formality, began to look for ways to embrace newly fashionable Romanticism. Formal avenues of pleached lime trees with their feet in raked sand, and parterres clipped to the accuracy of marquetry, please the eye they lead on through unfolding geometric principles. But their classical beauty is an Enlightenment virtue, based on measure and proportion. 'The infinite possibilities of Romantic inventions' on the other hand, are, according to the influential Parisian connoisseur and landscaper Claude-Henri Watelet in 1774, 'more vague, more personal. They belong to each individual, so to speak, and for that reason they lead more directly into a disordering of the imagination and errors of taste.' Still, his *Essay on Gardens* goes on to concede that there are exceptions, even among 'those founded on rather childish ideas':

One example might be a very wild place where torrents plunge into deep valleys, where rocks, mournful trees, and sound of water echoing through successive caverns bring some kind of terror to the soul. [. . .] Such images of a magic wilderness, a place made for incantations [. . .] can produce a romantic thrill.

Watelet's own taste in landscapes was for the naturalistic *jardin Anglois* [sic], the style Lancelot 'Capability' Brown had perfected in more than a hundred and fifty sites across England, not least when he became the royal Master Gardener at Hampton Court in 1764. Capability Brown's rolling grassy grounds, with their copses, lakes and eyecatcher bridges, began to appear in the 1740s. They developed the work of the former court painter William Kent, his mentor and boss at Stowe House from 1741 to 1750.

Some of the expansive landscaping of British country estates, then, was already being rolled out before the specific moment of Romanticism. They were part of the shift away from a more inward-looking model of the small-windowed, high-walled Tudor and Jacobean Great House; a declaration that, since the Restoration of the monarchy in 1660, privilege had nothing to fear from ordinary people. A declaration too of the end of the old feudal relations in which that house, with its traditional Great Hall and dais, was a very public, and so also somewhat accessible, locus of power. Now landowners' families were shielded from contact with ordinary people by wide skirts of landscaped grounds that, high in acreage, gobbled up the common lands on which local tenants had traditionally practised their subsistence farming. The processes of Enclosure, by which they created this new recreational space, simply accelerated during the Romantic era.

But the *pittoresque* itself was not an English idea. By the 1780s the English theorists of the new parkland aesthetic would be Humphrey Repton and Horace Walpole. Walpole's *Essay on Modern Gardening,* published privately as an annex to a study of painting in 1772, appeared in French translation in 1785 but, despite Walpole's companion role in developing the gothic novel, it fell to Watelet to note the developing Romantic influences in landscape design. At the time Watelet published his gentleman's guide to creating a *ferme ornée* in 1774, the available English texts, both practical in nature, were *Observations on Modern Gardening*, published by his near-namesake Thomas Whately in 1770 and, two years earlier, George Mason's *An Essay on Design in Gardening.* They theorised this kind of landscaping that was led from the drawing board by the 'big picture' contours and resources of the land rather than by close-up plantsmanship. 'The ground is like the canvas of the picture,' Watelet wrote. Rather than being resolved into a form by an artist, a landscape *itself* can form a picture, ready for the artist, or even bypassing him altogether. With this simple reversal the idea of the picturesque was formulated.

'Pretty as a picture,' the adults used to say when we were kids, 'Isn't that a picture.' Being an anxious child, I took note of the implied instruction about how to look. Prettiness was certainly part of the deal; austere tracts of the mid-Cambrians, all post-industrial rubble and rain, did not seem to come under the rubric. Also, I was a child, with childish tastes. I liked intricate, close-up, colourful things: a new summer frock, grandma's Kitchen-in-a-matchbox. As it turns out, this was oddly on the historical money. The British national idea of the picturesque has been substantially shaped – ironically, since the book itself is all but forgotten – by Sir Uvedale Price's 1794 *An Essay on the Picturesque, As Compared With The Sublime And The Beautiful; And, On The Use Of Studying Pictures, For The Purpose Of Improving Real Landscape*. That subtitle is lengthy but it does a good job of summarising its new approach: the picturesque was *not* the sublime or the beautiful, both already categories in the Romantic visual lexicon since Edmund Burke's *A Philosophical Enquiry into the Origin of Our Ideas of the Sublime and Beautiful* (1757), but something less elevated, having more to do with simple visual thrill.

Price wasn't alone in borrowing the French idea of picture-worthy 'landscape value', however. In 1782 his friend William Gilpin, clergyman and artist, published *Observations on the River Wye and Several Parts of South Wales, etc. Relative Chiefly to Picturesque Beauty; Made in the Summer of the Year 1770*. This bestselling illustrated visitors' guide, which Gilpin followed up with further hugely successful volumes, in turn triggered the entertainments of the Wye Tour. The Tour, an early model of mass tourism, was a two-day expedition up the Wye – far downstream from its source in the Welsh mountains – between Chepstow and Ross-on-Wye. This boat trip offered every picturesque cliché: cliffs, primeval woods, historic towns, castles, the night spectacle of the wire-pulling furnaces lining the steep valley of the Anghidi tributary, and the famous ruined Cistercian abbey at Tintern.

We've got so used to the idea of the picturesque that we scarcely notice it *is* an idea. It feels like common sense to be attuned to the beautiful, and to enjoy looking at what we find beautiful in the countryside. But something is not quite straightforward about this. Framing something as a picture places it away from us and *over there*. We aren't *in* the picture we frame. Besides, experiencing a place is more multi-dimensional than any image. Silence falls when a photo is *taken*: what happened to the rooks calling, the dogs barking, the tea-drinker odour of leaves or the nip of gnats?

My mental shorthand has the picturesque down as overworked with detail. After the early morning passage through the Cambrians, after the Builth Wells water meadows and Abergavenny, where old men in caps walked the middle of the road ignoring traffic because they'd done so since boyhood, my dad would take the winding A466 through Tintern on the way to the Severn Bridge. The Wye valley here held onto the rain: it looked narrow and impoverished, but also ancient. I'd square up Tintern Abbey, receding there into its darkling background, between my fingers. Today, standing denuded in a bed of tightly mown grass, the Abbey overlooks the organised bleakness of a car park and visitor centre. But when I was a kid its ruins, cross-hatched with damp and ivy, seemed of a piece with dark woods massing across what was still the 'sylvan Wye' of Wordsworth's 'Tintern Abbey'. I knew I was supposed to find its famous 'steep woods and lofty cliffs,/And this green pastoral landscape' beautiful. And yet – I couldn't make it happen in my own mind's eye.

I didn't experience such an imperative to visual obedience again until years later, at Yangzhou in the east-central Chinese province of Jiangsu. A spring poetry festival was being held in historic pleasure gardens at Slender West Lake. I lit the fire in the ceremonial cauldron to mark New Year and later, puttering round the lake in a dragon boat, viewed a succession of bridges, teahouses and pagodas that record the park's apotheosis as an imperial playground designed for the Qing dynasty emperor Qianlong.

A boatload of poets is always in danger of resembling a Ship of Fools. At every pause, the Chinese guides at our Western elbows arranged us in order that a particular view could fall into place. If we took a step to the side they charmingly rebuked us and then, smiling with embarrassment at our ignorance, explained to us what we could see. We witnessed, for example, light shining on the water. But the way the pale water matched the pallor of sky that came to meet it was not to be seen. We could see the colours of the azalea blooms, but not that their evergreen foliage was somewhat drab. We might be enjoying a daytime visit, but the *significance* of Five Pavilion Bridge lay in the way that on moonlit nights the moon is reflected fifteen times through the structure's fifteen decorative punctures and arches. After a while I began to understand that it was wrong to try and see this kind of Chinese landscape art, which is called Enframed Scenery, for myself. My subjective impulse wronged both each particular view, and the historic culture it was part of. *This* eighteenth-century landscape was indeed picturesque, in the sense that it composed views. But it was a picturesque very far from any Romantic, Western idea of a landscape created to release subjective experience.

Later, in the windowless red and gold banqueting room of a local restaurant, I thought about how this much older landscape culture than my own has resisted Anglocentric, global-cultural assumptions about individual agency. I rolled a tannic green tea around my mouth. All the same, I realised, to the Western eye

Slender West Lake looks absolutely Romantic, because it combines all the elements of the classic Willow Pattern ceramic design, which dates from that era. As a child I'd passed the time before I was allowed to get down from long adult meals dreaming myself into those blue landscapes busy with detail, lovebirds and gnarled tree roots, where a boat oars forever across the white water, while someone crosses a bridge with an intricate balustrade to the pavilion on an island. Yet now that I was actually here in Yangzhou, I found such dreamy wandering was prohibited. Even setting foot on the grass was not allowed. I was and was not *inside* a landscape. Of course: the cheap china I'd spent those hours daydreaming over is not a Chinese but a British image, dreamt up in the English Potteries in the 1780s. Though it combines elements from Chinese ceramic decoration in a kind of fantasia on Qing dynasty themes, Willow Pattern was dreamt up not somewhere like Slender West Lake but in a Romantic reverie.

Orientalism has always had this forked tongue. It's easy to spot when it speaks a self-knowing language of greed, theft, cruelty and destruction. This was the language barked out by the East India Company when the British Army concluded the first Anglo–Sikh War by massacring Sikh forces at the Battle of Sobraon, 'winning a victory at the cost of blood and tears', as Elizabeth Barrett Browning put it. Or by Lord Elgin between 1801 and 1812, when he ordered his men to hack off the Parthenon frieze and other Acropolis marbles and ship them to England to decorate his home near Dunfermline. (Some had to be salvaged after a ship transporting them, the Mentor, sank in 1802, incidentally taking with it among other treasures William Martin Leake's topographical survey of the lower Nile.) But Orientalism is also a language of enthusiasm and admiration, a *sotto voce* of life-long study or one of Edward Lear's light-filled watercolours, which means to do nothing but good – yet can't accept it damages the cultures it admires by framing them from its own perspective.

Small: far away. Framing isn't necessarily just a way to manage visual material. It can be a power relationship too. Romanticism coexisted with the accelerating British imperial era, when the east-west flow of resources and power became overwhelmingly unidirectional. Yet, choosing a dumpling from the lazy Susan at our Yangzhou banquet, I'm reminded that this was far from the only imposition of geographical will going on in what the West calls the eighteenth century. The Qing Emperor Qianlong, born in 1711 CE, ruled China from 1735 to 1796. When he visited Slender West Lake, he had to be seduced into favouring the area, and the story is that Yangzhou's inhabitants faked his fishing catch. I think of them grubbing in the marsh mud, holding their breath underwater and waiting to fasten another carp onto the imperial hook and line. Huddled below the waterline and making history happen, the way ordinary people do.

The lake shore remains dotted with eighteenth-century structures that celebrate the emperor's resulting patronage: Five Pavilion Bridge (built in 1757), Little Jin Mountain, the Fishing Terrace. At least, their appearance remains – tiled roofs, fretwork eaves, walls that turn into sliding shutters – even if they have in fact been mostly rebuilt, as our guides on the dragon boat revealed. However they managed the matter of survival, these structures continue to punctuate their land-scape, just like the neo-Classical eyecatchers at William Kent's

Stowe, or Henry Hoare's Stourhead, that are their contemporaries and their kin: fellow statements of cultural tradition,
matching signatures of ownership on a curated landscape.

Today, standing by the car in the heart of the Cambrians,
I can spot no eyecatchers: neither accidental ruin nor picturesque invention. I've brought us not along the A44 but over
the other, older, east–west mountain pass: a single-track lane
following the course of the Elan. The small river winds through
this high, shallow valley towards the notorious series of res-
ervoirs with which it, and the equally diminutive Claerwen,
supply the water needs of Birmingham. P and I have parked
at the western end of the pass, above the long descent to
Cwmystwyth, and although it's August a keen, clean breeze
is racing up from the valley below. We're more than 1,200
feet above sea level, in the massif of the Cambrian mountains.
Everything here is pared down to its essential form. Even the
colour palette's parsimonious, a Whistleresque study in greys,
yellows and browns that ranges from the whitening grass to the
deep graphite of the tarmac lane, then offers up a surprising
mustard yellow in the lichen splattering the faces of boulders
in infinitely slow motion. I shiver as I lock the car.

At first glance our surroundings look primaeval. Of course,
they're not. This old pass links two sites of Romantic history
in a story about the lost, great houses of eighteenth-century
Ceredigion. Hafod Uchtryd, below us and out of sight at
Pontrhydygroes, is where for decades Thomas Johnes framed
feats of artistic patronage in the extraordinary picturesque
landscape which he created, and which today is all that remains
of his endeavour. Behind us and to the east Nantgwyllt, now
under the waters of Garreg-ddu Reservoir in the Elan Valley,

was one of the places Percy Bysshe Shelley lived with his first wife, Harriet.

We call the dogs from their fossicking in the verge and turn that way. At that other end of this high straight, the OS map records around eight kilometres of 'Ancient Road' running south-west from the Elan to the Claerwen. This archaic route leaves the valley at the ridge where the road skirts Craig Goch reservoir, on what's intriguingly called House Scarp (Esgair y Ty^). But we're not going to walk that far, just to Abergwngu and Esgair Dderwen, Oak Scarp. Only there are no oak trees there now, just a modest modern farmhouse sitting back across the river. The only settlement visible from the road in this wide landscape (though two other farms shelter in the lateral pleats of hills), it's a mnemonic for loneliness. This is hill farming country, whose open grazing land or *maes* has been smoothed to the stone by generations of sheep.

Silence. Only a pair of buzzards float above us almost at cloud level, mewing. The couch grass that fastens the scree and hedges the rock faces is pallid and hardscrabble. The faded blue of P's jeans, the red and orange stripes of the dogs' leads, make unignorable notes of colour. The dogs strain ahead, finding nothing to sniff in the roadside grass. Yet the name Esgair Dderwen carries a memory of human settlement – in this high country a stand of oak, or particularly a rowan tree, often betrays a lost homestead – and the drone's-eye view on Google Earth captures sgraffito lines of discoloured vegetation spelling out the foundations of houses or byres and sheep folds. But wet flush, where we could sink up to our knees in bog, cuts us off from that higher ground, and as we walk all we can see is its beard of bracken.

By the lane, reeds sport pale bobble-flowers. There are clumps of cotton grass, and near the shining edge of the river the modest, rather pale and veiny blue bells of ivy-leaved bell-flowers. Tawny with peat, the ankle-deep water itself is brisk and inviting. Rounding a shingle beach, it inflects into parallel wavelets. In November 1854, George Borrow's walking tour of Wales brought him into the Cambrians just a few miles north of here. At the highest peak, Pen Pumlumon Fawr:

> A mountainous wilderness extended on every side, a waste of russet-coloured hills, with here and there a black, craggy summit. No signs of life or cultivation were to be discovered, and the eye might search in vain for a grove or even a single tree. The scene would have been cheerless in the extreme had not a bright sun lighted up the landscape.
>
> 'This does not seem to a country of much society,' said I to my guide.
>
> 'It is not sir. The nearest house is the inn we came from, which is now three miles behind us. Straight before you there is not one for ten miles, and on either side it is an *anialwch* to a vast distance. Pumlummon [*sic*] is not a sociable country, sir; nothing to be found in it, but here and there a shepherd.'

Even today, the Elenydd is 'not . . . a country of much society'. These roughly five hundred square miles of mid-Welsh mountain landscape are dominated by the five Pumlumon peaks, which rise to 752 metres above sea level. But the region has taken its name not from them but from the little upland river we're walking alongside, since at least the twelfth century, when 'Elenydd' appeared both in Gerald of Wales's topographies and in the *Mabinogion*. In the Romantic era Anglophone visitors, who seem to have been thrilled by its austerity, began calling the region instead the Desert of Wales.

Percy Bysshe Shelley was only eighteen in July 1811 when he responded to an uncle's invitation to come and stay at his house, Cwm Elan, in the heart of the Elenydd. After a month the young poet rushed back to London, in order to elope with his first wife, Harriet — but not before he had taken in the scenery:

> Thou rock, whose bosom black and vast
> Bared to the stream's unceasing flow,
> Ever its giant shade doeth cast
> On the tumultuous surge below!
> [. . .]
> And whither this lone spirit bent
> The footstep of a wild intent —

This fragment comes from 'The Retrospect', a poem in his early manuscript, the *Esdaile Notebook*. In letters written from the house Shelley enthused,

> This country is highly romantic; here are rocks of uncommon height and picturesque waterfalls. I am more astonished at the grandeur of the scenery than I expected. [. . .] I am not wholly uninfluenced by its magic on my lonely walks.

Since buying Cwm Elan (the name means 'Elan Valley') two decades earlier, his uncle, Thomas Grove, had converted '10,000 worthless acres [. . .] into a paradise'; the 'romantic' features the young poet admired had been curated, if not created, by the new idea of picturesque landscape. Shelley's correspondence during his stay reveals him mulling this idea:

> Rocks piled on each other to tremendous heights, rivers formed into cataracts by their projections, & valleys clothed with woods, present an appearance of enchantment—but <u>why</u> do they enchant, <u>why</u> is it more affecting than a plain, it cannot be innate, is it acquired?

Five years later, in his 'Hymn to Intellectual Beauty', Shelley would evoke the 'awful Loveliness' of a different mountain landscape: 'Spirit of Beauty, that doth consecrate/With thine own hues all thou dost shine upon.' Already in 1811 the possibility of 'consecration' by an essential, given principle was more than simply an aesthetic matter, since he had recently and very publicly renounced Christianity. His refusal to deny authorship of *A Defence of Atheism*, the tract he had co-written with his friend Thomas Jefferson Hogg and published anonymously, had caused him to be sent down for good from Oxford. His struggle, in that letter written in Cwm Elan a few months later, to find some sort of guarantee underlying the 'appearance of enchantment' reads like a desire to believe in the material world at least; to find something on which belief could catch: 'But *why . . . why . . . ?*'

In reaching the conclusion that its attractiveness 'cannot be innate' Shelley puts his finger on what differentiates the picturesque from other Romantic views of the countryside. The picturesque, whether composed by planting and shaping the landscape itself or in framing representations of that landscape, has been created for consumption. Unlike the sublime and the beautiful, those earlier-established Romantic categories with which the young poet would have been more familiar, the picturesque has to do not with innate or spiritual – perhaps supernatural – value, but with the human act of looking itself.

All his life, Shelley's poetry would be more engaged by the sublime and the beautiful, by what elsewhere in the 'Hymn' he calls the 'awful shadow of some unseen Power', than by the picturesque. But that didn't stop him enjoying the 'magic' of his uncle's Cambrian estates. When he returned with Harriet to look for a home in Wales the following spring, he came first to the Elenydd, and rented Nantgwyllt, a slightly smaller and older manor in the next valley. Nantgwyllt was situated near the confluence of the Claerwen and Elan rivers; like Cwm Elan it had lawns sloping down to the water, with views of craggy hillside beyond. Percy Bysshe and Harriet fell frankly in love with the place; but it was the summer seat of the Lewis Lloyd family, who wisely refused to sell, and eventually the young couple moved on.

While they were still here though, in April 1812, Percy wrote to a mentor he had yet to meet, William Godwin:

The cheapness, beauty, and retirement, make this place in every view desirable ... Nor can I view this scenery, mountains and rocks seeming to form a barrier round this quiet valley which the tumult of the world may never over-leap without associating your presence with the ideas, that of your wife, your children [. . .] to complete the picture which my mind has drawn to itself of felicity.

The intensity of his fantasy must have communicated itself. By late 1814, when one of those 'children', Mary, had supplanted Harriet and was on her way to becoming Percy's second wife, she would refer to Nantgwyllt as to a touchstone fantasy of the good life:

Oh how I long [to] be at our dear home where nothing can trouble us neither friends nor enemies [. . .] But Nantgwllt do you not wish to be settled there at a home you know love – with your own Mary nothing to disturb you studying walking & other such like amusements – oh it's much better [I] believe not to be able to see the light of the sun for mountains than for houses.

Her hopes came to nothing, and today nothing of either house remains. The huge simplification of a reservoir has obliterated both Cwm Elan and the neighbouring *cwm*, where Nantgwyllt House stood opposite the church at the head of the Claerwen Valley. Caban Coch and Garreg-ddu have replaced the homes and fields, village and wildlife of those valleys with a level surface of grey water. Superstition says the bells of Claerwen Village can sometimes be heard ringing, and that Cwm Elan still stands underwater, a beautiful submerged house like a kind of dream. But neither fantasy is true. The Victorian engineers razed the buildings they flooded, and in drought years all that's exposed are Cwm Elan's naked foundations.

The section of the Elan valley we're walking today is shingled with slate scree. A few bracken-capped pillow mounds on the slopes immediately above us are traces of a mediaeval rabbit farm. But when I lift my phone to take a picture, the lens flattens them almost completely. Up here in the highest strata of Silurian outcrop, there are none of the post-industrial ruins, remains of slate and lead mines, that scar the settlement of Cwmystwyth, hidden in the lower valley to our west. There's almost no trace either of the intensive farming of the warmer early mediaeval period – gone already by 1530 when John Leland, on his great *Itinerary in Wales*, saw the open *maes* used for common grazing, as it is today:

Al the montaine ground bytwixt Alen [*the river Elan*] and Strateflure longgeth to Stratefleere [*belongs to Strata Florida Abbey, at its south-western perimeter*], and is almoste for wilde pastures and breding grounde, in so much that everi man there about puttith on bastes as many as they wylle without paiyng of mony.

'Nothing beside remains,' as Shelley would write, in his sonnet 'Ozymandias', five years after he left the Elenydd for the last time. 'Boundless and bare/The lone and level sands stretch far away.' The writing Shelleys, and later George Borrow, imagined an emptiness here at the heart of Wales, which they pictured as ready to be filled with their own impressions. Such Romanticism both averted its gaze from the surrounding poverty, and at the same time exoticised it. Whether on the Elenydd or in Thessaloniki, it was her unmodernised costume and bare feet that made the peasant girl picturesque.

I should know better, but as we walk I keep turning and squinting through my camera-phone for some feature to create perspective or frame a view; Lear's 'foreground or middle distance'. 'Lonely, lonely, lovely Elan,' wrote the poet John

Fairfax, a latter-day Romantic if ever there was one, in *Adrift on the Star Brow of Taliesin* (1974). 'Autumn rising in your long voice.' At a time when it was still unfashionable, Fairfax carried out the neo-Romantic project of moving to deep countryside in order to write poetry. In doing so he helped create a national institution, the Arvon Foundation; and a movement. He understood both slow living and this kind of 'long' landscape, where there's little picturesque detail to snag the restless eye.

But as we get back to the car another mountain river flashes white among its rust-and-black rocks like a signal. This is the little Ystwyth. Because it runs the other way off the plateau, not inland but down to the sea, it's escaped the fate of the Elan and Claerwen and has not been dammed by Birmingham's civic fiat. Now it gives me an idea. We load the dogs into the car – and fifteen minutes later we're in the Ystwyth valley immediately below, pulling into Fforest carpark by Hafod Church. Here kids crowd wooden picnic tables, and car boots stand open to air dogs, in a cheerful welter of noise and movement. This is not the spooky Hafod that I remember from childhood, when long car trips would bring us at last to dim clearings between rhododendrons, rubble-strewn grass, and the smell of damp mortar and wet leaves. Something's being understood and used here in an altogether new way.

Fashions change. At the end of the eighteenth century Richard Payne Knight, friend of both William Gilpin and Sir Uvedale Price, made the third in their trio of influential British advocates of the picturesque, both through the land-scaping he undertook at his own property, Downton Castle in Herefordshire, and through publication. *The Landscape: A didactic poem in three books Addressed to Uvedale Price Esq.* (1794) summarises the new art:

> How best to bid the verdant Landscape rise,
> To please the fancy, and delight the eyes;
> Its various parts in harmony to join
> With art clandestine, and conceal'd design;
> T'adorn, arrange;——to sep'rate, and select
> With secret skill, and counterfeit neglect

It was Knight's cousin, Colonel Thomas Johnes, who inherited the twelve hundred acres of Hafod Uchtryd in 1780. A hafod is a summertime dwelling, a country home or hunting lodge; the 'Havodychdryd' which belonged to Strata Florida Abbey, in the neighbouring 'valley of the flowers', had traditionally been the latter, and was acquired by the Herbert family in the mid-sixteenth century after the dissolution of the monasteries. A little over two centuries later, Johnes started work to replace the building which had come down to him with an extraordinary Gothick mansion. The house he started building in 1786, to the designs of Bath architect Thomas Baldwin, was transformed a decade later by John Nash's pair of virtuoso additions: an enormous conservatory, where Johnes propagated rare species, and a great library, which he filled with a priceless collection of books and early Welsh manuscripts. In 1807 the entire extravaganza was destroyed by fire.

But Johnes rebuilt. In portraits, this man of appetites appears bullish, puffy jawed, indeed overweight. His grandfather's iron-foundry fortune was just two generations old, and as its heir he seems to have been determined to be equally an agent for change. And so he created a paradise to be shared, where tenants had proper pay and decent stone-built homes. He reforested the bare valley he had inherited, created a model farm with a specialist dairy, and even established the first private press in Wales, in its own premises at nearby Pwll Peiran, which published his translations from the French. He would eventually plant a total of around three million trees, work for which the Society of Arts awarded him five gold medals in silviculture. This was both cheeky – since he also planted up 7,000 acres of Crown Land – and a celebration of passionate direct action since the Crown had left that land deserted and bare.

Exemplary practice; and also a kind of advocacy. Visitors were welcomed – a practice which continued in the decades after its creator's death – though those without an introduction stayed at the Hafod Arms Hotel at nearby Devil's Bridge. Johnes himself had this constructed in 1792–3. By 1795 he was receiving up to forty visitors in a day. In 1796 his friend George Cumberland addressed this growing market, publishing the influential *An Attempt to Describe Hafod*, with a map engraved by William Blake (one of the sequence of such commissions Cumberland put the artist's way). One of these visitors was George Borrow, who made his 1854 hike over the Elan valley from the Hotel, an 'immense lofty cottage with projecting eaves' whose fluent commercialism he bashfully disguised in *Wild Wales*, calling it a 'hospice'.

Today this institution has become the Devil's Bridge Hotel. Within four years of Borrow's visit and before he had even published his book, it was advertising a high degree of comfort and accessibility:

Table d'hote daily at [. . .] half-past Three o'Clock [for day trippers coming] to view the magnificent FALLS OF THE MYNACH AND RHEIDOL and to visit the picturesque GROUNDS OF HAFOD, Tickets to view which can only be had at the Bar of the Hafod Arms Hotel.

Those who paid their 3s. fare 'There and Back, Inside or Outside' for the 'new and well-appointed omnibus' would have found a Hafod much as Borrow describes it:

The scenery was exceedingly beautiful. Below [me] was a bright green valley, at the bottom of which the Ystwyth ran brawling, now hid among groves, now showing a long stretch of water. Beyond the river to the east was a mountain, richly wooded [. . .] near the lower part of the valley the road tended to the south, up and down through woods and bowers, the scenery still ever increasing in beauty. At length [. . .] I suddenly beheld Hafod [. . .] on a rising ground, with a noble range of mountains behind it.

A true fairy place it looked, beautiful but fantastic [. . .] At the southern end was a Gothic tower; at the northern end an Indian pagoda; the middle part had much the appearance of a Grecian villa. The walls were of resplendent whiteness, and the windows which were numerous shone with beautiful gilding.

This valley paradise has always been both concealed and wide open, a local secret known proprietorially as *The* Hafod, as if there could only ever be this one. Today a little under half the parkland and deciduous woodland Johnes planted are held in trust by the Hafod Estate, and the winding paths he laid out have been reconstructed. So now we find ourselves walking a palimpsest landscape as we set out along a 'ladys—walk' mentioned in the first published account of Johnes's Romantic project: the second, 1789 edition of William Gilpin's *Observations on the River Wye*. Gilpin and Johnes were friends and, though Gilpin never visited the estate, Johnes had visited him, in April 1787; persuasively bringing along to his meeting with this famously influential architect of the picturesque movement and the tourism associated with it, 'a large portfolio, full of paintings (on paper) of a variety of views around his house. They were done by [Thomas] Jones, a pupil of [Richard] Wilson.'

Though Uvedale Price recorded privately, and somewhat cattily, that 'there are some picturesque scenes, and a very pretty cascade but I think the place has been over-rated,' Gilpin's account of Hafod's delights was followed by numerous other published and personal accounts until the estate's cost became too much for Johnes in 1814. Many of these describe recognisably the same views we glimpse now when the Ladies' Walk takes us across Middle Hill. The planting we cut through is still broadly recognisable from landscapes painted twenty years after Gilpin by John 'Warwick' Smith. Three years after the 1807 fire, as rebuilding came to a conclusion, these were reproduced as etchings by J. C. Stadler, to illustrate Sir James Edward Smith's *Fifteen Views Illustrative of a Tour to Hafod in Cardiganshire, the Seat of Thomas Johnes Esq, MP* (1810).

These estate walks have been opened up again using such contemporary sources. For much of the post-war era they were lost in the maze of animal tracks that I remember from childhood, and that still thread the thickets of rhododendron and azalea, the overgrown stands of ash and sycamore. These the dogs powerfully appreciate, disappearing on mazy divigations of their own. We regroup at some artful tree bole seats above a prospect of valley and woods. *But oh! That deep romantic chasm.* It's beautiful but, looking out over the plump heads of trees below, I'm not exactly sure what we can see. Are we glimpsing Johnes's internal vision, or following in the footsteps of those throngs of distinguished visitors and later, mid-nineteenth-century omnibus day-trippers? Can I still see with the proprietorial eyes of a local, as I did when I was a kid?

Versions of the Hafod slip and merge in a ramifying picturesque. I find myself trying to explain to P how I used to think of it as high Romantic cultural monument untenably superimposed on wild countryside: the Strawberry Hill Gothick of its lost windows and domes an idiom too delicate to survive the locale. Now I realise Johnes was in fact embracing, and artfully cultivating, this very wildness. P has no difficulty recognising this orthodoxy of the picturesque landscape movement. But I can't quite experience the Hafod as a cultural historical phenomenon because I got to know it as a child, with a child's literal-mindedness. For me it *is* the lost paradise it was designed to evoke, and I believe its rusticated wilderness. To be true to itself, I need it to continue to be half forgotten, visited only by locals, its terraces and caves hidden like rumours among the overgrown trees and shrubs. For me it's a kind of dream; a stage-set for the unconscious.

In one local rumour, Hafod was Xanadu in Samuel Taylor Coleridge's dream of 'Kubla Khan':

And here were forests ancient as the hills,
Enfolding sunny spots of greenery.

But oh! that deep romantic chasm which slanted
Down the green hill athwart a cedarn cover!
A savage place! as holy and enchanted
As e'er beneath a waning moon was haunted
By woman wailing for her demon-lover!
[. . .]
It flung up momently the sacred river.
Five miles meandering with a mazy motion
Through wood and dale [. . .]

The same rumour maps his 'sunny pleasure-dome with caves of ice' onto Hafod's dome library and riverside kitchen icehouse, or the tunnel and cavern behind a waterfall that Johnes had blasted out of a plain slate bluff. Myth upon myth. Coleridge, who completed the poem in 1797, passed close to here in 1794, when on a walking tour with a university friend, Joseph Hucks. But as Hucks records in *A Pedestrian Tour through North Wales*, published the following year, there was in fact no trip to the Hafod itself, only to the falls at Devil's Bridge; no stay with the Johnes, but only a 'miserable hole' of an inn in Tregaron, 'in which however we were constrained to sleep, and to break the windows in our bedrooms to let in the fresh air.'

The Hafod is a collective dream. Even the name of this trail we're on, Ladies' Walk, makes a palimpsest of ghostly parasols and invisible, brushing hems. 'Meandering with a mazy motion,' we follow it through the tilting, low-walled enclosure of Mariamne's Garden. This hillside patch, today violet with heather, was created for Johnes's adored daughter – his only child to survive to adulthood – who was a gifted botanist. Its meagre topsoil and oddly arbitrary setting make it seem merely patched-on to the valley. It's hard to imagine rare or delicate species doing well here. Delicate herself, Mariamne died unmarried at twenty-seven, and was buried in the small church Johnes had built further up the valley. In 1932 a second Hafod fire, getting as far as the church, damaged her monument too.

The slightly sticky shadow of Mariamne's sickliness combines with these fires like a spectre of failure. Yet Johnes did not fail. Mariamne's early death, though sad, wasn't unusual in 1811. Indeed it's a reminder of how, that same year, Percy Bysshe Shelley's first stay at Cwm Elan, just ten miles away over the shoulder of the massif, had an edge of austerity and risk. Even house fires were not particularly rare in the era of open fires in every room, though Johnes committed the cliched error of being underinsured. When he ran out of money, in 1814, he retreated to Devon. He died there two years later, and the estate stayed locked in chancery until 1832 – though it remained staffed, and visitors continued to be welcomed. But the landscape he had created remained, as it was in one sense bound to do, and for more than another century the house he built had a series of proud owners, even though a clumping Victoriana would be unleashed up on it. In *Murray's Handbook* (1860) 'The contrast between the old house of Nash, with its puerility of design, and the Italian roofs and terraces of the new portion, is very striking and almost ludicrous.'

Arriving by what Blake's map, in Cumberland's book, calls the 'return of 1st walk', we've come to the parting in the rhododendron wings that should reveal the mansion. Rabbits scutter into the bushes as we crunch the gravel drive. Here suddenly is a meadowy lawn, grazed by sheep, spreading southwards and down in a rather incongruous apron from a paved terrace. Only the house itself is absent. Inhabited till around WW2, some dozen years later it had become derelict and, like many other mansions around Britain, was demolished in the out-with-the-old fashion of the fifties. The work was executed with such cursory contempt that today the rubble's still heaped in the middle of this upland pasture, which was once lawns. We circle the blurred foundations and, as I do every time I visit, I peer through the locked grating to see the brown glass of smashed nineteenth-century bottles still littering the floor of the abandoned wine cellar. Delicious frisson: not Knight's 'conterfeit neglect', perhaps, but still a manmade ruin. Johnes was a generous host, renowned for lubricating the visits of many admirers both at the house itself and at the hotel. The cellar suggests an establishment wrecked in mid-gesture, as if his arm were still raised to summon another bottle.

In fact, by the time it was destroyed, the site had been looted for years. The artist John Piper, who visited in 1939 as his own romantic vision of ruin and place was developing, recorded:

Tragedy, on the whole, has triumphed at Hafod. In the house some of the original Gothic fireplaces remain. [. . .] Plants wither in pots on the decaying shelves in the Gothic glasshouse. The woods up the valley are dishevelled; their paths overgrown and often impassable [. . .] But the beauty of the whole place in decay is overpowering.

Photographs taken in 1950 by the architect photographer Edwin Smith capture this 'beauty . . . in decay', as well as its erosion by a hundred small acts of greed. A cottage greenhouse incorporates a gothic window stripped from the house. In the mansion itself, an internal doorway with its frame of wooden panelling ripped entirely away opens onto a fireplace undressed to the bare brick, and above it an eighteenth-century oil landscape painting, still in its heavy gilt frame, from which someone has hacked out a foreground detail. Bare plaster shines through the hole in the canvas.

Edwin Smith's pictures of Britain are beautifully wide in range, but are linked by a sense of nostalgia and loss, of places as the footprints of communities and ways of life that have always just left the frame. It's as if he somehow knew he would die prematurely, of a cancer diagnosed too late. Still his sensibility, so perfectly adapted to the gothic love of ruin, mystery, regret and distance, found its ideal subject in this ruined Romantic landscape. That same year Elizabeth Inglis-Jones published *Peacocks in Paradise*, her evocatively titled history of this romantically occluded spot, which John Claudius Loudon's 1822 *An Encyclopaedia of Gardening* had long before called a:

secluded basin, among high mountains: the approaches to it full of beauty and contrast, the numerous walks displaying waterfalls, precipices, prospects, cultivated scenes, rude spots, seats, buildings etc., singularly romantic and sublime.

Inglis-Jones's book captured Welsh public imagination for decades, and by the time I was a child the adults around us seemed curiously in thrall to the place. Friends' parents would bring us out on afternoon trips to what I privately thought of as that Creepy Valley. Whatever the time of year, the turbulent River Ystwyth seemed swollen by rain. After the complicated, sick-making drive up into the Cambrian foothills, the adults would swing open the back doors of their family estates and urge us out onto muddy laybys in amongst the dripping trees with the instruction to 'run off and explore'. But we kids stood around. It was hard to get your bearings; mist muffled our voices. It felt as if just beyond the roadside trees, the valley was deleting itself and might take us with it. I suppose there must have been some hippy magic to the place for that cohort of young parents. They were (I see now) a gang of provincial college tutors and accountants, self-conscious in their jeans and denim jackets and with the new freedoms these clothes represented. Looking back, I wonder what actually was being smoked as rain pattered on the rhododendron leaves.

Landscapes can be excavated like buildings. The hillsides we glimpse in the background of Edwin Smith's photographs are almost as bare as the ones that Johnes — or his neighbour Thomas Grove, ten miles east up at Cwm Elan — had first decided to cloak with trees. The 'paradise' Shelley's uncle created disappeared under the reservoir waters. But Johnes's picturesque paradise had simply gone underground, waiting in the mild soil and seepage of west Wales as roots and seeds, plant stock and ground works. Today, from the Alpine Bridge we see how oak, beech and birch once again line the banks of the Ystwyth that winds between them, cluttered with rocks and stones. They're pale above the waterline, golden-brown below. The August river's running shallow, and the dogs pull us onto the waterside shingle as they splash about, drinking and barking and swimming a few strokes. Moss thickens on the ground from which the trunks of larch spring up around us, pale as driftwood. Above a rocky outcrop opposite, an acre or more of fireweed, *Chamaenerion angustifolium*, has turned to seed. Its long feathers lean into the light. Sun bleaches the far slopes of Cwmystwyth. As we turn back, we see the almost luminous green grass of the old house lawn, dotted with masonry, sheep and clumps of reed, 'Its various parts in harmony'.

The eighteen-year-old Shelley worried whether nature forms our tastes, or our tastes distort nature, when we find 'rivers formed into cataracts by their projections, & valleys clothed with woods, present an appearance of enchantment—' Pausing our way back to the car at a bench by the Bedford Monument, I flick through the day's photos on my phone, and realise with dismay how conventional what I've seen really is. My enchantment is just too nicely composed. Even in this last shot. Look how I've placed the obelisk and its railing in the foreground as a frame for the distant prospect – an artless strand of ivy blurring as it reaches too close to the lens – so as, in Edward Lear's words, to 'make this wild, simple picture alive with interest'.

Walks 2: Elan Valley and Hafod Estate. National Cycle Route 81 from viewpoint, OS: SN 8539275812 to Esgair Dderwen; and from Hafod Forest carpark, Hafod Estate, Pontrhydygroes, Cwmystwyth, Ystrad Meurig SY25 6DX on the Hafod Estate Ladies' Walk, OS Grid ref SN 7677072280.

St Augustine's Priory.

Third Walk

Surveying

> every space that a man *views* around his
> dwelling-place
> [. . .] such space is his universe

WILLIAM BLAKE, Milton

S t Rumwold's Bonnington stands alone on a lane I'd always believed must peter out in the low ground beyond it. But now, unfolding the map, I see the road goes on, crossing the Military Canal and doglegging south between fields towards Dymchurch and the English Channel. On this northern rim of Romney Marsh you step out of the car into muggy dazzle. Even in October the air, warmer here than in the rest of the country, is faintly odoriferous. The Marsh makes an almost bestial presence, always surprisingly close-at-hand. Dark water standing in what locals call sewers reminds me of the viscous, barely grasped material of dream.

Today the lane is empty, and there's a salt edge to the air.

On my map, local roads zigzag from drain to drain; abrupt perpendiculars that chart not so much rights of way as an opportunistic water-world still shifting beneath the soil. With its empty grassed levels, its concealed dykes and verges grown higher than the car roof, this is a landscape it would be easy to get lost in. All the same, here I am, where a literal cross marks the spot on the OS map. Bonnington's stockily built parish church stands outside the village itself, surrounded by fields that lie empty in every direction. They look, this morning, a little dowdy. Weak sunlight shocks against white-bladed grass; outsized camomile daisies cluster at the verge. Ash keys idle down onto the roof of the car. As it must have every autumn since mediaeval times when this first became sheep country, a breeze from the south combs the tussocks in the paddocks, 'Fluttering the sear leaves on the blasting lea/That litters under every fading tree' – just as it does in the Northamptonshire Octobers of John Clare's *The Shepherd's Calendar* (1827).

Bonnington church is two-chambered on a compact Norman pattern – chancel, nave, but no expansive transepts. Only a pennant weathervane flies from the jaunty lead-gabled belfry. It looks not so much as if the community it serves shifted away from it over the centuries, but as if this lonely site on the brink of what's now the Military Canal, though it was once tidal marsh and sea, were somehow itself significant. Churches built in such exposed, seaward spots have a tendency to hunker down, becoming more ark than oracle: I think about the seventh-century chapel at Bradwell-on-Sea on the Essex marshes, or the ruins of St Non's Chapel in Pembrokeshire. Perhaps St Rumwold's turns inward to contemplate the mysterious child to whom it's dedicated? This seventh-century son and grandson of pagan kings lived, according to the eleventh-century *Vita Sancti Rvmwoldi*, for only three miraculous days. My guidebook tells me he was born professing Christianity, baptised at his own demand, and on the third day preached a sermon to his presumably startled parents before expiring.

Dusty and foxed, printed on spongy old paper, my guide also has plenty to tell me about itself. The Foreword by the incumbent at the time of publication, the Revd W. T. Sampson, commends its:

> reliable information in respect of my three parishes of Bonnington, Bilsington and Falconhurst [. . .] intended both for the casual visitors, who are always most welcome in our churches, and also for our own parishioners and their friends.

In the next paragraph, my grandfather goes on to thank his 'younger son', my dad, for the 'considerable time and pains' of his research and authorship. There's a glimpse in this of the public formality of their relationship that makes me realise how little I know about how they were together: about this part of my own prehistory.

Old things come down to us undone and open for interpretation. Maybe that's one reason the Romantics, valuing the freedom to create their own meaning out of personal experience, found ruins so attractive. Another was the fashion for the picturesque. The gnarly detail of remains like, say, the ruined church at Yazor in Herefordshire have just the aesthetic character picturesque landscaping strove to achieve. It happens for example that the landowner at Yazor was that movement's advocate, Sir Uvedale Price. He both preserved the site as a landscape feature, in part by building a new church elsewhere, and constructed a Ragged Castle folly in response nearby.

We could dismiss such tinkering with history's material record as mere orchestration. But after all a tradition of story-telling clings to such places: ghostly superstitions long predate the Romantic movement. Ruins have a not-to-be-taken-for-granted quality; a narrative character. Maybe that's because, by making evident that buildings are in process, they disrupt our everyday assumption that what was here yesterday will also be here today, and tomorrow: that our surroundings – and our lives – are immutable . . . Not that it's all existential doom and gloom, as the gleeful spookery of a thousand B movies reassures us. My favourite *Fronkunsteen* movie, for example, remains Mel Brooks's *Young Frankenstein*, whose fibreglass spooky castle glori-ously complements the Deco kitsch of the laboratory set Brooks repurposed from James Whale's iconic 1931 *Frankenstein*.

Besides, a tower among grassed-over mounds, a solitary gable-end, or a relief map of foundation walls all carry what's missing alongside and within themselves, like a series of blanks for us to fill in. When I was a kid visiting my grandparents at Bonnington, I told myself stories about Kentish yeomen and long-lost Marsh smugglers which were based on the books I borrowed from the library. These volumes were considerably older than I was; their soft brown pages and crinkly plastic dustjackets made me feel as though the stories themselves were coming to me from deep time. Bored in the back of the car, or during meals, I refurbished and repeopled the oasts and pillbox guardhouses, the windmills with missing sails and the broken-down wharfs that surrounded us.

The narrative space of ruins also makes room for compassion. As the eighteenth century came to an end, William Wordsworth repeatedly visited the trope of the abandoned cottage, 'a ruined house, four naked walls/That stared upon each other,' as he put it in 'The Ruined Cottage', and the human calamity such nakedness recorded. Written in 1797–8, 'The Ruined Cottage' was later folded into 'Book One: The Wanderer' of *The Excursion* (1814). Here, and in 'Michael: A pastoral poem' (1800), Wordsworth chooses to repopulate the countryside of his poetry with the actual rural poor he knew and lived among, whose lives literature had so often deleted or overwritten with chiffon and ribbons, nymphs and swains. His 'Wanderer' is no Romantic thinker at leisure but a tramp who took a risk on freedom, as no labourer then could, and tried (and failed) to live as a Pedlar:

> I see around me here
> Things which you cannot see: we die, my Friend,
> Nor we alone, but that which each man loved
> And prized in his peculiar nook of earth
> Dies with him, or is changed; and very soon
> Even of the good is no memorial left.

Buildings in a landscape shrink, grow and are swallowed up again. Amid this mutability, sometimes only trees outlast both them and us:

> I rose and turned towards a group of trees
> Which midway in that level stood alone;
> And thither come at length, beneath a shade

Of clustering elms that sprang from the same root
I found a ruined house[,]

In the late twentieth century, this kind of rueful nostalgia
for hopes gone astray would – at least as formulated by the
post-punk theorist Mark Fisher – turn for evidence to urban
and cultural settings, often using rediscovered film and sound
recordings or old-fashioned consumer goods; and, repurposing
a term from the French philosopher Jacques Derrida, it would
come to call itself hauntology. In the eighteenth century it
called itself Gothic and became particularly fashionable in
fiction and architecture, where it licensed a gleeful borrowing
from other times and places.

Gothic fiction and architecture collide at Strawberry
Hill, near Twickenham, where from 1749 Horace Walpole
embarked on creating the 'little Gothic castle' that would
give the emergent building style its name. From this apt and
extraordinary home, Walpole also launched the English Gothic
novel with his *The Castle of Otranto* (1764), which combined
historical settings (it was, after all, named for a mediaeval
architectural style as well as for the German 'Goths') with the
supernatural. It was a genre designed to produce wonder as
well as terror. In Germany itself the contemporary equivalent,
the *Schauerliteratur* or shudder literature, doubled down on the
terror, often dabbling in necromantic fantasy. An example
famous in the history of English literary Romanticism is the
Fantasmagoriana read together by the Byron and Shelley house-
holds at Villa Diodati in the summer of 1816. This collection
of ghost stories, in a French translation by the Romantic geog-
rapher Jean-Baptiste Benoît Eyriès, inspired Byron to propose

the writing competition that led, eventually, to Mary Shelley's *Frankenstein* and John William Polidori's *The Vampyre*.

At the turn of the nineteenth century, the uncanny offered a way to talk about the past. But it was also charged with a sense that the contemporary world might be alive with as-yet-obscure forces. Since the 1780s the Italian anatomist Luigi Galvani, followed by his nephew Giovanni Aldini, had given public demonstrations which seemed to prove that animal and human bodies were powered by electricity and could be brought back to life by an electric current. Now, Alessandro Volta realised that this wasn't the case; the bodies weren't generating electricity. Nevertheless, he named this new field of electrophysiology 'galvanism'; and it too featured in the discussions at Villa Diodati. In the Introduction to her 1831 edition of *Frankenstein*, Mary Shelley records how they debated:

> various philosophical doctrines [. . .] among others the nature of the principle of life, and whether there was any principle of its ever being discovered and communicated [. . .] Perhaps a corpse would be reanimated; galvanism had given token of such things.

In the process of writing her novel, and in the hands of her most famous creation, 'the principle of life' becomes 'the instruments of life'. *Frankenstein* was and remains a lightning rod for anxieties about who would play God if the secret of life were indeed discovered. More than a quarter of a century earlier – and four months after Galvani published his research as *De viribus electricitatis in motu musculari commentarius* – the scientist Joseph Priestley's home and laboratory had been destroyed by a mob in the Birmingham Riots of 1791. The immediate trigger for these three days of violence was Priestley's tactless public celebration of Bastille Day. His subsequent inability to re-establish a life in London, so that in 1794 he sought exile in America, also stemmed from this action, which carried in it a suggestion of treason. But the fanatical tone of the riots make it hard to forget that Priestley was conducting electrical experiments when to do so could readily seem to be meddling with 'the principle of life.'

He was certainly meddling with future ways of living; though that cannot have been so apparent to contemporaries. The unfolding Industrial Revolution was primarily steam-driven, but harnessing electricity would be among the enduring legacies of Romantic science. Alessandro Volta invented the electric battery in 1800. Within a decade Sir Humphry Davy was using it for experiments with electrolysis that added a number of elements to the periodical table. Other devices, which the era initially evolved for popular public demonstration, have since disappeared into discrete specialisation. Today's digital electrometers, for example, bear little resemblance to the version developed by the Alpine geologist and physicist Horace Bénédict de Saussure in 1766, whose fine gold leaves were used to register an electrical charge.

These early electrometers revealed, with delicacy and precision, the slight differences between the electrical charge of different locations. But such delicacy did not make for visually dramatic demonstration: instead, the popularity of electrometry when first discovered had to do with *what* it measured. That a particular place might be especially charged is after all a fundamental religious sense — all those Classical sacred groves and Celtic springs – as much as it is the basis of ghostly superstitions. As I cross the lane and unlatch the gate to St Rumwold's churchyard, I find myself thinking that, when they built on pagan religious sites (I picture those give-away circular graveyards that dot the Welsh Marches) early British Christians surely had in mind not just cultural capital – establishing a strategic continuity between beliefs – but some sense that they might redouble a sacred charge that actually already existed there.

Romney Marsh, too, believes itself to be a special kind of place. Loitering at sea-level, these 260 square kilometres feel remote enough from anywhere else – including from nearby Canterbury and the rest of Kent – to call themselves the Fifth Continent; at least, according to the Revd Richard Barham in 1837, in his pseudonymous *The Ingoldsby Legends*, a popular sensation of the Romantic era. This last, or first, corner of Britain executes a flamboyant turn in the English Channel, from whose choppy waters it wasn't fully reclaimed until the thirteenth century. That sea itself may be scarcely visible, at least until you're actually standing on the foreshore at Dymchurch or Dungeness, but it's present everywhere – threat or promise – in the innings and sewers that crisscross the marshland fields.

And there's the ubiquitous marine light. Even today, when the wide sky is pure silver, light seems to press down on everything with a weight I find almost physical: it's like a kind of eye-strain. Here at St Rumwold's it keeps returning my gaze to the stretched-out horizon. Brightness accumulates – the way a meniscus fattens at the rim of a glass – at that terminal line, which seems to the dazzled eye almost to flex. 'The sky is an immortal tent,' as William Blake says in his epic poem *Milton*:

And on its verge the sun rises and sets, the clouds bow
To meet the flat earth and the sea in such an order'd space:
The starry heavens reach no further, but here bend and set
On all sides, and the two Poles turn on their valves of gold[:]

Blake is making the *echt* Romantic act of faith, using poetry
to crown science transcendent. There *are* no 'valves of gold'
turning the world on its axis, of course, but visionary impulse
leads past the measurable world. No gold here in Bonnington's
modest churchyard, either. The gate is just a wooden wicket,
and the churchyard enclosed – just for now, or so it seems – by
wooden stock fencing. Momentarily, the breeze lifts the dried-
cod odours of salt marsh and dyke.

St Rumwold's was built in the twelfth century, rebuilt in
the fourteenth; but the site itself is thought to predate the
invasion of 1066, which took place only thirty miles along the
coast from here. I like to think that it's haunting the twenty-
first century in infinitely slow motion. Inside, cool white walls
and fourteenth-century trefoil tracery carry windows of clear
glass. There's a pulpit with tester, and the east end is pierced
by a trinity of Norman windows, clenched so tight against the
weather that they almost assume the martial form of lancets. At
the back of the church, below a high, clumsily vernacular gallery, hangs a framed list of vicars dating back to the fourteenth
century. I find my grandfather near the foot of the second
column: *Revd William T. Sampson 1947–1963*. It's very peaceful,
dusty and elegiac to sit for a while in a pew, remembering him
leading a service here.

'Nothing beside remains'. My grandfather was no
Ozymandias, but the Marsh is good at making things

disappear. 'Boundless and bare / The lone and level sands' . . . impoverished, underpopulated, and less than thirty miles from the French coast at Cap Gris-Nez, this is ideal smuggling country. 'Watch the wall, my darling, while the Gentlemen go by!' carolled Rudyard Kipling in 1906, from across the county border at Burwash in Sussex: 'Brandy for the Parson, 'Baccy for the Clerk.' In the following decades, generations of English schoolchildren recited the 'Smuggler's Song' from his *Puck of Pook Hill*, and absorbed the belief that 'the Gentlemen' belong to the picturesque olden days. The impression was only reinforced by Russell Thorndike's seven Doctor Syn novels, published between 1915 and 1944 and recently brought back to life by a Disney re-release, where the old rogue exclaims with a wink and growl, 'Them that asks no questions isn't told a lie.'

Untrue of course. And it wasn't brandy being smuggled by the White Scanner, a small motorboat crammed with eighteen Albanian migrants, when it went down with all hands off Dymchurch on 28 May 2016; nor by the dinghy that capsized in mid-Channel on 24 November 2021, killing thirty people. The high point of contraband smuggling on Romney Marsh, though, did overlap with the Romantic era. It had developed in the 1730s and 1740s under the violently public rule of the Hawkhurst Gang: their village is seven miles this side of Kipling's Burwash. It culminated with another peak in violence in 1826 when the Ransley Gang, also called the Blues, was broken up. They came from Aldington, just a mile or so west of here. St Rumwold's, which stood on their route to the coast, is one of the Marsh churches where they're believed to have stored gear.

I step blinking out of the shelter of the church porch. Vigilante violence, murder, transportation, execution: the stakes were high, and it would have taken more than 'watching the wall' to keep on the right side of real-life smugglers, soldiers and excise men, even in handsome period costume. Yet the Marsh has traditionally contended with a still greater threat than organised crime. The proximity of France also heightens the risk of invasion. Romanticism was the era of Napoleonic anxiety; for a quarter century, the risk that France would invade Britain was real and close at hand. From 1789, Britain's ruling class feared that French revolutionary radicalism would spread across the Channel. But when in 1799 Napoleon engineered the coup that ended with him as First Consul of the new Republic, and in 1804 had himself crowned Emperor, the threat shifted. His international imperial ambitions were as audacious as his domestic arrogation of power. In 1812 he got as far as Moscow, some 2,800 kilometres distant, and more than seven times the distance from Paris as London.

Moscow led famously to rout and a harrowing winter retreat for Napoleonic forces; southward expansion, during which he installed his brother Joseph as King of Spain in 1808, led to the six-year Peninsular War and also ended in defeat. But Bonaparte's earlier, definitive successes in central Europe and Hapsburg Northern Italy had created a personal and geopolitical powerbase. Although overshadowed by the British naval victory at Trafalgar the next day, his 1805 victory at Austerlitz had effectively ended the Holy Roman Empire; while Jena and Auerstedt, just under a year later, subjugated Prussia. Even after his 1814 defeat and the loss of Paris to a coalition which included the British, Napoleon wasn't quite done. Banished

to Elba, he set to work building a personal army, and in
nine months had escaped to France, where he ruled for the
final Hundred Days until Wellington finally defeated him at
Waterloo, in June 1815. He spent his last six years exiled on St
Helena in the middle of the South Atlantic. Only then could the
bad dream of 'Bony', that capering skeleton in knee breeches
who had led Europe in a dance of death, finally end.

Such nightmarish images were the stuff of contemporary
political cartoons. James Gillray had helped shape not only the
genre itself but also the way Britain fantasised about Bonaparte.
For example, in 1805's 'The Plumb-pudding in danger', as the
childishly diminutive Frenchman who vied with British Prime
Minister William Pitt in carving up the world. Strangely,
Gillray died in the month of Napoleon's final defeat – almost
as if his services were no longer needed. But the Channel
remained the gateway to the continent, and all that implied of
difficult foreign affairs. In Kent, the proximity of the European
continent is a continual low rumble, like a bad conscience or
the *mauvaise foi* of jingoism. Low-slung and vulnerable on the
very front line, Romney Marsh has often feared itself to be
not protected so much as merely suspended between opposing
national forces.

In the Second World War, countrymen who remained
working the land in reserved occupations in place of being
called up to fight were recruited into the Auxiliers, who
would have formed the British Resistance. My dad used to
say that, after the war, older men in the village told him
they'd been trained to kill local community leaders in the
case of German invasion, in order to hinder the process of
occupation. I know now that as a vicar his own father would

have been on the list. And as I'm writing this I wonder: is it possible that my dad, whose December birthday kept him out of active service until the very last minute, in fact had this knowledge not from such shadowy 'older men', but from his own training? Would he – could he – ever have been expected to kill his own father?

The Auxiliers were a national force. They trained far from here in the Vale of the White Horse, and implemented national policy. But in the Napoleonic era the threat to Romney Marsh was specific and local. Until 1804, the British defensive plan in the event of invasion was quite simply to inundate the entire Marsh, on the grounds that it might be used by enemy forces as a bridgehead. As I saunter across the concrete road bridge with its cream-livery iron railings, and down onto the levels beyond the church, I feel again how vulnerable and modest this low ground is. Here and there are pylons: over-size and desultory. Hedges line the lane but have been kept low and blocky. Trees standing along them, mostly thorn and oak, have been whipped into fists by the sea wind.

In 1804 field engineers of the Royal Staff Corps, on Romney to make anti-invasion preparations, saw almost the same landscape; soon after arriving Lieutenant-Colonel John Brown was constrained to point out to his superiors in the military establishment – including that ultimate authority the Prime Minister – two major difficulties of defensive flooding. One was that it would take about ten days actually to flood the whole Marsh, giving the enemy plenty of time to redeploy. The other concerned false alarms. Any needless flooding would cause disproportionate damage to morale and infrastructure. Letting farmland and homes be inundated by the sea is very different from simply deploying dams and watercourses. Salt poisons the land for conventional crops. The legacy of marine flooding would be both long lasting and widespread, and it created a real potential for sedition. Romney Marsh prides itself on a rugged independence which it owes partly to proximity to the continent but partly also to the absence, on this relatively recently reclaimed land, of the old feudal reflexes.

Lt-Colonel Brown's suggested alternative, made at a meeting on 26 September 1804 with Prime Minister William Pitt the Younger and the Duke of York, who was Commander-in-Chief of the British forces, was for a kind of giant moat. It would follow the line of the Roman-era coastline where higher ground formed an additional natural defence. Perhaps surprisingly, Pitt and the Duke enthusiastically agreed the scheme and appointed a Scot, John Rennie the Elder, as Consultant Engineer.

Work started just a month later. In the British way, however, it was put out to tender by private contractors:

TO CANAL DIGGERS.

FOR THE DEFENCE OF THE NATION.

WANTED IMMEDIATELY, TWO THOUSAND WORKMEN, TO EXCAVATE A CANAL OF LARGE DIMENSIONS, AND FORM A MILITARY ROAD FROM SHORN-CLIFF ACROSS ROMNEY-LEVEL TO RYE HARBOUR. THE EARTH IS OF THE FINEST QUALITY, AND THE WORK WILL BE LETT *[sic]* IN LENGTHS OF ABOUT A MILE EACH. [. . .] A GOOD PRICE WILL BE GIVEN FOR THE WORK, AND EVERY ENCOURAGEMENT.

As a result, half a year later only six of its twenty-eight miles had been dug. Meanwhile, less than thirty miles away, Napoleon was sabre-rattling. During these months of stalled progress he was busily building up the ominously-named *Armée d'Angleterre*, dug in at Boulogne, from 200,000 towards an eventual 300,500 men. In March 1805 the Franco-Spanish fleet broke out of Toulon where it had been blockaded, making what was meant to be a first move in seizing control of the Channel. Unsurprisingly therefore, in May Pitt intervened in the management of this key defence project, sacking Rennie and his entrepreneurs and bringing the works into public ownership.

The result, completed in April 1809, became the third largest defensive structure in Britain after the antique – and, of course, picturesquely ruined – Hadrian's Wall and Offa's Dyke. The Royal Military Canal runs from Seabrook behind Hythe nearly to Hastings, cutting off the corner of Romney Marsh. As it was excavated, the displaced earth was formed into a parapet to support a canal-side military road. Stretches of this survive as paved laneway and, today, the Canal runs in distinctive kinked stretches across the Kent landscape. The double-bend salient still visible roughly every five hundred yards allowed a defender on the rampart to enfilade the whole of each stretch of water. These salients also acted as a sort of geospatial hinge, allowing engineers slightly to modify the angle into each successive straight so as to accommodate the irregularity of the old coastline.

The Canal was never put to the military test, and today its dimensions – which average five metres across, one and a half deep – seem hardly enough 'For the DEFENCE of the NATION'.

I squint along the near length of ditch and fantasise that I could be across it in three minutes. But I know this is anachronistic. Military engagements in the Romantic era came down to little, besides the cannon, more than men facing each other with muskets. Even in the Second World War, the waterway afforded a defensive line along which to position concrete pillbox blockhouses. It has had other uses too. It was an effective defence in the battle against smuggling, proving just as easy to patrol as it had been designed to be. Easier anyway than the coastline itself, with its dubious creeks and flats, its miles of easy-beaching shingle. The Canal also played such a useful part in the Marsh drainage system that it transformed the health of the district, which until then had been malarial. It was even used, though without great commercial success, for transporting goods. Finally, in 1877, the Crown handed use to the local magistracy, the Lords of the Levels.

I think about this line of water settling into the landscape and becoming local. As boys, my dad and his brother swam here. Days of newts and frogspawn, the shock of cold water, wet dogs galloping up and down the bank. What was the name of the dog my dad had as a kid? I'll find his old sketch and check on the back. *Flossie.* Today each bank's sharp diagonal makes clear that this waterway is regularly dredged and its margins are strimmed and sprayed. But I miss the dock and marsh marigold and pink campion, that untidy and generous variety here in my childhood. And where are the wild ducks, the geese and the gulls?

Poisoned waterways die. To left and right the light lies flat on an unvariegated surface. Between the splayed banks I glimpse cloud drifts of dead pondweed. This is what the fear of flooding looks like. Romney Marsh has been engineered to stay ahead of its water table – just, through constant management. If it seems to float on water, that's because today's green surface is mapped and bisected by an almost impassable maze of dykes and ditches. South and east, as far as Newchurch, St Mary in the Marsh and New Romney, its fields are boxed in by drains, just the way they're boxed up with hedges in other parts of the country.

When groundwaters start to flood they seem like some old cunning rising to the surface: forgotten contours and winterbournes cutting off first one route through the marshland and then another. Romantic engineering overcame such dangerously subversive terrain with new methods of measurement and construction. In 1787 Jesse Ramsden created the Great Theodolite, the first modern version of the instrument, which enabled the Principal Triangulation of Great Britain by the Board of Ordnance between 1791 and 1853, from which the maps of the Ordnance Survey originate. Meanwhile, between 1784 and 1830, a national network of mail coaches, post route and coaching inns sprang up after John Palmer secured prime-ministerial backing for his scheme to award Post Office mail contracts only to express coaches, which changed horses every hour to ensure maximum speeds. In 1816, John Loudon McAdam wrote up the durable crushed-stone macadam surfaces he had devised: they allowed for speedy and smooth progress and were much cheaper than the complex road structures Thomas Telford had been proposing since the turn of the century. McAdam's *Remarks (or Observations) on the Present System of Road Making* (1816) and his *A Practical Essay on the Scientific Repair and*

Preservation of Public Roads (1819) were so influential that by 1823 the first macadam road had already been constructed in North America.

These new roads and railways contracted space; eventually the era even managed to map time, when in 1840 it imposed standardised Railway Time on a shifting time-scape of dawn and dusk, sundials, and church bells. In this period of exponential development, the new mechanical technologies that research devised were swiftly enabled by developments in manufacturing – such as new ways of rolling glass – and so in turn enabled further research, for example through improvements in telescopes and microscopes.

New ways of looking allow for new ways of seeing. The chemist Sir Humphry Davy was one of the leaders of a shift that now occurred in scientific attention. As well as founding the science of electrochemistry, he applied his research in a series of inventions that laid much of the material groundwork of modernity. The Davy lamp radically improved mining safety, his experiments in using laughing gas (nitrous oxide) as anaesthetic helped transform the experience of surgery, and he invented the first arc lamp, precursor of streetlighting around the world. President of the Royal Society from 1820 to 1827, Davy also played a key role in popularising chemistry as a gentleman's hobby, including through public lectures such as those he gave at the Royal Institution in 1802, and through publications including his *Introduction to Chemistry*, which he first produced as an introduction to that series. *A Discourse, Introductory to a Course of Lectures on Chemistry, Delivered in the Theatre of the Royal Institution, on the 21st of January, 1802,* to give its full title, became so widely known, it's perhaps not surprising that it appears among the preparatory works Mary Shelley read while she was writing *Frankenstein*.

Davy's popularising and persuasive summary of the history of scientific thought, and argument for its charms, opens: 'Chemistry is that part of natural philosophy which relates to those intimate actions of bodies upon each other, by which their appearances are altered, and their individuality destroyed.' I'm struck by the resonances of this stress on the 'intimate'. Immediately, it suggests not only the nature of chemical interaction itself, but the key role of close and detailed observation. William Blake's 'Auguries of Innocence', in which you could 'see a World in a Grain of Sand/And [. . .] /Hold Infinity in the palm of your hand', is thought to have been written the year after Davy's *Introduction*.

In 1803 microscopes with newly calibrated lenses, and optics of hitherto undreamt-of precision, might have seemed to both men, following their differing but contemporary paths in two very different parts of London, to make Blake's observable Infinity an empirical as well as a visionary possibility. But the chemist was interested not just in observation but in engagement. His *Introduction* is full of the importance of relationships – between observer and material, or between two or more materials – that are where things take place:

Natural history and chemistry are attached to each other by very intimate ties. For while the first of these sciences treats of the general external properties of bodies, the last unfolds their internal constitution and ascertains their intimate nature. Natural history examines the beings and substances of the external world, chiefly in their permanent and unchanging forms; whereas chemistry by studying them in the laws of their alterations, develops and explains their active powers and the particular exertions of those powers.

Davy draws the strongest of distinctions between empirical involvement and abstract thought, which for him is a retreat from engagement. The gigantism of generalisation loses the detailed attention which is his own art. Chemistry, he argues, 'consists of a number of collections of facts connected together by different relations':

> we can perceive, develop, and even produce, by means of our instruments of experiment, an almost infinite variety of minute phænomena, yet we are incapable of determining the general laws by which they are governed; and in attempting to define them, we are lost in obscure, though sublime imaginations.

It's a truism that abstraction is the enemy of concrete observation, and this morning, turning west along the canal, I'm of the observation party. You could barely describe the opposite bank as a rampart now. Yet there it lies, still legible in the landscape as a slight, broad-shouldered rise that's been left uncultivated. I assume it protects the land immediately to its north from the worst of seasonal flooding. Beyond the fields, at surprisingly regular intervals of roughly one mile each, the small churches of Bonnington, Bilsington, Ruckinge and Hamstreet mark out the old coastline.

I'm walking parallel to this old chain of settlements, and the mnemonic wind of John Davidson's post-Romantic ballad

'In Romney Marsh', written in 1894, seems to lift from the levels as I go:

> As I went down to Dymchurch Wall,
> I heard the South sing o'er the land
> I saw the yellow sunlight fall
> On knolls where Norman churches stand.

At Bilsington, St Peter and St Paul stands not so much on a knoll as on a bluff, snug up against a farm. As at Bonnington, there was a church on this spot in the Doomsday Book. Facing it across the Newchurch Road, the Bilsington Monument is a classical obelisk built from pale dressed blocks of local Kentish ragstone. It's visible for miles, always just there like a mote in the corner of your eye. When I was a child I thought it celebrated Napoleon's defeat. Possibly I even believed it marked the spot of a famous battle – although with another part of my mind I knew perfectly well that, apart from the expeditionary force who landed in Fishguard for three days in February 1797, Britain was never invaded by French revolutionary forces.

In fact the monument wasn't erected till 1835, and it honours an altogether more local Romantic radical, Sir William Cosway. A landowner who understood the consequences of enclosure for rural labouring families, he provided his tenants with housing, livelihoods, and education for their children. Bilsington Monument is also – symbolically? – a lightning rod, and in 1967 it was nearly destroyed by a direct strike.

On the Marsh, even autumn can be muggy. I remember this sticky thunder-air from my childhood. I used to find it so hard to sleep at night that days became blurred, as if the Marsh country was just a dream. My grandfather had retired before I was born, but he stayed on in his parish, among the isolated cottages and farms of Bonnington. Visiting for the holidays, I used to feel we were floating far out from daily life. In this remote place, things that happened seemed always to have been happening: games of catch that went on past bedtime, or tables standing perpetually ready for something on the grass beneath dark trees. Everything appeared infused with a meaning I couldn't quite grasp, like a Ruralist painting from the 1970s by David Inshaw. In his canvasses, as in dreams that are coming loose at the edges, figures balloon and shrink. When I tried to fall asleep in the hot attic at Bonnington, my dreams were interrupted by other dreams, or by hyperreal glimpses of the day just gone – Grandma in the garden, glacé cherries on a trifle, the car moving down a sunny lane – like tiny precursors of migraine.

For you can feel it in your body here, the way the country angles down to meet the continent of which it was till relatively recently a part. Three hundred thousand or so years haven't displaced a climate the Marsh still partly shares with its southern neighbours. Perhaps this explains my grandparents' particular interest in the barometer that hung above the telephone in their hall. But in fact their whole house was an introduction to the restless, ticking world of clockwork and measurement. In the dining room was a grandmother clock, with a sun and moon beautifully painted on its face along with the year it had been made, 1817. Its mahogany case amplified the 'tock-tock' counting off each comfortable, orotund second. The barometer was also a Romantic survival, but more mysterious and not nearly so handsome. Or perhaps I didn't like it so much because I didn't understand it. Mounted on a panel of oak were a palimpsest of glass tube with brackets, a brass plaque whose commentary – 'Low. Chance of showers', 'Very low. Rain forecast' – was engraved in fine copperplate, and at the centre of this apparatus a tiny, almost illegible line of mercury. 'Mercury's falling,' Grandma would say over the breakfast eggs, 'Better take an umbrella': and I expected to see the silver liquid surge, or at least shift before my eyes along the notched ladder of the rubric. It never happened, but every morning I craned at my grandfather's elbow as he tapped the glass 'to settle it'.

We had no barometer at home. In fact we didn't have a clock in the house, apart from our watches and the bedside Westclox alarms. My dad resisted technology, even if it dated from the eighteenth century. Yet at ninety-four he would be amazed and delighted by YouTube footage from a drone circling in the sunshine over St Rumwold's Church. 'Beautiful,' he exclaimed, as the remembered Bonnington landscape came back to life for him in digital colour, like a demonstration that his life there had been real after all. On the night before he was rushed to hospital, he sat in the wingchair by the fire, playing the clip over and over.

Walk 3: St Rumwold's Church Bonnington, Ashford, TN25 7BW, OS reference 51.071999 N, 0.934314 E, west by public footpath along the south bank of the Military Canal to Tar Pot Lane.

Fourth Walk

Eating

Ah, did you once see Shelley plain,
And did he stop and speak to you?

ROBERT BROWNING, 'Memorabilia'

Their letters tell us how, one summer evening in 1847, Robert and Elizabeth Barrett Browning broke their own recently established routine. Since arriving in Florence two months earlier, they'd caught the local habit of sauntering out to buy an ice-cream from the palatial Caffè Doney, just shy of the Santa Trinita Bridge on Via de' Tornabuoni, and viewing the sunset along the Arno. 'We go about, sit on the bridge and see people pass, or take an ice inside Doney's, after the vulgarest fashion,' as Robert put it. But in late June, while (I assume) sunset was staining the city stucco, the way it does every fine evening during the *passeggiata*, the couple instead joined an informal *'sans façon'* soirée in one of the smartest homes in Florence.

Their hosts were Richard Belgrave Hoppner, retired British consul to Venice, and his Swiss wife Marie. As Elizabeth wrote to her sister Arabella next day:

> There was a table cloth on a table, & tea & bread & butter just as if we were on English ground again, and a good deal of talk about poor Shelley & his wife, & how they passed three weeks, with the Hoppners once at Venice, & how on their arrival they ate nothing except water gruel & boiled cabbages & cherries, because it was a principle of Shelley's not to touch animal food, & how Mrs Hoppner did, as she said, 'seduce' him into taking roast beef & puddings . . . 'Dear Mr Shelley, you are so thin.' (Fancy all this said with a pretty foreign accent.) 'Now if you wd take my advice, you would have a very little slice of beef today—You are an Englishman & you ought to like beef—A very little slice of this beef, dear Mr Shelley'—And so, she said, by degrees, he took a little beef & immediately confessed that 'he did feel a great deal better'—'Why of course he did. He was so thin'.

The scene Mrs Hoppner was recalling had taken place almost thirty years earlier, in the autumn of 1818. Yet in the retelling we, and Elizabeth, suddenly 'see Shelley plain', seated at that long gone dinner table: the delicate-looking but attractive young man whose face we know from the famous portrait Amelia Curran would paint a few months later in Rome.

Elizabeth would have been able to picture the same image, albeit passed through an engraver's hands, thanks to its use as a frontispiece to early editions of Shelley's poems. Today,

Curran's original hangs in the National Portrait Gallery, in the room dedicated to paintings of the Romantics. Against pale aquamarine walls the twenty-seven-year old, all doe eyes and curls, looks younger than his actual age. As he poses in his frame, cherub lips parted and ever-so-faintly phallic quill in hand, it's easy to see him as the kind of man women fuss over. That turned-up collar and sweeping, Aussie Rules footballer mullet are perfectly pitched to elicit feminine care and attention. It makes every sense that his wife, though five years his junior, should have called him her 'sweet Elf'.

As he accepts a 'very little slice of this beef', Marie Hoppner's vignette catches what's recognisably the same man, allowing himself – not for the first or last time – to be charmed out of his principles by feminine suggestion. 'Dear Mr Shelley, you are so thin': how this flirtatious challenge, with its teasing reference to the body itself, would have cut through the formal good manners, the splendid silver and glassware, of that Consulate dinner.

More than a hint of such grandeur must still have clung to the Hoppners in retirement. Elizabeth had initially resisted their invitation; she had to be argued into it by Robert. Even at forty-one, she remained unusually shy. But the surprise of her excited letter home – 'You will never guess where I was, last night' – is how much, once she got herself to the salon, the encounter evidently meant to her. She was star-struck, not just at one remove but by her hosts themselves, 'the Hoppners mentioned & written to in Lord Byron's letters & I think Shelley's.'

Perhaps all writers are cannibalistic: 'mature writers steal', as T. S. Eliot would write of the Jacobean dramatist Philip Massinger, in *The Sacred Wood* (1920). At any rate, Elizabeth's reaction is immensely recognisable. What *is* so special about meeting our heroes in person? It's a slightly embarrassing question, one that seems to me to hang around biography, in particular, for all the world like a whiff of body odour. If the Shelleys were already out of reach in the mid-nineteenth century, they're more remote still in the twenty-first, when there's no chance of encountering anyone who met the Brownings in Florence in 1847, leave alone 'saw Shelley plain' in Venice in 1818. Yet we catch the occasional glimpse, even so. There is a spooky recording, for example, of Robert Browning stumbling over the opening lines of his own 'How they Brought the Good News from Aix to Ghent' in 1889, which is like someone coming back to us through time, through the aural storm of crackle and warp.

When the recording was unveiled on the first anniversary of his death, at a meeting of the London Browning Society, the *Times* called it an 'extraordinary séance [. . .] The voice of the dead man was heard speaking. This is the first time that Robert Browning's or any other voice has been heard from beyond the grave.' As Browning raises that voice almost to falsetto to impress it upon Edison's wax cylinder, on a May evening in the last year of his life – a coup organised by Edison's sales manager Colonel Gouraud – we hear in its reediness the actual old man, living with fame through long years of a distinguished widower-hood. As for playing the revenant, in the middle of the twentieth century Browning was apparently still dictating poems down the 'clairaudient' line to one Mary Stephenson Barnes of California. She published *Encore, Browning,* a fifteen-page pamphlet of her 'transcriptions', in 1948.

In the midst of death we are in life. In Somerset this morning

I keep noticing how, even frozen into *nature mort* by a run of below-zero November nights, food defines the countryside. Late crab apples, and the leaves of coppiced hazels, hang damply in hedges. Tractors are harvesting potatoes and beet beside the river. At the turn of the nineteenth century, even a confirmed city-dweller like William Blake understood this. Blake knew where his food came from. Born and raised in Soho, he was a Londoner for most of his life. Nevertheless, food and its origins were simply part of the furniture of his thought. In his *Proverbs of Hell*, for example, 'The rat, the mouse, the fox, the rabbit watch the roots; the lion, the tiger, the horse, the elephant watch the fruits.'

At the other end of the Romantic social scale, Lord Byron probably didn't know how to boil an egg. But he must almost certainly have come across laying birds among the more glamorous creatures that at various times made up his menagerie: the bear, the half wolf-half dog Lyon, the hounds, horses, monkeys, cats, fox, geese, peacocks, guinea hens, crane, eagle, crow and falcon that he and his friends wrote about – not to mention whatever other roaring, squeaking or twittering has been lost from the record. He clearly found animals a delight; even though conceivably, and as with his women, he sometimes forgot to ask himself whether they were equally happy with the way he kept them. And he seems to have been no fan of eating these pets. His geese, for example, acquired on literally a passing whim – the scene a roadside in 1822, *en route* from Genoa to Pisa – were rescued from becoming roast dinners not just at the moment of purchase but for the rest of their lives. They lived on after his death to become a full-fledged administrative nuisance, enduring tokens of aristocratic whim.

Still, it can't have helped more delicate stomachs that, in the era, meat's identity with living beings was so crudely apparent close to the moment of ingestion. Eighteenth- and nineteenth-century butchery meant the naked animal stripped and displayed as a carcass; the purchase of body parts without any of the euphemisms of packaging. In Charles Dickens's *Oliver Twist* (1838), London's Smithfield market makes this hellishly proximate:

> It was market morning. The ground was covered nearly ankle deep with filth and mire; and a thick steam perpetually rising from the reeking bodies of the cattle, and mingling with the fog, which seemed to rest upon the chimney tops, hung heavily above. All the pens in the centre of the large area, and as many temporary pens as could be crowded into the vacant space, were filled with sheep; tied up to posts by the gutter side were long lines of beasts and oxen, three or four deep.

Sold on the twig, in pod, or bunched with leaves, fruit and vegetables too displayed the connection with their origins in fields and orchards: locales that were familiar even to town dwellers in an era when the urban remained porous, and city streets opened into rural margins. Mud and cold permeated the early nineteenth-century city, traces for many of a country life they had only recently left, under duress from Enclosures and the need to find work in the new industries. Just as in the favelas of the developing world today, this shift from rural abjection to an urban existence, in which happenstance could exist only within extreme poverty, would have entailed ambivalence and regret, those mnemonic emotions.

After all, even the odour of frost can be evocative. Today's chill dawn, coming in misty after a clear night, outlines every detail in forensic white, as if on the trail of crime. As we pass through Nether Stowey, frost sharpens up kerbstones along the little stream that tracks the pavement. In gardens beyond the village centre, it stiffens and polishes the low-slung bean rows, sprout stems caught on a tilt. We ate breakfast at home in the ghostly predawn, and we seem to have been driving for hours, far out from the known. But now, according to the satnav, we're about to arrive at Great Wood, in the Quantock Hills of west Somerset.

Between 1796 and 1798 the Wordsworth siblings and Samuel Taylor Coleridge often walked here, with visitors who included Charles Lamb and William Hazlitt. Two centuries on, National Forest status means whole stretches of its treescape remain pretty much un-tinkered-with; an eighteenth-century landscape. As we climb the Quantock scarp, foggy Adscombe Lane closes round us with its All Souls atmosphere. Low gear. At Over Stowey I open my window to let the windscreen clear. The draught is a shock of chill damp. Under the surrounding trees everything appears indeterminate; smudged like the start of a story before you know where it's taking you. There's a burnt, school-morning smell of freeze. Suddenly, with the immediacy of childhood, this trips a memory: my old fascination with the Charlotte Moberly–Eleanor Jourdain incident. I recall the entire story; how, one afternoon in summer 1901, two Edwardian educationalists, the distinguished Principal and Vice-Principal of St Hugh's College Oxford, stumbled upon ghosts of the Romantic-era court of Marie-Antoinette, *les fantômes du Trianon*, in the grounds of Versailles. Or at least, so they came retrospectively to believe. A decade later, as Elizabeth Morison and Frances Lamont, they published their account of *An Adventure* (1911) and became, pseudonymously, a *cause célèbre*. In the cold morning car, I think with envy of them walking the famous park as it shimmered in summer heat.

Surely they were as full of unacknowledged sensibilities as the Englishwomen in an E. M. Forster novel – Lucy Honeychurch, Adela Quested. As I ease onto packed red earth in the Forest Enterprise carpark, I feel again the jubilantly shivery sense I had, as a child, of the vast presence of Versailles's 800 hectares waiting at the back of their experience. How it infuses their story with an hallucinatory quality, the out-of-time sense of summer afternoons when everything takes on new, deeply shadowed significance. I choose a parking spot under a silver birch that seems, alone among the surrounding trees, to be shivering mildly to itself. If the explanation – first mooted in Philippe Jullian's biography of the decadent poet and Versailles resident Robert de Montesquiou – that Moberly and Jourdain had stumbled on a fancy-dress house-party is true, perhaps some thundery feeling of the uncanny was what stopped them from recognising the fact. This morning, for the first time, their experience strikes me as not simply *unheimlich* but specifically Romantic in the way they trusted to sensibility, placing their feelings and reactions ahead of their education.

We open the car doors with relief. Supernatural possibility is a Romantic trope; and its association with rural forays no coincidence. You must leave the cosy and familiar behind, after all, if you want to seek out gothic thrills in the 'many a listening chamber, cave, and ruin,/And starlight wood' of Percy Bysshe Shelley's 'Hymn to Intellectual Beauty'. But the stillness we step out into makes me shiver again. At this time of day the forestry carpark remains almost empty, and there's a floating sense of unreality in the clearing. A clouded, late-autumn sky flattens the colours of the trees.

In 1814 Percy Bysshe borrowed his lover Mary's journal to record nights of ghostly storytelling. On 7 October, 'Our conversation, though intentionally directed towards other topics, irresistibly recurred to these. Our candles burned low, we feared they would not last until daylight.' As for his partner in ghostly crime, soon to rename herself Claire Clairmont:

> her countenance was distorted most unnaturally by horrible dismay – it beamed with a whiteness that seemed almost like light; her lips and cheeks were of one deadly hue; the skin of her face and forehead was drawn into [. . .] the lineaments of terror that could be contained; her hair came prominent and erect; her eyes were wide and staring[.]

Two years later, on a summer night above Lake Geneva, Shelley would outdo himself. One June evening, a group of friends who had gathered at Lord Byron's rented villa 'really began to talk ghostly' after midnight. It was one of the famous sessions at Villa Diodati that would eventually lead to the composition of both Mary Shelley's *Frankenstein* and *The Vampyre* – whose author, the young doctor John William Polidori, records what happened next: 'L[ord] B[yron] repeated some verse of Coleridge's 'Christabel' [. . .] and Shelley, suddenly shrieking and putting his hands to his head, ran out of the room with a candle. Threw water in his face, and after gave him ether.' When he came round, Percy Bysshe claimed he had hallucinated that Mary's nipples were eyes: an image borrowed, whether or not consciously, from an early draft of Coleridge's poem itself.

Which seems somewhat worked up. At any rate, it probably reveals more about the man himself than about the supernatural realm. Under stress Shelley habitually hallucinated, suffered night terrors, sleepwalked. In the frenzied last weeks of his life in summer 1822, living in a half-converted former monastery built out over the sea at San Terenzo, near La Spezia, he suffered such graphic nightmares about drowning that it's tempting to call them premonitions. Sleepwalking and screaming, on 22 June he saw the Shelleys' housemates, his lover Jane Williams and her common law husband Edward, 'in the most horrible condition, their bodies lacerated – their bones starting through their skin, faces pale yet stained with blood.' The spectral Edward – the man he was cuckolding, and with whom he would in fact drown just over a fortnight later, on 8 July – commanded, 'Get up, Shelley, the sea is flooding the house & it is all coming down.'

Fear death by drowning. We lace on our waterproof boots, turn up our collars against the November damp. There's also, of course, the question of Shelley's own 'ghostly' posthumous existence. In 1847, the proxy immediacy of Mrs Hoppner's story clearly stirred both the Brownings. Two years later, Robert in low mood 'seemed to have a fancy for Spezzia and the sea' and the couple even explored the possibility of renting near Shelley's last home, where they 'never saw the olive grow so magnificently like a forest tree as in this country, nor the vines so luxuriant,' but 'found the prices *enormous*.' It's possible, however, that Robert had been less charmed than his wife by ebullient, come-as-you-are Marie. At least, so his much-quoted poem 'Memorabilia' seems to suggest: although he never publicly attributed its genesis to her.

'Memorabilia' was first published in *Men and Women* in 1855, seven years after that Florentine soiree:

> Ah, did you once see Shelley plain,
> And did he stop and speak to you?
> And did you speak to him again?
> How strange it seems, and new!

This opening stanza is a bold invocation to resurrection, summoning the drowned Shelley back 'strange [. . .] and new' from his 'sea-change', in the cognate words of Ariel's Song from *The Tempest*. As Browning knew, those are the lines carved on Shelley's gravestone in the Protestant Cemetery in Rome: 'Nothing of him that doth fade,/But does suffer a sea-change/Into something rich and strange.'

Indeed the whole of this apparently simple four-stanza lyric is brought to life by thrilling traces of the supernatural. We almost hear Mrs Hoppner's laughter echoing in the background of the second stanza, as if in ghostly protest:

> But you were living before that,
> And you are living after,
> And the memory I started at—
> My starting moves your laughter!

If the second half of the poem appears to walk away from this encounter, it walks the trope home again through metaphor:

I crossed a moor, with a name of its own
And a certain use in the world no doubt,
Yet a hand's-breadth of it shines alone
'Mid the blank miles round about:

For there I picked up on the heather
And there I put inside my breast
A moulted feather, an eagle-feather—
Well, I forget the rest.

'I forget the rest': the strikingly dismissive line with which the poem ends returns to that secondary ghost, the mutual interlocutor, whose 'living before . . . living after' is nothing but 'blank'.

Ever since I first heard it, I've thought it odd how this poem turns on itself with a kind of rancour. Over his shoulder P, who's got hold of both dogs and is preceding me up the forestry track, agrees. Browning's interlocutor has 'a name of [their] own/And a certain use in the world no doubt,' yet remains unseen and unnamed – why? Is their ghostly laughter remembered *as mockery*? Did Robert Browning, at 34 arguably less handsome, less of an aristocrat and, in particular, less poetically distinguished than the Shelley of 1818, feel slighted in comparison with his precursor? Notice perhaps that *he* was not being flirted with and helped to extra beef, or indeed extra attention of any kind? Jealous, even, of that poetic ghost? Is it in fact Robert who feels blanked out in that moment in the poem?

Or does 'Memorabilia' simply pivot on the dismissive belief that a mere literary 'civilian' is unworthy of a poetic great? The Brownings kept faith with the idea of a poet's life as a kind of empyrean soaring, from which an anecdote like Marie Hoppner's could count as nothing more than 'a moulted feather'; and on the evening when they 'picked up' her story, their own upward trajectory must have seemed to echo the Shelleys' own. After all, they too were poets building a new life, on their own terms, in Italian exile.

In that case, 'Memorabilia' would make a statement of poetic identification by Browning with Shelley that crosses through – and seems to *cross out* – their mutual interlocutor. It reminds me of Marina Tsvetaeva's 'An Attempt at Jealousy' ('*Popytka revnosti*'), written in 1924 and addressed to a lover who had left the poet for an 'ordinary woman'. A lifetime after Browning's shining eagle, and a whole century after the Russian Romantics – Alexander Pushkin, Mikhail Lermontov – the idea of poetic gift as 'godhead', 'magic' or 'sixth sense' still had traction in the national tradition in which she wrote:

> How is your life with an ordinary
>   woman without godhead?
> [. . .]
> More to your taste, more delicious
>   is it, your food?
> [. . .]
>   Now you are grown cold to magic,
> how is your life with an
>   earthly woman, without a sixth sense?

In Elaine Feinstein's English here, Tsvetaeva is coruscatingly dismissive of her 'earthly' rival. And this sexual, domestic rivalry brings us back to food, that intimate imperative. It stands as both practical domesticity and symbolic, even super-natural, succour.

The same bifurcated symbolism is at the heart of the Christian traditions by which both Tsvetaeva and Browning were formed, and which infused the Romantic era. The 'staff of life' of the Old Testament Book of Isaiah becomes in the New Testament the broken bread – the sacrificed Christ – of Last Supper and Mass. Food and death. Food *as* death, in the sacrificed body of the saving Mass; and every bit as much in the peripheral folk practices that have grown up everywhere like half-digested understanding around it: Yorkshire sin eaters and their little cakes, sugar skeletons on 2 November for the Mexican Day of the Dead. Communion was the part of Anglican orthodoxy my father, and *his* clergyman father, most tried to avoid; perhaps because of its literal viscerality.

Yet guilt and pleasure speak to each other far beyond the Christian tradition, as Sigmund Freud was not the first to point out. In their continuing, universal conversation we can glimpse an origin story for the twenty-first-century West's alienation from food, which it seems increasingly to treat as mere enter-tainment or commodity.

The dogs are on the scent of game birds in the underbrush: an appetite for sport, or real hunger? Because of our depend-ence upon it, food must always be both an issue of trust – how clean *is* the takeaway kitchen? – and a form of giving. Its rela-tionship with death surely arises from this animal vulnerability of ours: in the ecclesiastical year All Hallows, with its mourn-ing and its ancestor worship, follows on the heels of Harvest Festival, that annual celebration of food. Christian culture internalises the notion that offering the means of subsistence is at least partly transcendent, a gift is both unconditional *and* conditional. The Lord's Prayer makes the link explicit: 'Give us this day our daily bread, and forgive us our trespasses'.

In school, we sang:

> We plough the fields and scatter
> The good seed on the land
> But it is fed and watered
> By God's almighty hand.

And every year I was puzzled anew. The adults around us sang, 'All good gifts around us/Are sent from heaven above,' among stacks of baked beans tins and surplus pumpkins that we'd *seen* them bring in and arrange. Above their heads the high Victorian windows revealed clouds swarming and bumping, an active reminder of the countryside itself waiting outside.

But then, 'We plough the fields and scatter' wasn't written as a hymn. It first arrived in English in 1862, translated by a London vicar's daughter called Jane Montgomery Campbell. Its original is a Romantic poem, *'Wir pflügen und wir streuen'*, composed by Matthias Claudius in 1782. He was then in his forties, and serious illness had precipitated his return to the faith in which he was raised. But like other young intellectuals of his day (he was born in 1740) he had been an atheist in his twenties: Christianity, after all, presented an important target to Romantics. Claudius was already a well-known poet and editor when he wrote *'Wir pflügen und wir streuen'*, but it would be another quarter century before a composer two Romantic generations his junior, Franz Schubert, made his 'Death and the Maiden' into an enduring Romantic landmark. Schubert first set '*Der Tod und das Mädchen*' in 1817 as the early *lied* D.531. In 1824, when he already knew he was dying, he took the theme of that *lied* up again for the variations that form the second movement of his String Quartet number 14 in D minor D.810. Here the chordal song becomes a lamenting *passacaglia* over which the first violin, miming the 'maiden', works variations of astonishing, yet never quite transcendent, delicacy.

There's a pheasant tailfeather by the path. Damp has turned its colours smoky. I pick it up quickly, before the dogs get to it. Not 'an eagle-feather' but handsome all the same, this skinny, tobacco-coloured quill that's almost as long as my arm, shoulder to wrist, yet no wider than my finger at the top. I twirl it between thumb and forefinger. Perpendicular from the rachis, at roughly centimetre intervals as if along a primitive measuring rule, go wobbly black bars set in what seem like gold-luminous highlights, but which close up are simply the absence of panels of speckle. Twirl again and the speckles darken, the whole reverse a darker brown. Even at the purplish fringe, its tongue-and-groove barbs mostly still zip together, sign that it was likely shed, not lost in some fierce territorial duel.

There are plenty of pheasants in the brakes along Quantock Combe this morning. As the dogs sniff them out, they explode from their forms in the long grass and bracken, crackling away. Tamed by hand-rearing and daily feeds, they're easily spotted, even by the human eye – not really 'sport' at all. A decade ago when we lived next door to Johnny, a gamekeeper, we ate pheasant every week in winter. While the Rayburn roared companionably, we worked our way through those chewy Sunday roasts, picking fluff and shot from between our teeth. Their dark gaminess seemed to me to say that the birds we were consuming had lived well and freely. Now I'm not so sure. Brilliant red masks bob above outsize bodies that labour in flight; they can hardly make their bodies *go*. As they fuss between the bracken ahead of us, the urgent nod they give with every step seems less comic than a gesture of frustration, like a toddler rocking her carry seat to make the car speed up.

Until we moved to live in the middle of a keepered shoot, I didn't truly associate *Phasianus colchicus* with the living landscape, nor even with the countries where it's indigenous: Asia, the Balkans, Georgia — which the Romans called Colchis and from where the bird gets its name — but with that historical elsewhere, eighteenth- and nineteenth-century cuisine. 'Pheasant' was a food rather than a creature; it belonged on the pages of historical novels along with port, stilton and, in that plausible phrase of the eighteenth-century satirist Henry Fielding, 'The Roast Beef of Old England'.

As the 1743 etching by Jonathan Wild reveals, by his late thirties Fielding was already the Brobdingnagian bon vivant who would die of gout and cirrhosis at 48. Perhaps it's not surprising then, that according to his popular theatrical singalong:

When mighty Roast Beef was the Englishman's food,
It ennobled our veins and enriched our blood.
Our soldiers were brave and our courtiers were good
Oh! the Roast Beef of old England,
And old English Roast Beef!

But since we have learnt from all-vapouring France
To eat their *ragouts* as well as to dance,

We're fed up with nothing but vain complaisance
Oh! the Roast Beef of Old England,
And old English Roast Beef!

This helping of Little-Englanding combines nostalgia for a hearty, and fictional, 'yeoman' past with insistence that international cultural or even diplomatic negotiation, 'vain complaisance', is somehow wrong. But its cultural history is as inaccurate as its sentiments were dangerous. Britain has a long and famously enthusiastic relationship with both stews ('ragouts') and 'all-vapouring' steamed food. Suet, a seventeenth-century culinary innovation, was already a favourite in Fielding's own era, which crowned Plum Duff first among equals in the great repertoire of British steamed puddings.

I feel hungry at the thought. But we've a distance still to walk, and now we come across parked-up cherry pickers and lorries, spectral in mist. Trees are being cleared to stamp out ash die-back disease, part of the mortal collapse of so many species from wilt and gall, canker and processionary moth, blight and dieback and the acute declines of stress. We've already passed several areas where woodland must have been felled just this year. The last autumn streaks of green – fireweed, bramble – show where regrowth has already occurred, and slopes are staked out with those serious, if ugly, white cylinders that protect replacement slips. Woodlands, as the Estonian poet Jaan Kaplinski said of life, are 'a constant work of repair.'

Two generations after Fielding's literary gourmandising, when Coleridge and Wordsworth were walking here in Great Wood, Mary Shelley's own parents were among the many British writers and intellectuals who discovered a sympathy with revolutionary, 'all-vapouring France'. In 1794, four years after publishing the first printed riposte to Edmund Burke's influential, conservative *Reflections on the Revolution in France*, her mother Mary Wollstonecraft was actually living in revolutionary France when she gave birth to Mary's elder half-sister, Fanny. Her father William Godwin's *An Enquiry Concerning Political Justice* (1793) and *Caleb Williams* (1794) inspired the next generation of radicals, including the young Percy Bysshe Shelley. Before either Mary or her future husband were even aware of the world around them, Godwin and Wollstonecraft were leaders of an emerging radical, antimonarchist feeling — or, as conservative and Establishment opponents saw it, political subversion and treason — that successive British governments struggled to control. It was a struggle that would culminate for the young Shelley couple in 1817, when Westminster returned, after a gap of eighteen years, to a favoured legislative technique of earlier times, suspending Habeas Corpus and the right to a fair trial. The following spring the couple emigrated to political safety in Italy — where later the same summer they would pass into the freeze-frame of Mrs Hoppner's Venetian anecdote.

At Seven Wells Wood, logging trucks have zipped maroon S-bends up and down the slopes on either side of the valley, but we're following a grassy trail just wide enough for a quad bike. When we come out between pale, contorted trunks of indigenous oak, lichen and sunlight create an alternating, piebald effect that's almost dizzying. It's like the zipcords of morning light between curtains or through blinds when you have a hangover. Had Henry Fielding lived another half century, he might have felt his prejudices vindicated by the Shelleys' 'vapouring' food choices, which excluded not only roast beef but all meat and fish, dairy, and fermented drinks of any kind. In this the old satirist would have found common cause with Lord Byron, who maintained that the family diet risked the health of the Shelley children. Whether or not it was responsible – perhaps weakening mother and infant – their daughter, twelve-month old Clara, had indeed fallen ill with what was originally a teething fever, developed dysentery and died just days before Percy's flirtatious exchange over the roast beef. This tragic reason for the family's presence at the consulate has vanished from Mrs Hoppner's story, at least as recounted by Elizabeth Barrett Browning.

Admittedly, Byron was scarcely disinterested. He was making his argument against the Shelleys' vegetarianism in the context of securing custody of his own daughter Allegra from their household, where her mother Claire Clairmont was ensconced. But whatever the causes of Clara Shelley's death, he may well have been right. Much nineteenth-century vegetarianism was every bit as restricted, and nutritionally under-informed, as the 'water gruel, boiled cabbages & cherries' of Marie Hoppner's recollection. Percy Bysshe's argument for this diet, which he had published in 1813 in the Notes to his 'Philosophical Poem' *Queen Mab*, is quite evidently based on philosophical principles rather than empirical observation. The tone of the Notes, which he republished in 1813 as a freestanding polemic, *A Vindication of Natural Diet*, ranges from a secular pulpit rhetoric to crank cure advocacy:

There is no disease, bodily or mental, which adoption of vegetable diet and pure water has not infallibly mitigated [. . .] Hopes are entertained that, in April, 1814, a statement will be given that sixty persons, all having lived more than three years on vegetables and pure water, are then *in perfect health*. More than two years have now elapsed; *not one of them has died*.

We associate vegetarianism with health: but not like this. Twenty-first-century vegetarian diets are backed by science (in the west) or long tradition (elsewhere); western vegetarianism, enriched by world foods perennially in season, runs the gamut of those seasonal proteins, nuts and legumes. A gamut of flavours, too. In 1813 even Shelley seems to realise the problem of tastiness forces him onto the back foot:

The pleasures of taste to be derived from a dinner of potatoes, beans, peas, turnips, lettuces, with a dessert of apples, gooseberries, strawberries, currants, raspberries, and in winter, oranges, apples and pears, is far greater than supposed.

'Greater than supposed' doesn't exactly have the ring of conviction. But much more problematically, the young aristocrat clearly has no idea that turnips and lettuces, apples and strawberries, simply aren't in season at the same time as each other. The disengagement from food itself is fundamental – is fundamentalist.

I think about last night's supper. How we piled onions, seethed to orange with olive oil, lemon juice, sumac and za'atar, onto baked aubergines. The way the skins shone, vulgar and tasty as wet-look plastic: food is life. The kitchen was full of smells and colours, light pooling between roof beams.

Bananas and avocados, pears, garlic and red onions tumbled voluptuously together in the bowl on the table beside us – not *nature mort,* but nature alive. Read with a full stomach, Shelley's disgust at what he calls 'unnatural appetites' for 'animal food and spirituous liquors' seems like trouble with food itself. He condemns cooking food as 'an expedient for screening from [our] disgust the horrors of the shambles.' Apparently, since we stopped eating everything raw:

> Man, and the animals whom he has infected with his society, or depraved by his dominion, are alone diseased. The wild hog, the mouflon, the bison, and the wolf, are perfectly exempt from malady, and invariably die either from external violence or natural old age [. . .] The super-eminence of man is like Satan's, a super-eminence of pain, and the majority of his species [is] doomed to penury, disease, and crime.

This vocabulary of disgusted condemnation – *infected*, *depraved*, *diseased* – is more familiar in the context of sexuality than at the dining table. Was this really what the handsome young poet was thinking about as he flirted between the cut glass and gleaming cruet sets at the Venetian consulate?

In the five years since he had published these views, Shelley had not become renowned for sexual continence. He had however managed successfully to restrict the intakes of the women in his entourage – both his wives, Harriet and Mary, as well as Claire Clairmont – even when they were pregnant or nursing. Whenever I return to this story I ask myself: was Mary Shelley also offered 'a very little slice of beef'? Did her need cross Marie Hoppner's mind? Or, as she mourned the death of her baby girl, was Mary absent from the feast both symbolically and in person? Did that absence occur, either, to the woman who was as it were sitting in her place three decades later, as a recipient of the Hoppners' hospitality; a woman who had lost her own first child to miscarriage just two months earlier? As a teenager, Elizabeth Barrett Browning had been such an admirer of another *Vindication*, 'Mrs Wolstonecraft's system', that her mother had warned her off developing the '*singleness of will &c*' that might leave her an 'old maid'. Freshly married, did she remember *The Rights of Woman* that Mary Shelley's mother had framed?

I've never had much truck with dieting myself, presumably because I turned out to be a skinny kid. But this morning, rinsed by tiredness and with coffee still thrumming in my ears, I'm feeling almost as attenuated as the November daylight we're walking through. Percy's disgust makes me think again about food's double function in the imagination as something both practical and symbolic and, whether offered or withheld, always controlled. His food fetishes may not quite have been anorexia by proxy, but they don't seem far removed from it. They parallel the calorie restricted diets some now believe increase longevity; yet Shelley's rhetoric seems to face not towards a future stretching ahead, but backwards to a lost Edenic purity – an Eden that, as a declared atheist, he did not believe in, yet reproduces in pseudo-scientific form:

I hold that the depravity of the physical and moral nature of man originated in his unnatural habits of life. The origin of man, like that of the universe of which he is a part, is enveloped in impenetrable mystery. His generations either had a beginning, or they had not [. . .] The language spoken, however, by the mythology of nearly all religions seems to prove, that at some distant period man forsook the path of nature, and sacrificed the purity and happiness of his being to unnatural appetites.

To conflate spiritual purity with bodily health like this is indeed to echo repressive responses to sexuality as a site of desire and disease. 'O Rose thou art sick,' William Blake had written in *Songs of Experience,* which he published in 1794. 'The Sick Rose' is a lyric – or an anti-lyric – that evokes entropy and decadence. It also reads precisely as a hymn of horror at sexually transmitted disease. At a woman's genitalia:

> The invisible worm
> [. . .]
> Has found out thy bed
> Of crimson joy:
> And his dark secret love
> Does thy life destroy.

Both Blake and Shelley lived at a time when syphilis was untreatable and fatal, as of course were many diseases that had not been sexually transmitted. Shelley's disgusted desire to shed 'morbid action in the animal system' and return to a vegetarian state of nature, 'a continued pleasure, such as we now feel it in some few and favoured moments of our youth' resembles a kind of magical warding off of sickness and danger – Suddenly, a buzzard we must have surprised at its kill flaps rustling up from between gorse bushes right in front of us – Shelley's diet also reads backwards, I realise, as a secular expression of older Christian traditions of self-mortification, those desperate attempts at self-purification though which believers tried to escape from their Original Sin, the rotten-ness of embodiment.

It reads forwards, too, to today's self-sculpting weight-loss diets, or purging. In that phrase, 'few and favoured moments of our youth,' we glimpse this married adult as the 'Elf' who is 'so thin' that he seems to be warding off adulthood; rather like an adolescent whose self-starvation expresses terror of growing up. Of course, the idea that Shelley was a 'Peter Pan' doing badly with practical and moral responsibility, is noth-ing new. By the time of the Hoppners' dinner, he had wed his second wife after the convenient suicide of the first. He has also just been arguably implicated in the death of his own infant daughter, whose rushed and exhausting trip across Italy he had forced, despite the little girl's illness, in order for her mother to chaperone and protect his relationship with Claire Clairmont. However he formulated these events to himself, by 1818 it was also undeniable that he had missed some of the coming-of-age milestones customary for his time and class. Having been sent down, he never graduated from Oxford. Nor (though this was hardly his fault) did he come into his inher-itance. His violently disapproving father, Sir Timothy Shelley, would long outlive him.

'The proselyte to a pure diet must be warned to expect some temporary diminution of muscular strength. [. . .] But it is [. . .] succeeded by an equable capability for exertion.' If a hos-tile father – who once even threatened to commit his schoolboy son to an asylum, and now keeps him on an unusually tight financial rein – represents mature masculinity, mightn't the son reject signs of such maturity in his own body? Reading the passages in the *Vindication* which seem to struggle with adult male physicality, calling 'the premature arrival of puberty' a 'mental and bodily derangement,' I don't only wonder what they mean by 'premature.' I can't forget that their author was locked in an Oedipal financial struggle which involved literally being able to put food on the table.

This morning there's a hungry, hyperreal quality to the views we glimpse between the Great Wood trees. The light still hasn't fully resolved itself. Theatrical firs mass on the higher slopes. Below, an untidy pencilling of weeds gives way to birch, blackthorn, shrubby new planting. We catch sight of the grid of fields and hedges riding the red Quantock flanks: the Agricultural Revolution's great eighteenth-century mapping of agricultural will onto the landscape still being iterated today. It's a mnemonic for how fundamentally the Shelley family depended upon landowning wealth. A generation later, Elizabeth Barrett Browning had also grown up on a country estate with its own Home Farm, 'cottages' and 'Timber'.

For county gentry like the Barretts of Hope End, the Agricultural Revolution that, during the Romantic era, 'tied up [fields] with hedges, nosegay-like,' as she would put it in *Aurora Leigh*, substantially increased their income from farming yields. Yet little changed at their actual dining tables, where roast beef – and pheasant – remained staples of a long slumberous continuity, as in some conservative postprandial dream. Both the Shelleys and the Brownings pushed back against the fantasy of social timelessness that dinners of this sort rehearsed daily, using food as one way to differentiate themselves from the familial conventions they rejected. For the Brownings, though, such differentiation wasn't about a vegetarian rationing, but about adventures in sensuous pleasure. It wasn't just those ice-creams by the Arno. The Mediterranean diet was full of possibilities. In a letter she sent eight months before her evening with the Hoppners, Elizabeth contrasts the 'Herefordshire cold' of her upbringing with her new home in Pisa, where:

> Everyday I am out walking while the golden oranges look at me over the walls, .. & when I am tired R. & I sit down on a stone to watch the lizards. [. . .] We have our dinners from the Trattoria at two oclock, & can dine our favorite way on thrushes & Chianti with a miraculous cheapness—& no trouble, no cook, no kitchen . . . the prophet Elijah <or the lilies of the field> took as little thought for their dining— which exactly suits us—It is a continental fashion, which we never cease commending. Then at six we have coffee & rolls of milk— made of milk, I mean: & at nine, our supper (call it supper, if you please) of roast chesnuts & grapes—So you see how primitive we are, & how I forget to praise the eggs at breakfast.

Admittedly, there's something a little childish about this. Newly arrived in Italy, she's boasting to an old friend still living in Herefordshire, her former neighbour Julia Martin. And I suspect that the newly-weds didn't dine on those flagrantly luxurious, definitively un-British 'thrushes & Chianti' every night. All the same, colour and flavour were flooding into a life that had been restricted for many years: even the childishness of this boast is part of the Brownings' great adventure into the unknown and the possible, a world of new behaviours in which unfamiliar foods are both symbol and experience.

We're coming to the end of Rams Combe. We've been walking downhill for a while, and the air's warming. The dogs have calmed now there are no more birds to flush out, and they trot ahead of us with tails high. As he sold his pheasants over the fence to us, Johnny used to grumble, 'I hope you're not going to cook any foreign muck.' By which he meant in part, *I hate the smell of garlic*. Half a century earlier, before Elizabeth's letter to Julia, Mary Wollstonecraft's *Letters Written in Sweden, Norway, and Denmark* (1796) records the Scandinavian trip she made the year before from a more cosmopolitan perspective. Time in France had evidently introduced her to the pleasures of the table. She takes apart Gothenburg cuisine:

Their tables [seem] a caricature of the French. [. . .] Spices and sugar are put into everything, even into the bread; and the only way I can account for their partiality to high-seasoned dishes is the constant use of salted provisions. Necessity obliges them to lay up a store of dried fish and salted meat for the winter; and in summer, fresh meat and fish taste insipid after them. To which may be added the constant use of spirits. Every day, before dinner and supper, even whilst the dishes are cooling on the table, men and women repair to a side-table; and to obtain an appetite eat bread-and-butter, cheese, raw salmon, or anchovies, drinking a glass of brandy. Salt fish or meat then immediately follows, to give a further whet to the stomach [. . .] then a succession of fish, flesh, and fowl for two hours, during which time the dessert – I was sorry for the strawberries and cream – rests on the table to be impregnated by the fumes of the viands. Coffee immediately follows in the drawing-room, but does not preclude punch, ale, tea and cakes, raw salmon, &c.

That such a radical thinker should burst out in food snobbery is a joy. The approach also resembles a very modern kind of anthropology: as she observes Scandinavian eating habits, Wollstonecraft locates her own self – whether as hungry traveller, sufferer from indigestion, or simple passer-by – in relation to them. Travelling further, north of Gothenburg, she mixes fashionable observations of the picturesque with a pragmatic, socio-political alertness that's clearly her own:

The rocks which tossed their fantastic heads so high were often covered with pines and firs, varied in the most picturesque manner. Little woods filled up the recesses when forests did not darken the scene, and valleys and glens, cleared of the trees, displayed a dazzling verdure which contrasted with the gloom of the shading pines. The eye stole into many a covert where tranquillity seemed to have taken up her abode, and the number of little lakes that continually presented themselves added to the peaceful composure of the scenery [. . .] The farms are small [. . .] No gardens smiled round the habitations, not a potato or cabbage to eat with the fish drying on a stick near the door. A little grain here and there appeared, the long stalks of which you might almost reckon.

As if paralleling this passage, we too have reached pasture-land beyond the 'shading pines' of Great Wood, and now the path is tilting us down, and down again, to Crowcombe Park Gate at the bottom of a long, dry valley. On the other side of the lane parkland trees stand around, yellow-tipped, in the mist. Mary Shelley's own first book is a work of travel writing which borrows both her mother's epistolary structure, and its strategy of sometimes recycling private correspondence for print. *History of a Six Weeks' Tour* (the very trip on which, incidentally, she and Percy Bysshe read her mother's *Letters Written . . .*) was published the year before she found herself at the Hoppners' dinner-table. In it, she records how, in the desolate battlefield village of Échimines, these ostensibly vegetarian travellers consume:

> plenty of milk, stinking bacon, sour bread, and a few vegetables, which we were to dress for ourselves. As we prepared our dinner in a place, so filthy that the sight of it alone was sufficient to destroy our appetite, the people of the village collected around us, squalid with dirt.

But this is food as circumstance rather than sensation. Far from being placed within the writing frame, her narrator has become disembodied; and the author herself, as part of the coming trend among women writers, anonymous.

History relates intellectual and emotional, rather than bodily, experiences. It uses awe to smooth out the rugged details of embodied travel and guide the reader towards abstraction:

the snowy Alps [. . .] reach so high in the heavens, that they look like those accumulated clouds of dazzling white that arrange themselves on the horizon during summer. Their immensity staggers the imagination, and so far surpasses all conception, that it requires an effort of the understanding to believe that they indeed form a part of the earth.

Percy Bysshe Shelley's poetry isn't about being there *in the flesh* either. 'Mont Blanc' is his cognate reaction, on the same visit, to Alpine scenery:

> Over whose pines, and crags, and caverns sail
> Fast cloud-shadows and sunbeams: awful scene,
> Where Power in likeness of the Arve comes down
> From the ice-gulfs that gird his secret throne,
> [. . .]
> Dizzy Ravine! and when I gaze on thee
> I seem as in a trance sublime and strange
> To muse on my own separate fantasy,
> My own, my human mind, which passively
> Now renders and receives fast influencings,
> Holding an unremitting interchange
> With the clear universe of things around;

I find affinity in the couple's early work, this shared struggle towards transcendence, immensely telling. It's a salutary reminder, too, that Percy's *Vindication* of vegetarianism was important in their courtship. During the weeks immediately preceding their elopement, when Mary was grounded in the parental home, one of the few books he managed to smuggle to her was a copy of his *Queen Mab*, including these Notes on vegetarianism.

Mary turned eighteen in 1815, the year Lord Liverpool's Tory administration enacted the first in a series of protectionist Corn Laws that raised the prices of those British staples, wheat, oats and barley, entirely out of reach of the poor, and uncomfortably high even for those who, like her, were neither poor nor rich. By the time the last Corn Law was enacted, in 1846, she would be a widow of forty-nine. That same year the Brownings left a smoggily austere, even hungry, London for Italy. For this later pair of newly-weds, travel was an encounter with abundance *both* intellectual and sensory: of art, architecture and history alongside the flora and fauna of a populated world. Like Percy Bysshe, although for different reasons, Elizabeth associated the diet she now chose with good health. It was part of the bodily resurrection that her surprising late marriage had accomplished. Part, too, of a robust physical intimacy, for which it could stand as decent metonym in letters home: after all, it was in the intimacy of their shared hotel room that the couple, 'Have our dinners from the Trattoria at two oclock, & can dine our favorite way.'

For all the political activism that she would embrace in future years, when it came to food Elizabeth, unlike Percy, didn't expect to change the world, but only herself. The piercing pleasures she describes to fellow writer Mary Russell Mitford are no universal panacea:

> an immense dish of oranges . . . two hanging on a stalk with the green leaves still moist with the morning's dew . . . every great orange of twelve or thirteen with its own stalk

& leaves. Such a pretty sight! And better oranges, I beg to say, never were eaten, when we are barbarous enough to eat them day by day after our two oclock' dinner.

They represent an art of domestic attention.

The Elizabeth who attended the Hoppners' salon in June 1847 was a new wife, making her home in a new country. But this quality of attention, to the close at hand rather than what was awe-inspiring but risked generalisation, was also a writerly technique she was already making her own. With it she was refreshing Romantic poetics, turning them first back towards a Wordsworthian engagement with the texture of the inhabited landscape and eventually, as she embraced her own ethical poetics in works such as *Casa Guidi Windows* (1851) and *Aurora Leigh* (1856), forwards towards a rapidly changing contemporary society. Romanticism was already becoming a story from the past.

Robert took up this poetic approach in 1855's *Men and Women* as well as the works that followed it. Among the poems in that collection is 'Memorabilia', in which, as I read it, I see a ghostly Shelley offer his plate again and again for 'a very little slice of this beef.'

Walk 4: Great Wood to Crowcombe Park, starting at Great Wood car-park, Adscombe Lane, Over Stowey, Bridgewater TA5 1HN, OS Grid Ref ST179378.

Fifth Walk

Accelerating

... rapturous glance ...

WILLIAM WORDSWORTH, 'Is there no nook of
English ground secure from rash assault?'

Paddington was my first great terminus. I'd run up the stairs from the Tube to find myself in its giant echo chamber filled with the sounds of shunting engines, shouts, tannoy announcements and the clamour of drilling from perpetual roof repairs. On Friday evenings the Great Western Railway Paddington Station Military Band added top notes of clarinets and bugle to the din. Far overhead, the great glass and steel roof that Isambard Kingdom Brunel completed in 1854, five years before his death, was cloudy with diesel fumes. Its triple span seemed remote as the dome of some ancient, if secular, cathedral. The complex overlapping arches of the central aisle were lost in dimness, but the tulip curves of iron tracery at the end of each train shed remained, outlined by the daylight beyond.

Late on summer afternoons when the sun was directly to the south-west you caught a glimpse of the marvel the station must have been when it was new.

Brunel was de facto an artist. But he was also an engineer's engineer. Born in 1806, the son of French-born Marc Isambard Brunel – himself an engineer – he was educated in France, but found himself unable to attend the École Polytechnique because he was English. Instead, from the age of sixteen he served a kind of technical apprenticeship as assistant engineer to his father, who was building the Rotherhithe Tunnel. Early nineteenth-century engineering was a hands-on, material profession, at least in Britain: the teenaged Isambard Kingdom found himself not in some pen-pushing sinecure but under-ground with the tunnellers, where at twenty-two he was nearly killed by a flash-flood in the workings.

Five years later, in 1833, he was appointed Chief Engineer of the Great Western Railway and embarked on a programme of building the many miles of line (albeit with wide-gauge track that would later be replaced), stations and railway bridges that remain his signature on the British landscape. He also built to commission elsewhere. So it's no surprise that he should have been appointed to the Building Committee for the Great Exhibition of 1851, that national celebration which showcased technological innovations in a building that turned out itself to be an outstanding technological innovation. Here too he kept busy. For, while Joseph Paxton's vast steel and glass Crystal Palace was still being erected at the south-eastern perimeter of London, Brunel drew up plans for a Paddington station roofed with flying steel and glass arches of his own, and presented them to the GWR Board in December 1850.

He was equally unashamed in using Paxton's contractors. Over the next four years, both the wrought-ironwork fabricators Fox, Henderson & Co, and architect Matthew Digby Wyatt, whom Paxton had employed on the Palace, helped realise the station. Paddington is only half as long as the Crystal Palace was, but its central vault alone is half as wide again as the Palace's single span and, though it never became a national wonder like its precursor, when it was built it was the world's largest terminus. With a toughness born of practicality, it has remained in continuous use; unlike the Palace, which lost its purpose, underwent revival, and finally burnt down in 1936.

Still, Paddington is a cultural hybrid. The Great Exhibition was one of the lines that Victorian culture drew under Romanticism. It highlighted a breaking of the link between awe and the spiritual realm; a link that had remained even while Romantic atheism was shifting such awe from the field of organised religion to more general experiences of being in the world. The Exhibition substituted the braggadocio of human invention for the sublimity of, say, a mountain-scape. Yet at Paddington station the graceful, slender branches of Brunel's wrought-iron columns, their brackets pierced to relieve them of their own weight, seem to gesture back through time as they visibly adopt the Gothic proportions and splayed idioms of Horace Walpole's Strawberry Hill, or John Nash's lost orangery for Thomas Johnes at The Hafod.

In any case, the railway age had exploded out of Romantic era innovation in surveying and construction – to say nothing of its discovery of steam power. I think of Brunel himself as personifying this exponential expansion in our understanding of the possible: he allowed the nineteenth century's techno-logical revolution to surge forward from mere research and discussion. Dying in 1859, at the age of only fifty-three, he scarcely outlived the Romantic moment and – though he could be said to have outstripped that movement by the speed with which he drove urban and rural infrastructure out into a newly Victorian world – his work also shows him to have been capable of wonder. For, as they saw and did things that had never been done before, early nineteenth-century engineers found them-selves working with a natural world still capable of astonishing them – and of conjuring astonishments for their clients. Brunel experimented with highspeed vacuum railways capable of travelling at then eye-watering speeds of sixty-eight miles per hour; he designed suspension bridges whose struts and cables illustrate the elegance with which forces interplay. But he pub-lished no lyric exposition of ideas *about* this. His expressions of awe at the physical and chemical world that unpacked itself for him are the material work itself.

By the time I started using Paddington station, it was less a technological wonder than a human microcosm thronging with new arrivals, taxi-drivers, pickpockets, touts, the Praed Street girls and their pimps, and those lost souls who in every great railway station nurse solitary coffees in concourse cafes, or pace the halls as if searching for someone to hail. I loved it. Even as an unaccompanied child obeying the injunction not to linger, I felt the social web fraying and being remade around me. In the years since my delight hasn't diminished. I'm still intensely aware how, unlike the aseptic, gated spaces of an airport, railway stations are full of endings and beginnings, loose narrative threads.

Perhaps it's because the trains themselves are literally there in the room, or anyway the concourse. The transforming fact of travel sits noisily at every platform. Or maybe it comes instead from the concourse's own half-and-half indoor—outdoor character. Like a market square, or a cloister, it's a public space that has been differentiated by purpose, and something is shared even within the diversity that crowds around you. But while station concourses enclose, they don't shelter. You have to keep moving; and this imperative, so much a part of modernity, is what keeps Paddington shifting between joyful concatenation and grim *arte povera*; between gleaming glass or faux marble, and the puddles where pigeons and burger wrappers gather.

There's a blur of grey at the very centre of J. M. W. Turner's *Rain, Steam, and Speed — The Great Western Railway*, in which a train from Paddington races towards us over Maidenhead Railway Bridge. Like many of his later works, Turner's large canvas, which measures three feet by four, performs the trick of turning oil paint into water; or at least into the idea of water. It captures the drizzle and wet air of a summer storm and the swirling vapour of a steam train. The damp steel of his engine's firebox shines so brightly that it resembles a window into the cab's interior. Vapour threads across the image, making the landscape itself hard to read.

But the painting's predominant colour is gold. We glimpse, parallel with the railway viaduct, the golden, dressed-limestone arches of a road bridge. Its reflection in the still surface of the summer Thames makes it appear to stand twice as high above the water as it really does. Both of these bridges, thirty miles upriver from west London, are still in use today; absurdly, most trains in and out of Paddington still roar through this attractive and historic spot. Maidenhead is one of those places – like tracts of the most beautiful British coastline: south Devon, west and north Wales, the east coast of Scotland – where Victorian engineers had no compunction about driving their railway through whatever was in its path, with a kind of contextless zeal that they may well have characterised as purity of purpose. Brunel was guilty of a similar disfigurement at Dawlish and Teignmouth, where in 1847 the South Devon Railway was built to his specification along the seafront. Just under thirty years later, the South Devon Railway would amalgamate with the Great Western and these separate projects of his come under coordinated management. But to this day the line Brunel built along the rocky coves of south Devon cuts off the cramped esplanades of the little local towns from their beaches.

Turner's image of the express crossing the Thames in a gleaming cloud of *Rain, Steam, and Speed* was painted in 1844, if not before. The company had started running trains over this bridge in 1839 – after beginning service a year earlier – and by 1844 was doing so with royal patronage. Queen Victoria took her first trip on this line in 1842; thereafter she used the railway to travel between Windsor Castle and Buckingham Palace, and Brunel placed a royal waiting room on Platform One of his new Paddington station. But the first Paddington station was a neo-Classical structure built into the arches of Bishop's Bridge Road; it was this more modest building that Elizabeth Barrett Browning visited with John Kenyon in June 1846, to witness the trial run of a new, enlarged engine:

My head was still struggling & swimming between two tides of impressions received from the excitement & fatigue of the day. Mr Kenyon [. . .] took me to see the strange new sight (to me!) of the Great Western . . . the train coming in: [. . .] the rush of the people & the earth-thunder of the engine, almost overcame me . . .

The 'rush' and 'earth-thunder' are in Turner's painting too. Although he positions us looking straight at the train that steams towards us (where 'are' we? hovering in mid-air beside the railway line?) he gives us the sensory experience of the passengers who are actually on board the train's open carriages, and who face us. We glimpse them streaming towards us as a blurring of coloured dots, highlights on the dark body of the train. At the same time we also glimpse what they must be seeing and feeling: this mixing up of highlights and misted vision, all the sensations of displacement. Not only is the forty-plus miles per hour of the train faster than most of its passengers have ever travelled before, but they're speeding unprotected through the open air in its roofless carriages. Although it's summertime, they sit in a slipstream thick with smuts, smoke and vapour and, as they cross, the viaduct arches must make a resonating chamber for the engine roar.

The whole painting works like a great transferred epithet. Turner paints the 'Speed' of his title as a sort of involving rapture. Just as the shine of atmospheric damp seems to have been displaced into the engine cab, so the firebox seems to be glowing to the side of the train, as if sheer velocity has thrown it overboard. Speed has become another extreme experience through which to experience awe and wonder, those most

Romantic of emotions. Viewing mountains, falling in love, being astonished by innovation: by 1844 the Romantic search for intensity had for decades created experiences that might not be entirely enjoyable but which pushed the individual outside their comfort zone. As I stand looking at Turner's picture where it hangs, with historical inevitability, alongside canvasses by his great contemporary John Constable in the National Gallery, I'm swept up by its movement. It reminds me of watching people riding a rollercoaster; how we feel their rise and plunge in our own stomachs. The giant O of the weather swirling through his paint is like the Ooooh! of half-delighted, half-terrified screams rushing out from the cars. It's as if everyone in the painting has their mouth open to the wind.

Percy Bysshe Shelley's 'Ode to the West Wind', composed a quarter century earlier in the perhaps more glamorous setting of Florence's Parco delle Cascine, shares this mood of exhilaration:

> Thou on whose stream, 'mid the steep sky's
> commotion,
> Loose clouds like earth's decaying leaves are shed,
> [. . .]
>
> Angels of rain and lightning: there are spread
> On the blue surface of thine aery surge,
> Like the bright hair uplifted from the head
>
> Of some fierce Maened, [. . .]
> The locks of the approaching storm.

Poem and painting embrace weather as a form of rapturous momentum. In *Rain, Steam, and Speed* Turner has the motion of the Maidenhead train merge with the scudding of a summer shower, as it must in the passengers' experience. But Shelley's momentum is emotional and meteorological, not technological. Trembling on the brink of extremity, it feels close to another, apparently hidden source of Romantic motivation:

> Wild Spirit, which are moving everywhere;
> Destroyer and preserver; hear, oh, hear!

This gleefully pagan invocation is a reminder of how momentum is a symptom of underlying change: of how, once set in motion, a force will keep going, 'under its own steam' so to speak.

Both works reach forward to explore change itself. Every time is modern *at* the time, and to live in modern times can always feel vertiginous, whether you're Shelley, composing among the threshing trees of 1819 Florence, or Turner, sketching by a newly constructed Berkshire railway line in 1844 – or us, two centuries later. One response to this feeling that change might prove unstoppable is to secure the belt and braces of tradition. An alternative is to throw oneself into the 'steep sky' of the unknown; and we could read Shelley's life and work is as doing just this in order to forestall the vertigo of early modernity. Some of his best-known poems grapple with the risks and inevitability of continual transformation. In 'Mutability', 'We are as clouds that veil the midnight moon;/ [. . .] Nought may endure but Mutability.' In 'Ozymandias', our absence becomes deletion, the horizon a line ruled through human works and plans: 'Nothing beside remains. Round the decay/Of that colossal wreck, boundless and bare/The lone and level sands stretch far away.' Shelley's belief in social revolution, his love of sailing and notorious romantic infidelities, even his adolescent passion for amateur chemistry, could all be seen as aspects of a preoccupation with change and momentum. 'Ode to the West Wind' triumphantly transforms this anxiety into a manifesto, transferring private obsession to the external material world, and claiming a desire to 'share//The impulse of thy strength, [. . .] O uncontrollable!'

We can't be honest readers of this fourth section of the poem without noticing how grandiosely the poet compares *himself* to its 'uncontrollable' gale:

> A heavy weight of hours has chained and bowed
> One too like thee: tameless, and swift, and proud.

Or that a similar grandiosity runs through the poem's triumphant conclusion:

> Be thou me, impetuous one!
>
> [. . .]
> And, by this incantation of this verse,
>
> Scatter as from an unextinguished hearth
> Ashes and sparks, my words among mankind!
> Be through my lips to unawakened earth
>
> The trumpet of a prophecy!

But I'm not Shelley's therapist, and besides, the poet in me can't help but be seduced by this writing. That glorious, poetically transgressive polysyllable *unextinguished* takes such a long time to enunciate that it mimes the protraction within the state of *not-having-been-put-out*. The same word beckons, rhythmically and with that repeated *un-*, across the tercet to its equivalent opposite, *unawakened*, making us realise how these two adjectives of potential chime. In doing so, they reawaken the feeling of match-making that comes from the accompanying slant rhyme *hearth/earth* and — back in the previous verse, since this poem uses backward-looping, *terza rima* rhyme — *birth*.

A tremendous, vaunting desire for international reach — 'mankind', 'earth' — contributes to the momentum. At a distance, Romantic impulses can seem grandiose, at least in their tendency to exceptionalism. The notion that there could be alternative ways of living, and that to abide by social convention is unnecessary, undoubtedly produced working social microcosms, those local 'cottage' communities of the kind Mary Shelley celebrated in *Frankenstein* and *The Last Man*. But in some ways these social experiments were themselves a repudiation of the social contract. However irrationally a society is organised, to resist its forms of organisation — leave alone actually to believe in political revolution, as Mary's family did — is always a form of exceptionalism. A stepping out from the ranks to say, 'This may be all right for you, but it's not for me.'

There's little shift in tone between Shelley's somewhat grandiose self-portrait in 'Ode to the West Wind', and the pro-revolutionary vision of 'The Triumph of Life', the poem he left unfinished at his death three years later, in summer 1822. Nor does his image vocabulary change radically, though it's pressed into different use. In 'Triumph', the billions who down the centuries have lived obedient to empires and monarchies become 'earth's decaying leaves', who have individually failed to resist 'many a sceptre-bearing line/And spread the plague of blood and gold abroad':

> Numerous as gnats upon the evening gleam,
>
> All hastening onward, yet none seemed to know
>   Whither he went, or whence he came, or why
> He made one of the multitude, yet so
>
> Was borne amid the crowd, as through the sky
>   One of the million leaves of summer's bier;

It is indeed paradoxical that Shelley should have drowned in a sailing accident on the Ligurian Sea while working on a poem called 'The Triumph of Life'. But what makes the poem itself paradoxical isn't the evident irony of its title, but this way it frames action and passivity, suggesting that human passivity produces oppression, rather than being produced by it.

Such a belief in the scope of individual self-determination is partly the solipsism of privilege. Shelley was able to lead his radical life because he was heir to a baronetcy. But also at work is an idea which had passed from German into British Romantic thought, thanks in part to Samuel Taylor Coleridge's enthusiasm for the thought of Georg Wilhelm Friedrich Hegel. Born in 1770, Hegel was just two years Coleridge's senior;

when Shelley drowned in 1822, both men were still alive and working. The philosopher's *The Phenomenology of Spirit* had been published in 1807, and spelled out his idea of *Herrschaft und Knechtschaft,* the famous 'master/slave dialectic' in which two individuals develop a sense of self and other through their mutual struggle to master each other. In Shelley's 'The Triumph of Life' the individual fails in his struggle with political leaders, but he also struggles with the crowd around him, which threatens to defeat him by carrying him away – 'Swift, fierce and obscene/The wild dance maddens in the van' – though not to any particular destination. Aimlessly, the great mass of people, 'Like moths by light attracted and repelled,/Oft to new bright destruction come and go'. Poem and dialectical model share a notion of individual responsibility, in which the 'slave' has in some existential way assented to being 'mastered', and the trajectory towards annihilation, since successful mastery destroys the constituting dialectic.

Written into this Romantic philosophy is a sense of the importance of electing to live a certain way; and consequently of an elect who have, apparently, chosen well. Which seems to ignore how we always live situated within contexts. Hegel was writing philosophy of history; yet history *is* the particularity of how circumstances, including geography, society and beliefs, impinge upon choice.

'The Triumph of Life' is Shelley's *Divine Comedy*. Both long poems are written in *terza rima*, and while Dante's guide to the afterlife is Virgil, Shelley finds a guide in Jean-Jacques Rousseau. In Dante's *Comedy*, though, everyone assumes the position in hell, purgatory or paradise that accurately mirrors their behaviour in life; while Shelley's poem struggles to create an atheist cosmology that could replace these carefully calibrated tiers of wickedness and virtue. This struggle to create pattern and sense from often discordant motifs makes 'The Triumph' a precursor of literary modernism; it becomes explicit in the anguished dialogue between the poem's narrator and the ghost of Rousseau. There are also traces, in the narrative's bumpy hesitations, of modernist techniques still a century in the future: the way D. H. Lawrence's poetry and fiction *write out* their fail-again-fail-better attempts to describe the world afresh; or the layering of brushstrokes with which Paul Cézanne's impasto seems to wrench image, along with the understanding needed to create it in the first place, out of the blank canvas.

Unlike Dante's Virgil, Shelley's Rousseau is horrifyingly transformed by posthumous existence:

> . . . what I thought was an old root which grew
> To strange distortion out of the hill side,

> [. . .] the grass, which methought hung so wide
>   And white, was but his thin discoloured hair,
> And [. . .] the holes it vainly sought to hide

> Were or had been eyes:

Movement here is not agency, but mutability — and so it offers no escape from entropy. While Dante builds a conceptual structure in order to circle towards heaven, Shelley pushes everything and everyone out from the security of certainty into perpetual motion:

Figures ever new
Rise on the bubble [. . .]
We have but thrown, as those before us threw,

Our shadows on it as it passed away.

As he worked on the poem during his final weeks of life, Shelley was also fiddling with his new boat. The arrival of his *Don Juan* on 12 May, a couple of months before his death, had been rather overshadowed by that of Byron's much larger, faster vessel, the *Bolivar*. Competitively, Shelley had his own vessel altered with go-faster modifications – a false stern and extended bowsprit – that made it less stable, and harder to handle in the summer storm into which he would sail with fatal consequences on 8 July. The risks were only compounded by an exceptional compensatory ballast of almost an English ton of pig iron, and by its extensive rigging. The twin masts carried up to seven sails, including topsails: which made for wind-catching speed, but would have been difficult and dangerous to take down quickly in an emergency.

Speed is generally an expression of impatience. It might have been sensible for Shelley to try out the modified craft before making a trip of any distance. But his decisions in connection with sailing, long a hobby, seem generally to have been emotional rather than strategic: after all, he couldn't even swim. Besides, there was some masculine jockeying going on. At the start of the year, before either boat had been built, Byron, Shelley, the Shelleys' housemate Edward Williams, Byron's common-law brother-in-law Pietro Gamba and the adventurer, ex-Navy man and self-styled former pirate Edward Trelawny had taken to calling themselves the Corsair Crew and indulging in riotous behaviour. The name alluded not only to a general sense of themselves as dashing and piratical, but to the success Byron had enjoyed some seven years earlier with his verse novel *The Corsair* (1814), a composition of more than 1,800 lines in three cantos. Appearing before Byron's fall from social grace, and when the fame that the first two cantos of *Childe Harold's Pilgrimage* had brought him in 1812 had been further consolidated by other narrative poems like *The Giaour* (1813), on publication day alone it sold ten thousand copies.

Byron's eponymous corsair is his opening antihero: the opening Cantos of *Don Juan* (after which he had rather insultingly intervened to name Shelley's boat) would not be published until 1819. In this 1814 poem Conrad the corsair attacks a pasha's palace, loses the advantage while rescuing its harem, and is rescued himself by one of the enslaved women, Gulnare, who then assassinates the pasha herself so that the corsair won't have to kill in cold blood. Which would be dishonourable for a European male. Conrad displays his virtue further by not insisting on sleeping with Gulnare: 'He left a Corsair's name to other times,/Linked with one virtue and a thousand crimes.' It's a typically offensive piece of Orientalism. As a Turkish woman, Gulnare is beyond honour, both in being 'allowed' to kill in a way that's supposed to be dishonourable, and in her status as sexual booty.

More interesting, however, is the poem's rousing opening chorus 'that from the Pirates' isle/Around the kindling watch-fire rang.' It almost serves to define the Romantic embrace of 'wild life in tumult' in place of 'limits':

'O'er the glad waters of the dark blue sea,
'Our thoughts as boundless, and our souls as free,
'Far as the breeze can bear, the billows foam,
'These are our realms, no limits to their sway
– 'Our flag the sceptre all who meet obey.
'Ours the wild life in tumult still to range
'From toil to rest, and joy in every change.'

This is an evocation of both the restlessness – 'joy in every change' – that Shelley's 'Ode to the West Wind' celebrates and, though in very different terms from the junior poet's 'The Triumph of Life', surrender. 'Tumult' is exciting: at the same time, it strangely implies passivity, since it suggests something overwhelming. But after all, losing control can be thrilling, 'The exulting sense – the pulse's maddening play,/That thrills the wanderer of that trackless way,' as Byron's opening stanza goes on to say. And not just in orgasm: it's risk itself that is the beauty of 'the wild life'. If there's something of the Rock God about Lord Byron himself, there's something of The Who's 'I hope I die before I get old . . . ' in such ecstatic launching-off:

'Let him who crawls enamoured of decay,
'Cling to his couch, and sicken years away;
'Heave his thick breath; and shake his palsied head;
'Ours – the fresh turf, and not the feverish bed.'

To be carried along by sound and motion is rapture of a kind, as the GWR passengers Turner painted in 1844 knew. I've always loved the 'tumult of mighty harmonies' in a speeding train. When I was a kid being raced towards Paddington, I'd let my unfocused gaze catch on and release every passing tree and telegraph pole. The oldest carriages on that Gloucestershire line still had the post-war upholstery, green and red checker with a leather trim, and leather handles at their casement windows. They smelt of winter coats and stale cigarettes. On those mornings late in the last century Gloucester (where the train reversed) and Stonehouse were dim in the predawn. Past Stroud, with its high platform, a sequence following a canal and through tunnels led onto pretty, vertiginous Chalford. (We often went through these tunnels in the dark, seized by the chomping sound of the wheels on the rails beneath us, because a guard had switched the lights off when he went off shift.) At Kemble the daffodils of the iron station pillars were picked out in colour all down the empty platform. Then came the wide swerve of rails into the repairing sheds and marshalling yards at Swindon.

These rather plain stone and brick structures were the Great Western Railway's Swindon Works, officially opened in 1843, a year before Turner unveiled *Rain, Steam, and Speed* at the Royal Academy and three years before Elizabeth Barrett Browning was overcome by the 'earth-thunder' of a GWR engine that was probably built here. By the year of the Great Exhibition, 1851, around two thousand people worked here on repairs and engine building; and they were treated as skilled technical craftsmen. If GWR's origins were Romantic, it had managed to bring some of that movement's revolutionary egalitarianism forward into the Victorian age. Its Railway Village was among the first to bring the idea of the model country estate village to town, as good-quality housing for industrial workers. The variegated high Victorian and Arts and Crafts cottages of Bournville in Birmingham are deservedly famous, and prettier than the sturdily utilitarian terraces grouped in the shadow of the Swindon viaduct. But Cadbury's development came in the decades from 1893. Decades earlier, Swindon Railway Village already had its own school and chapel, and was pioneering insurance and free health care.

Remember how light arrives by stages in a morning train? First as a discolouration in the mirror of the window and then, little by little, as a competing image. Streetlights and houses appear: piecemeal, and then joining together as streets interlaced with hoardings, road signs and fences. Horses in a high field; rooks lifting from a roost. A motorbike. A kid on a paper-round, with asymmetric sack slung low. On board, passengers emerge from the sleepy privacy they brought into the carriage with them. Eventually someone speaks — then someone else — until the carriage fills with voices.

Yesterday it was the same as ever in the cramped and slightly nauseating Pendolino to Oxenholme. After a wait on Oxenholme's chilly platform, I caught the two-car Windermere stopper, whose windows stream condensation whatever the weather. Windermere town was called Birthwaite until it was persuaded to advertise its lakeside location by the advent of this tourist line. It's all stone houses and drystone walls, a pretty settlement dressed up in grey slate. It's also a tourist squeezebox, where the Kendal to Keswick road crosses the route that runs from Penrith and Ullswater down to the south Lakes, while buses converge at the region's only railway terminus. The Lake District is one of the most visited landscapes in Britain: in 2018 it had nearly twenty million visitors. But more than three quarters of them arrived by car and, behind its fudge shops and the waterfront crammed with pleasure craft, little Windemere town has become pretty much all traffic system.

This morning though, I've got to the eastern shore of Coniston Water. There's no one else here yet; I have the whole place to myself. The water pulses silver in the morning light. There's a nip in the air, yet the first earthy smells of the year have arrived, faint as autosuggestion. A tealeaf note of last year's leaves; the thick pepper base of damp soil. I'm standing on deserted shingle at Low Peel Near, and I can't resist nudging the toes of my boots into the very rim of the lake water. I can see peaty moss on the underwater stones. The water's so clear they seem hyperreal, as if no actual lake floor could really be so finely detailed.

Someone's had a fire on the smooth, hands-span stones of the shoreline beside me. The modest circle of leftover ash is still stubbled with burnt twigs. Moss on the trunks of the skinny waterside oaks and beech trees is mustard yellow new growth: February brightness. I pick a couple of stones to skim because I don't know how to express this unsullied feeling, of the water and of the morning, except by making a mark on it of some kind. The stones bounce twice – three times. The lake digests their ripples slowly.

I wonder whether to paddle. The water's going to be almost unbearably cold. But it's a way to claim something exquisite for myself; the freezing, endorphin-releasing shock of it on my skin. Otherwise I'm just going to look at the scenery. Which seems too passive, somehow, to figure as an encounter. I wave to a pair of kayakers paddling out across the lake. Wild swimming is a faff, but just taking off your boots and socks, rolling up your jeans? Easy. And soon I find myself hopping and slipping into the fierce water. Underwater, underfoot, fists of stone punching my bare soles.

And now it's nice sitting on the low wall beside the lane, rubbing my wet feet and feeling the blood glow and thump between the bones. I could wish I hadn't seen the kayakers, or at least the vivid highlights of their orange and blue weatherproofs, on such a palely dimpled morning lake. But anyway they've disappeared behind the wooded rock of Peel Island: which looks as though it hasn't changed since Arthur Ransome named it 'Wild Cat Island' in *Swallows and Amazons*.

At this moment the world of his 1929 children's classic seems as close as a trick of light on the water. Go back another century again, and so do the late 1820s, when Dorothy Wordsworth wrote about a 'Floating Island' that evidently looked much the way Peel Island does today. Created by erosion, her 'slip of earth,/By throbbing waves long undermined,/Loosed from its hold' will eventually be obliterated by the same means. Meanwhile it surrenders, as if in a mild ecstasy of its own, to the surrounding lake:

> Might see it, from the mossy shore
> Dissevered float upon the Lake,
> Float, with its crest of trees adorned
> On which the warbling birds their pastime take.
>
> [. . .]
> A peopled *world* it is; in size a tiny room.
>
> And thus through many seasons' space

This little Island may survive
But Nature, though we mark her not,
Will take away – may cease to give.

Perchance when you are wandering forth
Upon some vacant sunny day
Without an object, hope, or fear,
Thither your eyes may turn – the Isle is passed away.

Coniston this morning seems like everything William Wordsworth was desperate to preserve when, in 1844, he campaigned against a proposed Kendal to Windermere railway line, due to run through the heart of the Lake District. His sonnet, 'Is there no nook of English ground secure from rash assault?' appeared in the *Morning Post* on 16 October 1844:

And is *no* nook of English ground secure
From rash assault? Schemes of retirement sown
In youth, and 'mid the busy world kept pure
As when their earliest flowers of hope were blown,
Must perish; – how can they this blight endure?
And must he too his old delights disown
Who scorns a false utilitarian lure
'Mid his paternal fields at random thrown?
Baffle the threat, bright scene, from *Orrest head*
Given to the pausing traveller's rapturous glance;
Plead for thy peace thou beautiful romance
Of nature; and, if human hearts be dead,
Speak, passing winds; ye torrents, with your strong
And constant voice, protest against the wrong!

There's no measure by which 'Is there no nook' is successful verse, even if it does open with a question and that lift-off
'And . . . ', a strategy perhaps remembered across four intervening decades from William Blake's 'And did those feet . . . ?'
But 'Jerusalem', while it *is* another poem about despoiling the
British countryside, is also about the despoliation of British
society; the exploitation of working people in the 'dark satanic
mills' of his famous coinage. It too opens with a flourish of
rhetorical questions, but it manages to turn them into something visionary. Blake sees a Godhead 'Walk upon England's
mountains green'; Wordsworth pictures a retiree pottering in
his 'nook'.

One of the things that's gone wrong with the laureate's
sonnet is that this is argument in verse — and, unlike other,
younger poets who were by now publishing poems which
succeeded beautifully in storytelling (Alfred Tennyson) or philosophical thinking aloud (Elizabeth Barrett) — Wordsworth's
poetic strength lay not primarily in getting from one idea to
another, but in description. Still, within six weeks his rhyme
would be reprinted in more than sixty newspapers across the
country and, the day before the *Post* published it, he had already
enclosed it in a letter of protest he sent the Prime Minister. For
Wordsworth was no longer the twenty-nine-year-old cottager
who had moved with his sister into Dove Cottage, Grasmere
on 20 December 1799, intent on a radical new life. With his
marriage in 1802 to Dorothy's schoolfriend Mary Hutchinson
and the subsequent arrival of children, the Wordsworths had
first crowded and then outgrew the little roadside house,
which they left in 1808.

Romantic community was the Dove Cottage context. As if

to ensure continuity, Thomas de Quincey took the little house over in 1809. Between 1800 and 1803 Coleridge, who had followed the Wordsworths north, lived with his family in Greta Hall, just fourteen miles away on the riverbank at Keswick; he handed on that tenancy to Robert Southey, who remained there until his death in 1843. But by 1844 Wordsworth was a respectable gentleman in his seventies and, having succeeded Southey as poet laureate the year before, a figure in the land. He had moved into his comfortable home at Rydal Mount, high above Rydal Water and a couple of miles east of Dove Cottage, some three decades earlier, in 1813: 'Schemes of retirement sown/In youth.' Although the house and grounds were rented property and not, strictly speaking, 'his paternal fields.'

Rydal Mount is a pleasantly rambling house whose original, rougher vernacular has been smartened up with an early nineteenth-century façade. (A little, perhaps, like the poet himself.) Wordsworth's writing hut in its bosky grounds, a kind of loggia that he used until his death in 1850, mimicks in stone the wooden arbour at the top of Dove Cottage's steeply sloping garden. Alas, the campaigning sonnet he composed here in 1844 is bald nimbyism. It wields the language of Victorian domesticity – 'nook', 'retirement', 'pure' – against an outside world that threatens 'rash assault', 'random' and 'false utilitarian lure'.

This cosiness is precisely what Shelley excoriates for 770 lines in his 1819 lampoon of Wordsworth's 'Peter Bell'. No one could accuse Shelley of giving half measure in verse, and 'Peter Bell the Third' is strong stuff, the fury of a young man whose role model turns out to have feet of clay:

But from the first 'twas Peter's drift
To be a kind of moral eunuch,
He touched the hem of Nature's shift,
Felt faint – and never dared uplift
The closest, all-concealing tunic.

Yet it was only three years since Shelley had published his sonnet, 'To Wordsworth', which famously portrays the elder poet as a 'lone star' ecological visionary, who recognises in the natural world the mutability that was the younger man's obsession:

Poet of nature, thou has wept to know
That things depart which never may return:
Childhood and youth, friendship and love's first
    glow . . .

True, opinions are mutable too. But perhaps not everything in Shelley's thinking had changed that radically.

After all, 'To Wordsworth' reads like a eulogy to a poet already dead. The perfect tense comes close to suggesting the passé. Even in 1816, while placing his elder on a metaphorical pedestal and locating him within a special relationship to the natural world, Shelley at the same time confines him to a third location: the past. Now the charge has become selling out. 'Peter Bell the Third' weaponises its author's radical politics, represents worldliness as hell, and accuses the laureate:

When Peter heard of his promotion,
His eyes grew like two stars for bliss:

[. . .]

> He hired a house, bought plate, and made
> A genteel drive up to his door,
> With sifted gravel neatly laid, –
> As if defying all who said,
> Peter was ever poor.

If this weren't strong enough stuff, it also reproves 'Peter' with the loss of his poetic gift: a gibe both cruel and apt, since Wordsworth was indeed publishing mediocre work in the last decades of his life. (His inner eye, of course, was actually on his unpublished masterpiece, *The Prelude*.)

Like a naughty child, Shelley chants:

> Peter was dull – he was at first
> Dull – oh, so dull – so very dull!
> Whether he talked, wrote, or rehearsed –
> Still with this dulness was he cursed –
> Dull – beyond all conception – dull.

Childish: but not without foundation. The closing sestet of Wordsworth's 'Is there no nook . . . ' takes a turn into positively Shelleyian imagery, as if trying to *borrow* inspiration in lieu of an authentic music of its own: 'Speak, passing winds; ye torrents, with your strong/And constant voice, protest . . . ' And yet, these stormy forces are supposed paradoxically to 'Plead for thy peace thou beautiful romance/Of nature.'

The ill-chosen metaphor pushes and pulls uneasily. So does the one truly Romantic trajectory in Wordsworth's poem:

the 'bright scene, from Orrest head/Given to the pausing traveller's rapturous glance.' Walkers on Orrest Head just outside Windermere, a beauty spot 240 metres above sea level, do indeed have a stunning view not only of lake and fells but right across to the Pennines and Morecambe Bay. Today this panorama includes the railway that, though scaled down, did eventually open from Kendal to Windermere on 20 April 1847. But the poem's viewpoint is not *from* but *of* Orrest Head, 'bright' in the brief Lakeland sunlight and 'given to' some traveller below – the passenger on a train, say. Whose attention is briefly 'paused' by the sight even as, in that telling almost-homophone, they *pass* it. Just as in Turner's *Rain, Steam, and Speed*, experience and viewpoint are transferred. The 'rapturous glance', all speed and intensity, fleeting and yet utterly involving, is both the Romantic gaze – and the train traveller's unfocused stare.

Wordsworth's desire to exclude railways from the Lake District, which we could set down at least in part as early environmental protectionism, could not have envisaged the far worse pollution from twenty-first century traffic that would result. I find it discomforting for an altogether different reason. In October 1844, the *Morning Post* published not only his sonnet but, alongside it, a letter in which he objected to 'uneducated persons in large bodies' coming to visit the Lakes. To 'place the beauties of the Lake District within easier reach of these who cannot afford to pay for ordinary conveyances', he insists, would spoil its 'beauty [and] character of seclusion and retirement.' Bizarrely surprised that such snobbishness should have gone down badly with the very people he hoped to exclude, he wrote the *Post* again a few weeks later, on 9 December.

This time he enlarges an argument that 'temples of nature, temples built by the Almighty, [should be] left unviolated,' and that, in small local towns, 'the Sabbath day' should be protected from 'much additional desecration.' In other words, it is the working-class day-trippers who only have Sundays free who are his problem. He maintains they simply don't have the 'culture' to appreciate the beauty of the landscape:

> As for holiday pastimes, if a scene is to be chosen suitable to them for persons thronging from a distance, it may be found elsewhere at less cost of every kind [whereas] the perception of what has acquired the name of picturesque and romantic scenery is so far from being intuitive, that it can be produced only by a slow and gradual process of culture.

The laureate seems to have forgotten here the universalism that 'temples built by the Almighty' imply. Somewhat ironically, he is clumsily restating the very belief in an elite sensibility that the gadfly Shelley and his circle had often advocated: including ('Peter was dull . . . ') to mock Wordsworth himself.

It leaves a sour taste in the mouth. Which is why, on this morning of dazzle, I'm walking not around Rydal Mount or Dove Cottage but instead some nine miles away, along the shore of Coniston Water. I want to pay tribute to someone who in 1844 was thinking about landscape and art in profoundly different and more inclusive ways than the Wordsworth of the *Morning Post*. From 1871 until his death in 1900, the artist, writer and philanthropist John Ruskin would live at Brantwood, a level three-mile stroll along the eastern shoreline from my starting point at Low Peel Near. In 1844, however, he was living in south-east London and thinking about landscape painting as a search for truth; an argument he'd first made in Volume 1 of *Modern Painters*, published the year before. Ruskin just lived into the twentieth century. But it's his work with the urban poor, particularly in Sheffield, that peculiarly identifies him with Romanticism's industrial legacy. At heart an educationalist, he had no trouble assuming that workers in the city's steel industry both could, and must, respond to art just as much as Oxford undergraduates. John Keats's 'Beauty is truth, truth beauty' — insight from a poet who was himself the victim of destructive snobbery — would speak, for Ruskin, not to the elite nature of sensibility: but to its universality.

The influential *The Elements of Drawing* (1851) was based on Ruskin's lectures at the St Pancras Working Men's College, while students who enrolled in the School of Drawing he founded at Oxford University in 1871 would come under the sway of his belief that drawing is a particularly attentive way of seeing — for everyone. Over a century later, I learnt the same thing while standing at my father's elbow watching him draw. As his pencil nudged the paper, seeming to test and measure where and how to go, it showed me mark by surprising mark exactly how a corner joined to an elevation, a roofline to the contour of a hill.

The antidote Ruskin offers to the strain of elitism within Romanticism was surely explicit. For, although he was born twenty-seven years after Shelley and thirty-nine after Wordsworth, his thinking about art was deeply, and consciously, Romantic in its formation. 'The greatest thing a human soul ever does in this world is to see something, and tell what it saw in a plain way [. . .] To see clearly is poetry, prophecy, and religion, − all in one,' he famously wrote, in Volume III of *Modern Painters*. All five volumes of the work − the final published in 1860 − are passionate in their advocacy of the picturesque tradition and its heirs, particularly Turner. His method was Romantic too. He argued from and for experience and emotion rather than classical form in art and criticism: perhaps most famously in 'The Nature of Gothic', his great essay from *The Stones of Venice* (1851−53) which explores the intuitive and spontaneous character of mediaeval church ornamentation.

Like Wordsworth's Rydal Mount, however, Ruskin's own home at Brantwood is a comfortably substantial gentleman's residence, at the same time enviable and a little disconcerting. It sits on a small outcrop that lifts it proud from the fell behind and even seems to shoulder it out over the lake; its stucco glows in the onshore light. But as I approach I'm surprised to see the house isn't especially handsome: in fact, its exterior looks oddly incoherent. The pretty Regency and Georgian property Ruskin acquired, and so proudly photographed for his *Lectures on Landscape* in 1871, has been distorted by extensions like any bypass villa. And yet even these additions, built to house relatives, and a valet's family, reflect its occupier's values. Ruskin did not share Wordsworth's impulse to clear away 'those who cannot afford to pay', the better to enjoy the beautiful view with which he lived; on the contrary, he chose instead to share.

I can feel the sun on my shoulders. The morning lake has receded to a series of glimpses between the skinny trees of the shoreline. By the time I get past the car park and up the stone garden stairs Brantwood, as he would have wished, will be open to the public.

Walk 5: East of Lake lane between Brantwood and Low Peel Near, Coniston, LA21 8AD, OS Grid Ref SD307945.

Sixth Walk

Securing

Dear was the pause of life, and dear the sigh
That call'd the wanderer home, and home to rest.

WILLIAM WORDSWORTH, 'On Seeing Miss Helen
    Maria Williams Weep at a Tale of Distress'

In January 1787, a sixteen-year-old William Wordsworth published his first poem, the sonnet 'On Seeing Miss Helen Maria Williams Weep at a Tale of Distress'. It opens:

She wept.——Life's purple tide began to flow
In languid streams through every thrilling vein;
Dim were my swimming eyes——my pulse beat slow,
And my full heart was swell'd to dear delicious pain.

'Thrilling' stuff indeed, and right from the first line, where 'Life's purple tide' as a synonym for blood raises the stakes by identifying the imperial, imperious, quality of the life force.

Though the poet in me can't help noticing that 'purple' also scans better here than 'red'.

But that's clearly not the only thing going on in what is at the same time the 'languid . . . swimming' of private fantasy. The sonnet genre is as much a formal expression of masculine desire as is the nude in painting. And sure enough, this one completes the octet with a sigh of release:

> Life left my loaded heart, and closing eye;
> A sigh recall'd the wanderer to my breast;
> Dear was the pause of life, and dear the sigh
> That call'd the wanderer home, and home to rest.

The English sonnet has a particular tradition of doublings; of teasing the parallel lines of paradox, metaphor or riddle. Under his *nom de plume* of Axiologus, the teenaged Wordsworth cleverly plays with how the daydreamer most successfully summons up his fantasy object when alone – for example, in the nightly privacy of bed:

> That tear proclaims—in thee each virtue dwells,
> And bright will shine in misery's midnight hour;
> As the soft star of dewy evening tells
> What radiant fires were drown'd by day's
>   malignant pow'r,
> That only wait the darkness of the night
> To cheer the wand'ring wretch with hospitable light.

Which is to the point, because there *is* no literal seeing being invoked here. Axiologus has encountered his subject only in fantasy; with what, two decades later, he would famously call 'that inward eye/Which is the bliss of solitude.'

Conspicuous women magnetise sexualised attention as well as sexual opprobrium. I think not only of today's sexualised trolling of distinguished figures, but of reactions in Wordsworth's era to Mary Wollstonecraft, especially after her husband's *Memoirs of the Author of A Vindication of the Rights of Woman* (1798) revealed how she had practised the free love he and their coterie preached. And Helen Maria Williams was a perfect fantasy object for the young Wordsworth. When *The European Magazine* published 'On Seeing . . . ', she was already known as a poet and literary highflyer, who numbered Robert Burns among her well-connected friends. She had been publishing poetry for just five years, but was on the brink of adding to her literary repertoire translations, volumes of prose and even literary salons. Meanwhile her reputation as an abolitionist, a radical and a Francophile already placed her beyond the protection of convention, something that perhaps only added to her allure. That she was nine years Wordsworth's senior, a fact of which he may or may not have been aware, seems to have been largely irrelevant.

Four years later in 1791, at twenty-one, he followed in Williams's footsteps to revolutionary France. Here he tried repeatedly to meet her, but was unsuccessful. Instead, in the elegant Loire-side city of Blois, he fell in love with another young woman, also a little older than him, who despite the coincidence of her oddly homophonous name was Williams's political antithesis. Annette Vallon was a twenty-five-year-old Royalist and petite bourgeoise whose father had been a notary's clerk. Still, the poet remained enough of a radical not to marry, despite making her the conventional promises: even when, a couple of months after he'd left Blois for Paris, she gave birth to his daughter. In 1792, Romanticism found this sort of thing highly forgivable. As William Godwin would put it in his *Enquiry Concerning Political Justice*, published the next year:

> It is absurd to expect that the inclinations and wishes of two human beings should coincide through a long period of time. To oblige them to act and to live together, is to subject them to some inevitable portion of thwarting, bickering and unhappiness. This cannot be otherwise, so long as man has failed to reach the standard of absolute perfection.

And in 1793, as the French political situation worsened, the young man quit for England, simply leaving behind his lover and their baby, Anne-Caroline.

Godwin's *Political Justice* generalises, 'Co-habitation is not only an evil as it checks the independent progress of mind; it is also inconsistent with the imperfections and propensities of man.' But for Wordsworth – who like Godwin himself did go on to marry – it must have been slightly more complicated: a wager on his future feelings for Annette against the immediate danger from political violence, when both were unknowns. In the event, he chose England. He would return to France only a decade later, making the trip in 1802 to announce to his little French family the marriage with Mary Hutchinson that displaced them. In coming home, he aligned himself with what would come to be a peculiarly English Romanticism of concrete apprehension, rather than joining the more political and philosophical continental European movement.

Helen Maria Williams, on the other hand, remained in France, braving the Terror on which she would report for English readers in eight volumes of *Letters Written in France* (1790–96). She spent her final decade largely in Amsterdam, but upon her death in 1827 was interred in Père Lachaise Cemetery, by then laid out near Paris on the farmland that had recently been the setting of Jean-Jacques Rousseau's 'solitary walks'.

Williams and Wordsworth did eventually meet, in the French capital, in October 1820. The Englishman was once again in the country to visit Annette and Anne-Caroline; this time finally introducing them to his wife and sister. His note accepting Helen Maria's invitation to call, now held at the Archives and Special Collections at Amherst, appears frankly scribbled, and its twisty, awkward expression seems to imply some process of resistance or negotiation. Was this, perhaps, internal? Or could it have been on the part of those unusually respectable Romantics, the Wordsworth women?

Mr Wordsworth regrets, that owing to conditional engage-ments he could not reply to Miss Williams's obliging note before this morning.

He is now happy to say that it will be in his power to wait upon Miss Williams on Friday Evening; and to bring Mrs & Miss Wordsworth, his sister, along with him.

45 Rue Charles
Wednesday Morning

The benefit of hindsight, the future perfect tense that lets us spy on this emotional and political future, makes it tempting to read Wordsworth's 1787 'On Seeing Miss Helen Maria Williams Weep ... ' as sentimentally farseeing. In fact, its 'weeping' is purely literary, a homage to Williams's development of the new writerly technique of 'sensibility', which directed onto the page a highly tuned responsiveness to the writer's own experiences and to the experiences of others. This often produced political results. In 1784 Williams had published the long anti-colonial poem *Peru*, and in 1788 her 'Poem on the Slave Bill' appeared. By 1794, her hardworking titles include 'Imitation Of Lines Written By Roucher, Below His Picture, Which A Fellow-Prisoner Had Drawn, And Which He Sent To His Wife And Children The Day Before His Execution', and 'Imitation Of Lines Addressed By M. D——, A Young Man Of Twenty-Four Years Of Age, The Night Before His Execution, To A Young Lady To Whom He Was Engaged'; unsurprising then that in 1815, after some years of silence, she welcomed the fall of Napoleon with a verse *Narrative of the Events*.

But Williams also set sensibility to work on an intimate scale. 'To Mrs K——, On Her Sending Me an English Christmas Plum-Cake at Paris' impregnates the 'odorous cells' of a Christmas cake with Proustian nostalgia:

> For magic surely lurks in this,
> A cake that tells of vanished bliss;
> A cake that conjures up to view
> The early scenes, when life was new;
> When memory knew no sorrows past,
> And hope believed in joys that last! —
> Mysterious cake, whose folds contain
> Life's calendar of bliss and pain.

Her sonnets move repeatedly towards what John Ruskin would later call the pathetic fallacy, in which the natural world and the poet are apparently so in tune that they echo each other. 'Sonnet: To the Curlew', for example, opens at the seashore, where in good British fashion it can't quite settle on what the weather's doing:

> Sooth'd by the murmurs on the sea-beat shore,
> His dun-grey plumage floating to the gale,
> The Curlew blends his melancholy wail
> With those hoarse sounds the rushing waters pour.

While the responding sestet shows the narrator's sensibility rushing to respond:

> I love the ocean's broad expanse, when drest
> In limpid clearness, or when tempests blow.

It's tempting to dismiss Williams's writing as a historical byway. Yet she was opening up a royal road to social and interpersonal exploration; one we still take today. I can't help juxtaposing her stylistic advances with the significance, for the Britain of her time, of her eyewitness accounts of revolutionary France. She made of sensibility – a quality her culture tended reductively to identify as feminine – a literary strategy whose strengths included the authority of historical witness: and so helped shift a 'feminised' engagement with the world towards the cultural mainstream. The bridgehead that sensibility opened there has proved substantial: one undeniable heir is psychoanalysis, with its systematic attention to the unconscious logic of feelings. Another is fiction driven by characters' motives and emotions. Since the nineteenth century it's become the norm, and in the twenty-first still predominates in novel and film. It's also, increasingly, the narrative approach taken to nonfictional material, and even current affairs.

All of which makes me think about Jane Austen's 1811 debut, *Sense and Sensibility*. Since the 1790s, Austen had been working on a story to illustrate the dangers of being carried away by emotion (sensibility) instead of listening to reason (sense). Even this, her final version, retains strong affinities with the conduct book; although that mediaeval genre, aimed at mapping the world of female experience, was by the nineteenth century rapidly losing ground to the novel. *Sense and Sensibility*'s portrayal of 'sensitive' Marianne is not, in the end, wholly condemnatory. But it's hard not to read Austen's whole corpus as comedy of manners, in retreat both formally and tonally from Williams's 'sensibility'. *Northanger Abbey* (1817), for example, pokes explicit fun at Gothic novels. But Helen Maria Williams was no mere character from sentimental fiction. And it's her real-life political and cultural courage that I find myself thinking about today, as we stand on this headland facing south across the Channel to her elective homeland.

P and I are some 140 chalky metres above sea-level, on the south coast of the Isle of Wight. March sunlight keeps hammering off the waves, and a breeze lifts from the water below. We're near the midpoint of Tennyson Down, named for the great mid-nineteenth-century laureate who lived in the lee of its long back, and who walked here daily. But I'm not here to search for the kind of people Lytton Strachey called *Eminent Victorians*. I'm looking further back, to 1793 and the height of the Terror in revolutionary France. That summer the two newest volumes of Williams's series *Letters Written in France*, disclosing the full horror of the previous months, had to be published anonymously for her safety. In October she, her mother and sisters were arrested as British citizens and imprisoned for six weeks.

Meanwhile, in response to France's declaration of war on 1 February, the British Navy was mustering here off the Isle of Wight. Wordsworth would recall in Book 10 of *The Prelude* how, visiting for a month:

> I beheld the vessels lie
> A brood of gallant creatures, on the deep;
> I saw them in their rest, a sojourner
> Through a whole month of calm and glassy days
> In that delightful Island that protects
> Their place of convocation.

The fleet's first great engagement with the French Atlantic fleet wouldn't be till the Glorious First of June the following year. But meanwhile the forces that anchored here were being vastly enlarged. By the end of the Napoleonic Wars the British Navy would have more than doubled in size; and since already the large number of crew this required could not be voluntarily recruited, many of the men stuffed into those 'gallant creatures' anchored offshore were serving against their will, impressed by violent gangs or through the Quota Acts. Their forced 'convocation' was neither 'calm' nor 'protected'.

But these choppy straits – the Channel to the south of the island, and the Solent to its north – do afford a form of shelter.

Even today, the Wight retains a curious character all its own, simultaneously wild and kitsch. There's a piratical note to the way its 150 square miles hang back offshore, not tethered to the south coast of England by a fixed link of any kind. Poor weather still frequently cuts it off from the mainland. To reach the island even in good weather, you must cross the crowded shipping lanes of the tidal Solent, where continental ferries, yachts and cruise liners compete with container ships from the Port of Southampton. And here the whole experience of driving up onto a car ferry's clanging deck, or stepping into the bouncing cabin of one of the high-speed alternatives – catamaran, hydrofoil or hovercraft – makes it absolutely clear that you really are going to sea.

Nevertheless in 1793 this modest diamond of land, which seems almost to float off the Hampshire coast, was already a destination. Today's cul-de-sacs of bungalows spring straight from the Romantic fashion for its *sublime* views, like the one we're enjoying from Tennyson Down today, and *picturesque* chines. Many of the fine eighteenth-century houses on West Cowes esplanade, for example, were built as the summer resort of London establishment figures, including that 'Myceneas of the age', John Kenyon. Writer, salonist and literary man about town, Kenyon was a larger than life figure whose mentees included his own distant cousin Elizabeth Barrett, and the young, unmarried poet, Robert Browning, to whom he introduced her. So it doesn't seem surprising that in late summer 1856 the Brownings, already married ten years, should have come to stay on the island while Elizabeth corrected the proofs of her masterpiece *Aurora Leigh*, which she dedicated to Kenyon. More disconcerting is that they did so in part because, soon

after their arrival in London on one of their regular visits from
Florence, her father decided his Wimpole Street household
needed a few weeks away. The coincidental trip away was also
something of a regular occurrence: Edward Barrett Moulton-
Barrett had after all disowned his eldest daughter, and was
evidently keen to limit her influence on her siblings. Now he
rented for his own household Melbourne Villa, overlooking the
Channel at Ventnor on the south-east coast of the Isle of Wight.

Undeterred, on 23 August, Elizabeth and Robert took
rooms in nearby Milanese Villa:

> Thirty five shillings a week for an acorn of a sitting-room, a
> bedroom & dressing room, & Wilson's room upstairs. And
> it's to be dearer presently, in the winter – the winter being
> the season here. But I like the place much. The country is
> very English & beautiful of its class – & I enjoyed to my
> heart, the green dewy shadows yesterday.

Ventnor, as windy as its name suggests, today retains the
Victorian character of its rapid emergence in the quarter
century before the Brownings visited. Villas stand among
shrubberies and on precipitate cliff edges, facing out to the
same gleaming horizon we can see from the other end of the
island, here on Tennyson Down. Even if it's never described in
Aurora Leigh, this spacious view, full of changeability and possibility, cannot but have informed the poet's revisions, as she
executed them in those seafront rooms among her much missed
family, who were eager to be involved as critical readers.

However, after a week *en famille* the Browning couple moved
across the island to Cowes, to stay with John Kenyon. He was

by now mortally sick. As Elizabeth reported to a mutual friend, the art historian Anna Jameson:

> At first, dear Mr Kenyon struck me as much better than I expected to find him – he looks occasionally like himself . . . and his kindness & generous, patient sweetness are always himself, or more – But there are changes – he is feeble, and he suffers the burden of life painfully . . . and I grow gradually sadder about him – Still, if he were younger, I should hope. There is no proof of organic disease of the heart, though abundant proof of symptomatic disarrangement of it. The want of breath is very painful – & plainly it is no asthma. He dines with us everyday, but has never been out since we came, – & complains of increased feebleness, &, every now & then, desires aloud to pass away & be at rest –

Still, the place itself was charming. We think of the nineteenth-century Isle of Wight as a Victorian invention: between 1845 and 1851, Queen Victoria built Osborne House just across the River Medina from Cowes. But by the time she did so Cowes had already been on the Establishment map for decades.

Today the little town remains as cosy as it is bracing: all coloured stucco, hip-roofed eighteenth-century brick and tile houses, mixed in with skinny flat-fronted terraces. By the mid-nineteenth century the Royal Yacht Squadron, of which Mary and Percy Bysshe Shelley's son Percy Florence was a member, had long since founded the annual regatta that sent tall-sailed craft scudding up and down the bumpy waters of the Solent. (Percy Florence evidently inherited his father's passion for risky sailing.) In 1826 this had become Cowes Week; in 1854 the

Squadron would move into Cowes Castle, positioned centrally on the Esplanade and still its home today. In a note mailed to Ventnor, Elizabeth described to her sister Arabella how:

> Mr Kenyon's house overlooks the parade (which is immediately under the windows!) and the sea touches the parade — so that the view of the shipping, American steamers, &c &c is in our very eyes, & shifting all day & night — [. . .] We sit out on the balcony furnished with chairs & telescopes —

In clear maritime light, these telescopes would have easily picked out details on the tree-lined shoreline of the mainland, less than two miles to the north. Her old friend's balcony must have deliciously resembled a kind of box in some fantastic outdoor theatre.

This morning Cowes is out of sight over the shoulder of the West Wight downs, which roll down to the Needles. Up here there are none of Ventnor's 'green dewy shadows'. Not even a gothic shading of pine or blackthorn, though in the valley below trees and shrubs cluster round Tennyson's Farringford House, which Elizabeth's sometime rival for the laureateship purchased in the very same year that she visited the Island. Farringford stands behind and overlooking Freshwater Bay, where a Victorian bohemia would later coalesce around the photographer Julia Margaret Cameron's home at Dimbola Lodge, and later still be famously satirised by Cameron's great-niece Virginia Woolf in her 1935 play *Freshwater*. But it also faces backwards, to the Romanticism that necessarily formed this consummate Victorian, born after all in 1809.

Tennyson's home is not hefty High Victorian shlock but a delicate, Strawberry Hill Gothic mansion, built in 1806. Its parapet crenelations, and the long arched loggia and balcony that define its north front – creating a sense of horizonal space and movement not dissimilar to the decks of an ocean liner – had been added in the 1830s. Perhaps most Romantic of all in spirit, though it would not be constructed until 1871, is the private staircase that gives from the poet's upper-floor study directly onto the Downs, allowing him to escape the worldly demands that accompanied his fame.

This morning we're heading away from Freshwater, uphill and west. The downland grass growing tight underfoot is part of an ecosystem shaped by the sheep grazing around us, although environmental management has reduced their numbers in recent years. Tennyson Down is triply designated: a Site of Special Scientific Interest held in trust for the nation by the National Trust within an Area of Outstanding Natural Beauty. Cropping helps the clover and those low creeping vetches, *Hippocrepis comosa,* horseshoe vetch, and *Anthyllis vulneraria,* kidney vetch, which can survive thin topsoil and scant irrigation. Come summer, nine species of orchid will reassert precarious tenure here, and from May even the rare early gentian, *Gentianella anglica* and, a month or so later, centaury, *Centaurium erythraea*, will be flowering. You have to pay attention to catch their flashes of purple and pink. But in the pallor of this March morning there's nothing growing this high up to match the outbursts of celandine and primrose in the banks and hedgerows of Freshwater.

The dogs are pulling us toward a skyline that – apart from the incongruous granite Celtic cross that is the Tennyson

Monument – describes a beautifully empty, clean horizontal. Downland always seems a landscape of gesture rather than somewhere to settle; although its sedimentary chalk, laid down over millennia, appears almost as a rebuff to the busy igneous revolutions, the granite and slate, beloved of Romanticism, that 'Ghastly, and scarred, and riven [. . .] scene/Where the old Earthquake-daemon taught her young/Ruin,' Percy Bysshe Shelley celebrated in 'Mont Blanc'. (The poet's own birthplace at Field Place, Warnham, lies ironically, of course, in softly rolling West Sussex, within the sandstone arc of Horsham Stone that lines the Weald Basin.)

The Wight's true paradigm, though, is indeed settlement, in the form of the bungalow crescent juxtaposing bright, disciplined gardens against a sea that roars just over the road, or beyond the corner shop. As a child of the British archipelago, I've a big soft spot for the vernacular of seaside kitsch: the plasticated closed verandas, the ornamental shells and varnished gnomes and pebbledash. I'm fond of the way moss on a concrete path, lozenges of mould on a water butt, make something picturesque out of the consolations of the suburban banal. I find these ugly, aspirational gestures – a glimpse of bold seventies geometrics through an open window, or a hot tub with junk evidently taken root on its cover – touching in their hopefulness. But I also remember how deeply, in my own coastal childhood, I loved falling asleep to gales that roared off the Atlantic and shook the roof. The contrast with my warm bed was a delicious intensifier: I suspect something of the same principle creates the paradoxical British seaside, which again and again sees cosiness pick a spot which might be bracing at its summer best but becomes badly godforsaken out of season.

This morning though, as our dogs browse among the sheep droppings – nibbling some, rolling in others, according to certain canine arcanae – it's not this kind of shelter that springs to mind. I'm thinking about a particular notion of asylum that owes its genesis to Romantic engineering, and to Romantic ideas about the sovereignty of the self.

When I was in my early twenties I came to the Isle of Wight to take up a job at what was then called Whitecroft. The three hundred-bed Isle of Wight County Lunatic Asylum had been built in 1896: a later date than most of the great nineteenth-century county asylums, because it was only required when the island ceased to be administered as part of Hampshire. But by the time I started work, the dissolution of the asylum system in Britain had begun. Whitecroft's name had already been softened from 'Lunatic Asylum' to 'Psychiatric Hospital'; soon, we would no longer refer to 'psychiatry' but to 'mental illness'. Later, we would shift from 'mental illness' to 'mental health'. Whitecroft itself was in transition too. The hospital farm had been sold and its market garden grassed over. Dotted around the grounds were empty, single-storey buildings of indeterminate character, their paintwork still gardener green. Built of red brick, with frosted glass in their metal framed windows, they were unprepossessing enough; in another context you'd assume they were changing rooms or tractor sheds. But here, where fireweed was beginning to break up the surrounding tarmac and a silence had settled under the Scots pines, they assumed an air of secrecy.

Our office occupied a ward that had fallen out of use. These wards were brick-built two-storey pavilions fanning from the hospital entrance in an Echelon Plan: a sort of three-dimensional filing system for the various ages and conditions of people who lived there. Psychosis, neurosis, learning difficulty, dementia: the system was blunt in its verdicts. The hospital had been designed by a Yorkshireman, Benjamin Septimus Jacobs. He had by the standards of Victorian asylums a somewhat austere approach to decoration. (Admittedly this was also true of the old Western Street synagogue in Hull, which he built in 1902 for his own congregation.) Additionally, in order to economise on land use, he placed his Echelon in a Compact Arrow formation, the wards stepping apart from each other but stepping into the spinal corridor that linked them.

Ours was the final pavilion of the northern wing of this formation, which meant there was no one else in hailing distance of the office. On winter nights when I was the last to leave, I'd run down the cement stairs and across the deserted yard to my car, full of gothic terrors the place seemed designed to generate. Yet during the long institutional afternoons, when wide-leaved sycamores soughed outside the windows, a tremendous sense of calm could float in these same high-ceilinged rooms, whose big windows gave onto a shoulder of downland, a seaside sky. You could succumb almost languorously to the routine of a place that ran, as the saying goes, like clockwork, and whose very scale encouraged your surrender.

The main corridor, a quarter-kilometre semicircle along which everything was conveyed, kept the hospital ticking over. But it also kept it turning away from itself. When you walked that tiled length, its curve created a perpetual concealment. The entrance to one ward had disappeared around its continual corner by the time you got to the next. Today this corridor, its black and white checkerboard floor tiles and its accretion of temporary wooden structures have all disappeared. Cut free, the ward pavilions have become small blocks of luxury flats, standing apart from each other in parkland: the entire twenty-acre site has changed its name to Gatcombe Manor. Only verticals give the game away. The old incinerator chimney now stands by itself in a communal patio, like a monument to the lives wasted here. The six-storey water-tower with its Tuscan pediment also remains. This at least Jacobs decorated, transforming it into a clocktower. The elegant ogee slant of its leaded roof – half-dome, half-spire – reminds me of the ornamental lid of a mantel clock.

When I worked at Whitecroft we always knew where we were in relation to the clock, which was visible everywhere, and the time it told, which we could hear as well as see. Its chimes announced the tea trolley, canteen visits, ward rounds, occupational therapy. Time, it pointed out every quarter of an hour, is where we live. For people consigned to the locked wards, sometimes for little more than a crime of nonconformity, often for years, time was part of the hospital's total control. 'Asylum' wasn't yet a word that had been pressed into service to somehow discredit refugee experience. But it had long shed any notion of shelter; it meant not 'safe place' so much as 'Bedlam'. Clock and corridor, mapped onto the site like nothing so much as the Masonic protractor and compass point, together traced out a design for impersonal control: one which had driven the design of workhouses, prisons and asylums for almost two centuries.

The idea that small numbers of staff could control large numbers of confined supervisees directly from a central observation hub such as a rotunda was developed by the Utilitarian philosopher Jeremy Bentham (1748–1832). He had come across a version of this arrangement, which he would come to call the panopticon, early in the Romantic era, in 1786–87, while visiting his brother in what is today Belarus. Bentham saw the innovation as an opportunity to persuade the British government to build a new National Penitentiary with himself as its Governor. Despite his argument that it offered a cheap and profitable way to hold prisoners, the sixteen years of planning and investment he directed to this ambition were ultimately unsuccessful. Nevertheless, the idea caught on. In 1791 he published *Panopticon, or The Inspection House*. The same year, Jean-Philippe Garran de Coulon presented his ideas to the French National Legislative Assembly. In 1821, a National Penitentiary was finally erected beside the Thames in London, on the Millbank site Bentham had purchased for his own prison.

Millbank, though vast, was a hybrid. Each of its six pentagonal wings was itself a panopticon, but at the centre of the structure was a courtyard with chapel rather than a watchtower. For detractors including Bentham himself, this hollowed out the supervisory principle, rendering it less efficient, and prevented the prison from being run for profit as a workhouse. Millbank's radial layout was in this sense decorative rather than utilitarian. It was Pentonville, completed in 1842 and designed from the outset for prison work, that would provide the model for future instantiations of a template planners eventually found so persuasive that, by the 1960s, a majority of British factories had their shopfloors, where the manufacturing labour actually took place, overlooked by raised, glass-windowed managers' offices. A total of 520 cells line the distinctive long landings of Pentonville's five radial wings. Each measures a tiny four metres by two and is designed to hold one man, cut off from his neighbours but visible to prison staff: his only relationship with authority.

The secret of panopticon surveillance is that, because inmates may be watched from the observation post at any time, at every moment they have to assume themselves to be under surveillance: they have to internalise *being-observed*. Bentham well understood this mechanism of coercive control:

> The Building circular – an iron cage, glazed – a glass lantern about the size of Ranelagh – The Prisoners in their Cells, occupying the Circumference – The Officers, the Centre. By Blinds, and other contrivances, the Inspectors concealed from the observation of the Prisoners: hence the sentiment of a sort of invisible omnipresence. – The whole circuit reviewable with little, or, if necessary, without any, change of place.

The panopticon 'gaze' uses a similar power dynamic and organising principle to the peep show. Of which the point is not just to *see* the body parts we all know women have, but to experience that thrill of asymmetry: the punters guaranteed privacy from which to peep, the woman granted precisely none. Contemporary digital assaults underline how looking is *the* primary gesture of power: women, prisoners, people living with mental health issues – and shopfloor workers – are socially subordinated groups; and non-reciprocal observation helps keep them so.

Whitecroft's clock could 'see' nothing. But, because it was more than three times the height of any other hospital building, anyone who *did* look out of its small roof windows could survey the whole site – without being seen. So the clockface became a kind of placeholder, mnemonic for those 'Inspectors concealed from [. . .] observation,' who might or might not be watching, 'hence the sentiment of a sort of invisible omnipresence.'

Utilitarianism was a radical philosophy that believed itself to be at some distance from Romanticism. However, in the course of these walks I'm regularly reminded of just how strongly Romanticism was orientated towards *seeing*. It understood that to see is to know. At Whitecroft, the locked ward doors, the ECT suite, the trembling fingers of the men on long-term lithium were all there for me to see. I witnessed the mind-numbing Industrial Therapy, where patients sorted screws by size for hours a day, and heard the life stories of women who had remained on the wards since being locked up as teenagers before the war for falling pregnant. But by the end of my time, life on-site had taken on an end of term feeling. As it wound down the hospital loosened its grip. As wards closed, the system ceased to be totalitarian simply because it was no longer total. The clock on the tower went wrong. Then it stopped, which meant that the bell-strokes marking the quarter hours ceased. Silence hung in their place like an ellipsis. Those staff who still moved around the hospital's emptied spaces seemed reduced too, the distinctive brown and blue check print of their uniforms appearing now oddly faded.

Times change, even on the Isle of Wight. As we hunker down in the lee of the Tennyson Monument to eat some chocolate and — to the dogs' disgust — gaze out at the beaten-silver of the Channel, I reflect how, by the time the Brownings visited in 1856, writers and artists had already worn a path to the island. William Makepeace Thackeray had holidayed here with his daughters three years earlier. John Hamilton Reynolds moved to the island on the recommendation of his close friend John Keats, who had himself visited for his health in 1817 and 1819. And, back in 1807, Charles and Mary Lamb holidayed in Cowes with a nephew of Fanny Burney's.

Nor was it the exclusive province of figures whose names we still remember. John Gwilliam dedicated two volumes of verse of somewhat mixed quality to the island: *Rambles in the Isle of Wight 1841–2* (1843) was followed by *Norris Castle: Or Recent Tramps in the Isle of Wight* (1845). In *Rambles*, Gwilliam contemplates Ryde landing stage from higher ground:

> How should I revel if, amidst these trees,
> I had some pleasant cottage of my own,
> With means sufficient for a poet's ease,
> And friends far diff'rent to the tribe I've known!
>
> I'd rather live amodst [sic] these elms and oaks,
> In some small cottage, than in Portman Square,
> For Nature here no jealousy provokes,
> Nor envies Art luxuriating there [. . .]
>
> Hence, when I sit upon thy mossy grounds,
> Thou fairy spot! and contemplate the sea,
> My heart with secret ecstasy abounds —
> I feel as happy as a bard needs be!

Beneath me lay the pleasant town of Ryde,
Whose terrac'd villas glitter'd through the trees -
Beyond them shone the undulating tide,
Where yachts and barques were waiting for a breeze.

Running far out into the azure sea,
The Pier display'd its fashionable throng,
Swells, dandies, nobles, sailors full of glee,
And nymphs as happy as the days were long!

There were the tourists from the boats alighting,
From Portsmouth some, and from
      Southampton others,
The ladies all so lovely and inviting,
You scarcely knew the daughters from their
      mothers [. . .]

There were the porters running up and down,
Making the place all noise and hurly-burly —
There Mr Smith was ogling Mrs Brown,
And Brown, her husband, looking rather surly.

But leaving these, and turning to thy groves,
How many happy moments have I pass'd,
Thou pleasing spot! where mem'ry often roves,
And finds herself at liberty, at last!

Leaving aside his difficulties with tense and tone, Gwilliam is bang on the money with his Romantic sentiment. There's a straight line back across the intervening two decades from

'Some pleasant cottage of my own,/With means sufficient for a poet's ease' to Mary Shelley's cottage-dwelling political idealists in her by-then widely-read *Frankenstein*, or to the group of like minds – Gwilliam's 'friends far diff'rent to the tribe I've known' – she pictures retreating from the world in *The Last Man*. Not that she was the first to cultivate the idea of this other form of asylum, the writer's retreat. Shelley was familiar in turn with Giovanni Boccaccio's book of tales, *The Decameron*, written in the aftermath of the 1348 Black Death, whose conceit is that ten young people retreat from the plague to a Tuscan villa, where they pass the time in telling stories of life-affirming voluptuousness. Equally well-known in her lifetime was how in 1571, 'at the age of 38, on the day before March, his birthday, Michel Montaigne . . . while still sound in wind and limb . . . retired to shelter where, in calm and total security . . . he consecrated this home and sweet retreat to freedom, tranquillity and leisure.' She would have been aware how, in the protective shadow of that declaration, painted over the study fireplace in his now famous tower at Chateau de Montaigne in the Dordogne, Montaigne produced his influential *Essays*.

Here on Tennyson Down it's easy to feel distanced from day-to-day worries waiting in the car park below. Straight ahead is West High Down, the last harrumph of the chalk scarp before it stutters into the sea. Wind whickers in my ears, as if I were being propelled very fast away from something. The water keeps on shining. Pushing through the turf we're sitting on are the ragged leaves and first bald flowers of groundsel, *Senecio vulgaris*. I pick a blade of grass and start to strip it. P is talking about how we've made what is after all a Romantic choice ourselves, living 'amodst [. . .] elms and oaks,/In some small cottage.' He's right, and I nod my agreement. But I'm thinking about something else. I hold the grass blade up to the sun and see its edges flush yellow. I think that I need to look clearly at my complicity in the notion of asylum. When I worked at Whitecroft, did I ever let myself step inside the viewing gallery of the psychiatry panopticon? Sometimes, for example, two-way mirrors were used in sessions I took part in; then I too was watching the people I was working with without being seen by them.

When I came to the island to work, I had everything straight in my mind: 'lunatic' and 'asylum' were technical words, which belonged together in the great heap of things that had been discredited. It was only once I actually arrived onsite that I encountered the physical and emotional seductiveness of a handsome 'Lunatic Asylum' built and equipped with what the nineteenth century believed to be the very best of facilities, from ballroom to farm. These good looks, and this attentiveness, complicated things by hinting at a lost ideal of safety and care.

Sometimes there was a kind of stillness in the hollow in the downs where Whitecroft stood. On sunny days the rooks seemed to float between the high beech and pine trees, which had been planted in the nineteenth century. Pigeons murmured on the roof. The tall windows let in the light and, above their frosted lower panes, expansive views of trees and skies. A comforting smell of dust rose from unpolished wooden floors. The institutional odours of chemical pine and lemon, polish and disinfectant, were reassuringly familiar. By eleven every morning canteen smells of steamed vegetables, gravy and custard seeped down the corridor. The clanging of steel canteens and the whirr of hospital trolleys, whistling porters and the almost-perpetual drone of a ride-on mower somewhere in the ground kept everything within reach and going on forever.

Yet something was so clearly wrong. What nineteenth-century authorities had remembered, in building hospitals like Whitecroft, was Bentham's Utilitarian principle of the convenience, for the social majority, of 'managing' people who seem incapable of managing themselves. What they had forgotten was asylum's elective nature. Safety and shelter can only be that if we choose them. Most people don't choose to be sectioned and held in locked wards. I was able to choose to enter the asylum and do the work I was involved in there. But it's only through this freedom that it could offer me the experiences – some shocking and brutal, others intimate and of almost transcendent beauty – I had there, and that I have never forgotten. At Whitecroft, I caught glimpses of a good dream behind the bad faith of the asylum movement. But I should probably have refused to look.

Walk 6: To Tennyson Monument on Tennyson Down, Isle of Wight, via Tennyson Trail from Freshwater Bay Long Stay Car Park, Freshwater Bay, Freshwater PO40 9QX OS Grid Ref SZ325853.

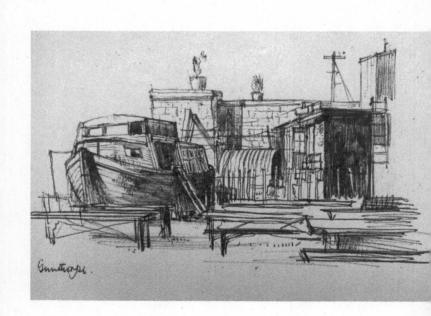

Seventh Walk

(Not) Belonging

. . . his stature, also, as he approached seemed to
exceed that of a man . . . the shape came nearer
(sight tremendous and abhorred!)

MARY SHELLEY,
Frankenstein

Traffic soughs down the Leiston road. As I swing it shut,
the five-bar gate catches the light between the pines.
Shadows of branches strobe the bright lane ahead; there's a
dewy smell of cut grass. Two golfers move purposefully over
the empty links opposite. Beyond them, incandescent gorse.

'Poetry without egotism comparatively uninteresting –,'
Coleridge noted to himself in 1795 or 6. I think he meant that
need we have to sense a poet's presence within the poem; to
encounter the human sensibility giving us its take on the world.
I don't believe this is only because of the seductiveness of *being
told,* our old desire to feel accompanied through a poem – as

through the world – by a narrator. It also has something to do
with recreating aliveness: that quality of the living world.

But what are the writerly equivalents of those 'instruments of life' which Frankenstein 'collected around me, that
I might infuse a spark of being into the lifeless thing that
lay at my feet'? Coleridge's note identifies the spark with
which, in Germany, lyric poetry had already been animated
by the Romanticism of, for example, Johann Wolfgang von
Goethe and Friedrich Hölderlin, and which he and William
Wordsworth would fan to life within the English tradition a
couple of years from now.

In 1798 the shorter first edition of their *Lyrical Ballads*
appeared; Wordsworth's Preface to its third, 1802 edition
includes that much-quoted definition:

What is a Poet? [. . .] He is a man speaking to men – a
man (it is true) endued with more lively sensibility, more
enthusiasm and tenderness, who has a greater knowledge
of human nature, and a more comprehensive soul, than are
supposed to be common among mankind; a man pleased
with his own passions and volitions, and who rejoices more
than other men in the spirit of life that is in him; delighting
to contemplate similar volitions and passions as manifested
in the goings-on of the universe, and habitually impelled to
create them where he does not find them.

This perfect encapsulation of Romantic thought places human
experience at the heart of its project, and at the heart of 'the
goings-on of the universe'. It sets these turning around the
individual self, much as in mediaeval times similar 'goings-on'

revolved round God. The God's-eye view has been replaced by a human viewpoint, but its existential significance remains.

Wordsworth borrows a language of neo-religious intensity: *enthusiasm, knowledge, comprehensive, the spirit of life, impelled.* In this benign, early configuration of the often-troublesome Romantic notion of an elite sensibility, the poet as a 'man speaking to men' (the usual gender disappointment) is 'endued with . . . more' than usual abilities. But this 'more' is instrumental rather than an end in itself: it's the difference that makes the poet and his work useful to society.

This relationship between society and that exception, the artist, is on my mind today, because I'm at the Suffolk coast as the guest of an institution that both promotes and examines the role of the artist in society. The Red House in Aldeburgh is where the composer Benjamin Britten and his partner and muse, the tenor Peter Pears, lived from 1957 until Britten's death in 1976. It's run by Britten Pears Arts, which the two musicians founded to bring music of the highest quality to their neighbourhood: and in doing so reciprocally to place this local community and landscape on the international artistic map. I'm staying in the grounds of the Red House, and my room looks out on both the old brick farmhouse itself – where a game of croquet is always set up on the lawn – and the serious modernist bulk of the Britten Archive, where at dusk the figures of scholars float in the illuminated windows. Of course Britten (1913–76) lived in the twentieth century, not the Romantic era. But it's his work with Romantic writing that I'm thinking about on this walk. It seems so provocatively to illustrate the way Romanticism remains embedded in British culture: allowing itself to be refashioned yet still carrying forward much of its own distinctiveness – and meanwhile intertwining itself with British ideas about countryside in a thoroughly 'organic' manner.

Coleridge's early note to self helped lead him to the *Lyrical Ballads*. But two decades later it also found an echo in the complex of ideas, about a work of art and the self who makes it, that he developed in 'On Poesy or Art'. Posthumously published as an essay, 'On Poesy . . . ' was originally a lecture given on 10 March 1818. It was the thirteenth in a series designed to introduce 'literary topics and the productions of the Fine Arts' to those who are 'altogether a stranger to subjects of taste', in order to relieve their allegedly low cultural self-esteem, that 'marked anxiety which men, who have succeeded in life without the aid of these accomplishments, shew in securing them to their children'.

'Altogether a stranger to', 'have succeeded in life without the aid of': I like this slightly ponderous phraseology, which is Coleridge's own. Yet the ponderousness also has a wandering, slightly avoidant note. It's as if those 'subjects of taste' are in fact rather hard to describe. Sure enough, Coleridge now views them as complex phenomena:

We all know, that Art is the imitatress of Nature. – And doubtless, the Truths, I hope to convey, would be barren Truisms, if all men meant the same by the words, *imitate* and *nature* [. . .] It is sufficient that philosophically we understand that in all Imitation two elements must exist, and not only exist but be perceived as existing – Likeness and unlikeness, or Sameness and Difference [. . .] the Artist may take his point where he likes – provided that the effect desired is produced – namely, that there should be a Likeness in difference & a union of the two – *Tragic Dance*.

This '*Tragic Dance*' is the interplay, within poem or picture, between identity and difference; the dialectic between one thing and another. Things are held together and apart by their difference from each other: the way presence and absence, or light and darkness, define each other. Right now, as I walk through the high-contrast morning shadows and sunlight, this dialectic play feels like plain common sense. It also helps me to think about the push and pull of influence between, for example, an original Romantic idea and its reception.

Yet even the very idea of such dialectic owes much to Romanticism. The technique of dialectical argument has been philosophical practice since Classical times; Socratic dialogue, which works through thesis and antithesis (statement and counter) to reach a conclusion, is the iconic example. Though, as Aristotle pointed out, the pre-Socratic Zeno of Elea, famous for his Paradox, was the real pioneer, since paradox is itself a pair of ideas that in pulling against each other create a particular position. Romanticism's great contribution to this intellectual tradition is the idea that forces within the world itself could work in this way too. The philosophers Immanuel Kant (1724–1804) and Johann Gottlieb Fichte (1762–1814) both embraced dialectic as a way of understanding the world. But it was their younger contemporary Georg Wilhelm Friedrich Hegel who developed not only the particular idea of *Herrschaft und Knechtschaft* but a wider understanding of history as a form of dialectical progress, achieved by the working out upon themselves of contradictions implicit in every moment.

Coleridge was so frequently implicated in British reception of European Romantic philosophical ideas that, in a notebook self-parody from December 1804, he advises the (imaginary) reader to 'read Tetens, Kant, Fichte, &c – and there you will trace or if you are on the hunt, track me'. By the time of his 1818 lecture on 'Poesy or Art' his reading had included *Wissenschaft der Logik*, which Hegel published between 1812 and 1816. In a marginal note on his copy, Coleridge objects to Hegel's highly schematic dialectical structure. Yet his own '*Tragic Dance*' brilliantly comprehends the doubled play of forces both within a piece of writing or art and in the process of creating it. The first dialectic he pinpoints – contrast within a unified text, that 'Likeness in difference & a union of the two' which is 'the effect desired' of good writing – is achieved by a second, the relationship between author and his text.

To avoid 'barren truisms', 'the Artist may take his point where he likes'. But wherever he does so he must insert the 'interest' of what Coleridge's earlier note had called 'egoism'. Writing which denies the resistances and partiality of the individual writing it, that 'check of difference', is lifeless. For Coleridge, this is as horrifying as any other form of lifelessness:

> If there be likeness to nature without any check of difference, the result is disgusting, and the more complete the delusion, the more loathsome the effect. Why are such simulations of nature, as wax-work figures of men and women, so disagreeable? Because not finding the motion and the life which we expected, we are shocked as by a falsehood.

I'm coming to the conclusion that my method on these walks is also a kind of dialectic. Now, for example, I'm crossing North Warren towards the sea, but I'm also thinking as I walk. The inner and outer worlds of my experience snag, or slip past each other. Far down the road, a white car seems to grow — yet dwindle — as I wait for it to pass. Is it flashing an indicator, or is that the sun glittering on its bonnet? This east coast light has a neuralgic quality. For Coleridge, 'Poesy' or 'Art' don't simply *describe* some element of, say, the natural world: the coconut smell of gorse blossom, or the golden-green woodpecker, *Picus viridis*, which just fired between the trees ahead of me. Rather, poetry and art *do as* nature does and, in both world and mind, beauty is an essential, because organic, formal principle: 'It is, in the abstract, the unity of the manifold, the coalescence of the diverse; in the concrete, it is the union of the shapely (*formosum*) with the vital.'

As the Coleridge scholar Seamus Perry points out, this is a response to F. W. J. von Schelling's 1807 essay, 'On the Relation of the Plastic Arts to Nature'. The philosopher's *System of Transcendental Idealism*, published in 1800, had already deeply influenced Coleridge who, the year before he delivered 'On Poesy or Art', had published *Biographia Literaria*. This great two-volume self-portrait of the artist as thinker is substantially a reckoning with his personal library of theoretical and philosophical influences, and it includes large passages of Schelling's thought — and sometimes his actual words. Thus, Coleridge writes about Schelling's dialectic:

In the same sense the transcendental philosopher says; grant me a nature having two contrary forces, the one of which tends to expand infinitely, while the other strives to apprehend or find itself in this infinity, and I will cause the world of intelligences with the whole system of their representations to rise up before you.

This bright April morning, the coast road is busy with people and dogs. Along the shingle beach towards Thorpeness trot old ladies with shivering terriers, dogs with studded collars walked by local heroes in biker jackets, a big guy in leathers with a pompom shiatsu, a red setter who tugs at his leash. They do 'rise up' like 'representations', and I miss my own dogs, at home on the other side of the country. But witnessing this flamboyant promenade, for once, makes me think of that incorrigible Parisian Gérard de Nerval (1808–55) walking his pet lobster.

Which was controversial stuff, at the time. The lobster's very existence has been both doubted and defended. Between bouts of madness Nerval's own take on the matter, as reported by Théophile Gautier, his fellow Petit Cénacle (Young Romantic), was that it was a question of the freedom to choose:

Why should a lobster be any more ridiculous than a dog? Or a cat, or a gazelle, or a lion, or any other animal that one chooses to take for a walk? I have a liking for lobsters. They are peaceful, serious creatures. They know the secrets of the sea, they don't bark, and they don't gobble up your monadic privacy like dogs do. And Goethe had an aversion to dogs, and he wasn't mad!

Hmm: well taking a lobster walking through the streets of Paris is a deliberative, not an unconscious act (though it is unconscionably cruel. The lobster is not in its natural environment), and there evidently was a real creature at one stage at least, which Nerval rescued from the pots at La Rochelle and named Thibault. Whether its later instantiation was a living creature or a fantasy, I think this proto-surrealist was offering up his lobster, to Paris as it were, as a symbol of his own Romantic artistic nature: setting it loose – though not *that* loose – in the world like any other artwork to do its work of symbol and integration. Next stop, the signed urinal.

Crabs figure in the zodiac, lobsters in the Tarot. Richard Holmes, biographer of the Romantics, points out that the eighteenth card in the Major Arcana, the Moon, that symbol so associated with the world of dream, is pictured drawing a lobster out of the watery depths to join – yes – two dogs howling on the shore. As if what could come crawling out of our unconscious, as out of the deep ocean, were bound to be grotesque. And here on cue are the fishermen's huts, wooden doors open wide onto refrigerated glass display counters, tills, chest freezers and chopping boards pink with fish guts. They stand above the tideline on Aldeburgh's terraced beach, snug against the promenade of Crag Path, all tar-black wood and tarred roofs. I don't quite want to think how the lobsters stirring in the fish-tanks I glimpse within them wear an exoskeleton that locks in all expression – and yet the creatures can feel.

Beyond the huts, today's shallow breakers seem like small gestures made without a care in the world. But their shingle fetch roars all the way north to Thorpeness and south, past Aldeburgh, to Shingle Street. I grew up with this sound. Even at the height of summer, my childhood shoreline heaved and settled, grumbled and exhaled with the Atlantic. It muttered a continual warning:

the ocean is dangerous, even when the sun's shining. In 1851 Matthew Arnold made 'Dover Beach' sigh for the retreat of faith from the 'vast edges drear/And naked shingles of the world.' But this sunny Sunday has another, springier rhythm. 'Sunday Morning', the second Sea Interlude from *Peter Grimes*, Benjamin Britten's 1949 opera set here in Aldeburgh is so good it's an ear worm. *Tang – tang – tang – tang* go his horns, pacing up and down their minor third as the syncopated changes ring out from the woodwind belfry. Their delicious sharp chimes aren't only church bells, but light struck from the morning's shining sea.

Britten took the story of Peter Grimes from George Crabbe's *The Borough,* a work he had discovered while living in the US. Crabbe's 1810 collection of narrative poems is set in a fishing community modelled upon his native Aldeburgh. Britten too was a Suffolk boy: he grew up thirty miles up the coast from here, in Lowestoft, and despite excelling in his London student days, was back in the county at twenty-three, converting the Old Mill at Snape, five miles upriver from Aldeburgh, into a home. In 1939, still only twenty-five, he had been seduced into visiting pre-war North America and toyed with building a life there. Yet into an exciting, worldly existence on that continent – staying with rich sponsors in idyllic parts of Canada, Long Island and California, spending time with Aaron Copland and W. H. Auden, being courted for broadcasts, premières and even a film – *The Borough* seems to have arrived like, well, like a peal of bells. 'I suddenly realised where I belonged and what I lacked,' Britten recalled in 1964. And again, slightly differently, a year later in discussion with William Plomer and Leonard Woolf: 'In a flash I realised two things: that I must write an opera, and where I belonged.'

Britten and Pears returned to the Old Mill in 1941, and the composer started work on *Grimes*. Even in rural Suffolk, the young, fiercely gifted couple were not isolated but part of a community of shared tastes and interests – sensibility, in the Romantic term – that reached out to them from the capital, and which they in turn persuaded out to the country. For example, Britten had been introduced to Crabbe by an essay by E. M. Forster, who would become a friend, published on 29 May 1941 in *The Listener*, the BBC magazine edited by Forster's Cambridge friend J. R. Ackerley.

The *Listener* piece opens, in suitably patriotic wartime style, 'To talk about Crabbe is to talk about England. He never left our shores and he only once ventured to cross the border into Scotland.' But I suspect it was other passages, exploring a complicated and very British ambivalence within Crabbe's work, that really spoke to Britten:

Crabbe knew the local almshouses and the hospital and the prison, and the sort of people who drift into them; he read, in the parish registers, the deaths of the unsuccessful, the marriages of the incompetent, and the births of the illegitimate [. . .]

He escaped from Aldburgh [sic] as soon as he could [. . .] He did well for himself, in fact. Yet he never escaped from Aldburgh in the spirit, and it was the making of him as a poet. Even when he is writing of other things, there steals again and again into his verse the sea, the estuary, the flat Suffolk coast, and local meannesses, and an odour of brine and dirt [. . .] he belongs to the grim little place and through it to England.

The Borough does indeed open with deprecation:

> 'Describe the Borough' – though our idle tribe
> May love description, can we so describe,
> That you shall fairly streets and buildings trace,
> And all that gives distinction to a place?
> This cannot be; yet moved by your request
> A part I paint – let Fancy form the rest.

Perhaps this is the privilege of the native. The son of a local schoolmaster, Crabbe was not only Aldeburgh-born but educated locally, in Bungay and Stowmarket; his first pseudonymous poems were published under the name of another local market town, Woodbridge. Yet he grew up to be bad with money and with vocations – trying first medicine and then the church – and at twenty-five resolved his increasingly anomalous social position within society by going to London to make good.

As in many ways he did. Crabbe was far from a one-book wonder. His other works include *The Village* (1781), *The Newspaper* (1782) and *Tales of the Hall* (1819), all of them group narratives that rattle along. Yet he never had a huge readership. He lived from 1754 to 1832, a comfortable fit with the Romantic era; but missed the Victorian age, which would be markedly more hospitable to such narrative verse. His true distance from the coming Victorian style, though, lay in his lack of overt emotion. He was a master of social observation; at the same time, his strikingly unsentimental verse keeps a wry, intelligent distance he learnt from the very Augustinian tradition that he was breaking apart, as he toppled poetry from its pedestal of elevated abstraction and Big History and brought it into world of the quotidian.

The Newspaper, for example, opens:

> A time like this, a busy, bustling time,
> Suits ill with writers, very ill with rhyme:
> [. . .]
> Since, then, the town forsakes us for our foes,
> The smoothest numbers for the harshest prose;
> Let us, with generous scorn, the taste deride,
> And sing our rivals with a rival's pride.
>
> Ye gentle poets who so oft complain
> That foul neglect is all your labour's gain;
> That pity only checks your growing spite
> To erring man, and prompts you still to write;
> That your choice works on humble stalls are laid,
> Or vainly grace the windows of the trade;

Such gifted debunking was never going to appeal to Victorian tastes either and, after his death, Crabbe's influence went underground. But he was *sui generis* in life, too. His mentors included Edmund Burke, Sir Joshua Reynolds and Samuel Johnson, none of them Romantics. Yet he was himself eminently a product of the Romantic era, without whose social revolutions he could never have participated in literary London. Besides, his writing is preoccupied by Romantic themes; it's just that he treats them from an unorthodox perspective. If there are no Augustan nymphs and shepherds in his work, there is no Frankenstein or Childe Harold either. Instead, he turned the Romantic absorption with individual selfhood, as experienced from within, into observation from without of how and why individuals act; he shifted from an embrace of elite, exceptional experience to dramatising representative and unprepossessing, uneducated or inarticulate selves. For all Romanticism's radical politics, this attentive, literary democratisation of selfhood fell outside its agenda.

Shingle beaches are entirely composed of detail. Aldeburgh's, crunching underfoot, stretches ahead of me south to Orford, Shingle Street and Felixstowe, and behind me north to Lowestoft, with a punctuation at sandy Southwold: a curving distance of some fifty miles. The beach footpath that runs beside the coast road has become a compacted track, but wander off it and everywhere the golden tawny stones, worn like nuggets, twist and roll underfoot. There is detail and abundance in Crabbe's work too. Yet ambivalence about the sum of that detail – about community per se – is central to *The Borough*. As it is to Britten's *Peter Grimes*.

Benjamin Britten's opera received its first performance in June 1945; after VE Day but before the end of the Second World War, and it seems in some ways a strange choice for this period of social solidarity. For *Grimes* is a story about community complicity in criminal activity – or in criminalisation. Peter Grimes is a fisherman whose apprentices, foundlings supplied – trafficked? – to him by the local workhouse, keep dying. Crabbe's Grimes is guilty of killing them, as he confesses on his deathbed. Britten's Grimes is a more ambiguous figure: is he guilty, or simply a scapegoat? The opera's 'Chorus of townspeople and fisherfolk' are attentive but unreliable narrators: happy to gossip and condemn, yet slow to rescue a child in need. Crabbe's poem raises similar doubts about collective probity: the Borough's understanding of Peter Grimes's criminality is slow to develop both because of his social bluster and because of the conservative desire to preserve respectability. The difference between these versions is, I suspect, the gap between two moments in British culture. One problem of the early nineteenth century was to find ways to articulate internal and emotional experience; one in the first half of the twentieth was whether such experiences and their articulations could count as 'true'.

Some fourteen miles north of Aldeburgh, Holy Trinity Church Blythburgh stands on a knoll above the estuarial Blyth. Yesterday I found an entire fifteenth-century community captured there as a series of finial pew ends, from the slothful rich man under his wrinkled bedcover to the petty criminal in the stocks. Among the Blythburgh figures are prosperous individuals in glorious hats, a glutton sporting his beer belly, villagers harvesting corn or collecting firewood faggots. Some seem almost angelic, others are clearly allegorical; but every one is about a handspan tall, and they line up together in a great equality of scale. As I walked up and down the sun-swept nave, looking at each in turn, I had a joyous intimation of how those early parishioners must have felt surrounded *by themselves* as they worshipped. At a time when fixed pews for the congregation were a luxury – most would arrive a century later, with the Reformation – didn't they feel like a chorus of the elect?

The Romantic preoccupation with individuation ruptured whatever the eighteenth century had retained of the mediaeval social contract, at Blythborough and elsewhere. But some precursor sense of the collective as a potentially monstrous entity had already led from Thomas Hobbes's emphasis on individual rights in *Leviathan* (1651) to Jean-Jacques Rousseau's *Social Contract*, published a century later, in 1762. In repudiating the Divine Right of Kings, and declaring that the population as a whole are sovereign, the *Social Contract* helped inspire the Age of Revolution, which saw democratic revolution and reform spread across Europe, from Italy to the Netherlands. Yet the sovereignty Rousseau envisaged was not mob rule and chaos, but a shared contract by which every individual surrendered and gained the *same* rights. Everyone might, for example, agree to surrender the right to murder with impunity, and so gain the right to live without being murdered.

In 1941 Benjamin Britten, who was pacifist and gay, ran a double risk of imprisonment. As he would tell *Time* magazine in 1948, when his opera was being recorded for the first time, *Peter Grimes* concerns:

> a subject very close to my heart — the struggle of the individual against the masses. The more vicious the society, the more vicious the individual.

Which seems to be offering another version of Hegel's master/slave dialectic, one in which society creates its outcasts. The musicologist Donald Mitchell records that Montagu Slater's libretto originally included sexual desire in the relationship between Grimes and his apprentices. Britten had the good sense and moral judgement to dispense with this plot thickener. There's hiding in plain sight and then there's not hiding at all: and Peter Pears himself was playing Grimes. The role had been written for him and he made it his own, not only at the première but in the first three, classic recordings made in 1948, 1958 and 1969. Besides, Britten and Pears were by now living in the actual Borough. In 1947 they had moved into a large property, Crag House, right on Aldeburgh seafront.

Crag House and later the Red House, where the Queen once came for tea, represented the other side of an ambivalent relationship with community. Britten's practice was strikingly outward turned. He made community musicmaking a major part of his work: writing extensively for and performing with children and amateurs, and working with Pears to create first a music festival, then a concert hall – Snape Maltings, which is in a way the Old Mill writ large – and eventually their foundation. When I first came to Snape as a nervous child violinist, although it was after Britten's death the parking bays by the office entrance were still marked BB and PP.

All these years later, in today's bright cold there's a queue at the ice-cream kiosk by Aldeburgh's model boating pond. Couples in beanies, and kids with their hoods up, stamp in circles, or huddle on benches to eat their cones. As we shiver and smile at one another we form a socially distanced community, in which nobody wants to be the outsider. Alienation is difficult to experience, to understand, and to portray. In Crabbe's 'Peter Grimes', for example, the nimble rhyming couplets occasionally linger into a third line, as if to finger revulsion:

There anchoring, Peter chose from man to hide,
There hang his head, and view the lazy tide
In its hot slimy channel slowly glide[.]

When Crabbe was a boy here, the Alde estuary behind Orford Ness, the shingle spit that by now extends the southern end of Aldeburgh beach for ten miles, formed a strategically important harbour at Orford – and was vulnerable to the Napoleonic fleet. Today, marshes clog the River Alde towards Snape at Long Reach, which has long ceased to be navigable. By 1810, when Crabbe published *The Borough*, spreading marshland was already beginning the squeeze that would reduce Aldeburgh to a fishing village. At the little community's northern perimeter, the heath and marsh of North Warren was emerging. Today, a little further north again along the coast are the radical and beautiful reserves of Minsmere and Dingle Marshes. There are wide, purple-plumed marshes to the south at Orford and Hollesley. At Snape they lie beyond the mown banks of the concert hall complex of Britten's Maltings as if they were the rough grazing beyond a parkland ha-ha.

Crabbe makes these tidal salt marshes Grimes's habitat, and gives them a deathly, rotten character that befits a killer:

> Thus by himself compell'd to live each day,
> To wait for certain hours the tide's delay;
> At the same time the same dull views to see,
> The bounding marsh-bank and the blighted tree;
> The water only, when the tides were high,
> When low, the mud half cover'd and half-dry;
> The sun-burnt tar that blisters on the planks,
> And bank-side stakes in their uneven ranks;
> Heaps of entangled weeds that slowly float,
> As the tide rolls by the impeded boat.
> When tides were neap, and, in the sultry day,

Through the tall bounding mud-banks made
    their way,
Which on each side rose swelling, and below
The dark warm flood ran silently and slow;
There anchoring, Peter chose from man to hide,
There hang his head, and view the lazy tide
In its hot slimy channel slowly glide;
Where the small eels that left the deeper way
For the warm shore, within the shallows play;
Where gaping mussels, left upon the mud,
Slope their slow passage to the fallen flood; –
Here dull and hopeless he'd lie down and trace
How sidelong crabs had scrawl'd their crooked race,
Or sadly listen to the tuneless cry
Of fishing gull or clanging golden-eye;
What time the sea-birds to the marsh would come.
And the loud bittern, from the bull-rush home,
Gave from the salt ditch side the bellowing boom:
He nursed the feelings these dull scenes produce,
And loved to stop beside the opening sluice;
Where the small stream, confined in narrow bound,
Ran with a dull, unvaried, sadd'ning sound;
Where all, presented to the eye or ear,
Oppress'd the soul with misery, grief, and fear.

This long passage is pure pathetic fallacy, of course. The real
dark bog is Grimes's own psyche. Yet what muddies it aren't
half-unknown crosscurrents of the unconscious. Crabbe's
protagonist is the complete Romantic individual, wholly
transparent to himself – and so, conscious of his own guilt.

This opens up a distance from Britten and Slater's portrait of a scapegoat who is conflicted not by warring motives, such as the desire both to belong to and escape from the Borough, but by aspects of his own self he doesn't even understand. More, in the opera Grimes is sacrificed by aspects of a communal psyche the townsfolk themselves don't fully understand either. Its Aldeburgh is a community of passionate sleepwalkers.

Crabbes's Grimes reminds us that the very act of lying acknowledges the truth it seeks to avoid – and so cannot. The guilty mind, as it turns this way and that, resembles the mazy waterways 'confined in narrow bound' within coastal marshland. Here at Aldeburgh Marshes, acres of reeds sough together in a single direction. Feathered maroon in summer, they're bleached to flax by the following spring. Today, when I step down among them where the mud has cracked and dried, the reed heads shiver overhead. What do they hide? Water. But also the freckled marsh dwellers, roe deer, bittern, newt. All that Gerard Manley Hopkins would in 1877 call, in a post-Romantic, newly religious fervour all his own, 'Pied Beauty'. Maybe an adder? No, the reedbeds are too cool and wet for them. Look out those old plaits of rope elsewhere, on sandy banks in the sun.

Two herring gulls glide overhead yoiking. Their yellow bills are crisp in sunlight. A man could easily hide in here: some creeping, stooping loiterer. Or else that stir in the reeds below the embankment is a twitcher with telephoto lenses slung around his neck. Yes. He strikes a characteristic pose: bins up, a khaki sunhat on his head. Some figures seem almost to be an emanation of the landscape they emerge from:

I suddenly beheld the figure of a man, at some distance, advancing towards me with superhuman speed. He bounded over the crevices in the ice, among which I had walked with caution; his stature, also, as he approached seemed to exceed that of a man ... the shape came nearer (sight tremendous and abhorred!) ...

It's Frankenstein, again, watching his rejected creation approach across the Mer de Glace in the French Alps. There's a filmic quality to Mary Shelley's writing in this passage; the sense of a figure moving raptly through silence. No birdcalls. We don't hear the breath of either protagonist rasp with the cold or the altitude. (Silently, today, water goes silver among the reeds towards a group of Scots Pines.) Like Grimes, Frankenstein's creature has been exiled by Romantic imperative to the wild, wide-open landscapes that lie beyond social settlement. But this wilderness is not freedom. Ostracisation traps both imagined scapegoats within a *mise en abyme*, a cycle of limitless recurrence because, as Britten put it in that 1948 interview, 'The more vicious the society, the more vicious the individual.'

Hegel's *Herrschaft und Knechtschaft* is a perpetual circle of domination and abjection. When Frankenstein's creature excuses himself for committing murder, he claims to have been turned by lovelessness – like Crabbe's Grimes:

Every where I see bliss, from which I alone am irrevocably excluded. I was born benevolent and good; misery made me a fiend. Make me happy, and I shall again be virtuous.

And yet for Mary Shelley the scapegoat's real burden is the scapegoater's own guilt. Frankenstein had envisaged creating not another self, but a fabulously loveable toy:

> My imagination was too much exalted [. . .] to permit me to doubt of my ability to give life to an animal as complex and wonderful as man.

His belief that he could exceed the conventions of human knowledge, and play God with the spark of life, is the shadow side that overshadows his creature's entire life.

I'm always struck by how the giant figure of the creature as he comes to meet his maker through the Alpine mist – that 'sight tremendous and abhorred!' – resembles the giant shadow of a Brocken spectre. A Brocken appears far away and gigantic but is actually the viewer's own shadow, cast onto cloud or fog by a light source at a low angle: for example, late afternoon sun on a foggy mountain. The clergyman who in 1780 identified the phenomenon, Johann Silberschlag, named it after a local peak, Brocken in the Harz mountains of Saxony, where many examples had been sighted. The peak had a spooky reputation in any case; in 1808 Johann Wolfgang von Goethe would make it the setting of the Walpurgisnacht revels in Scene xxi of his tragic drama *Faust, Part One*. That when we project our ideas or fears we create something exaggerated – and which we don't recognise as ours – is a psychological truism. In one beautifully schematic formulation, Carl Jung even dreamt that his own projections became a Brocken spectre. But then, clichés click because they're useful.

Marine light is always a little uncanny even when, as today, it's so clear it seems to shred everything in the landscape to glitter. In Britten's *Grimes*, unlike Crabbe's, story and verdict turn on the line between conscious and involuntary responsibility, just as they do in Mary Shelley's *Frankenstein*, where the doctor's twice-times fecklessness – pursuing his experimentation with insufficient expertise, and with no thought of consequences – shifts the novel from a simple parable about doing no evil into a series of questions about where complicity starts. Key to the tragic claustrophobia of Britten's opera is that the community who condemn Peter Grimes don't know whether he *is* guilty or not. His second apprentice meets with a fatal accident when the fisherman insists on going aboard during a storm: as audience we witness this embarkation, though not the offstage death itself. It means we must in effect decide on the nature of Grimes's guilt *on behalf of* the mob, which makes us complicit in the near lynching that ensues. 'Him who despises us we'll destroy,' the townsfolk sing as they hunt down the fisherman.

I've often wondered what the real life 'townspeople and fisherfolk' thought as they took part in the carnivals and festivals, concerts and broadcasts, that Britten and Pears brought to Aldeburgh and Snape over the years. Or about the affluence that's followed fame to the little town. I lift my shades. The midmorning sun blares its reproof. I drop them again. There's a smell of mown grass from the verge beyond the beach. In the sea's shifting glitter, bright points prick and slide. The swifts, back from their 5,000 km trip to sub-Saharan west Africa, race and turn low over the buzzing reeds, shooting across the embankment almost at my feet. Light flickers on blue-black iridescent feathers. Flying stars.

In abandoning his creature Frankenstein mirrors, for his

atheist author, God's abandonment of the human he has created. Shelley's novel takes its epigraph from the passage in John Milton's *Paradise Lost* (x. 743–5) where Adam accuses God of punishing him for the very flaws created in him:

> Did I request thee, Maker, from my clay
> To mould Me man? Did I solicit thee
> From darkness to promote me? –

Frankenstein's creature too has been created naked. Like Adam – at least according to Milton – he is abandoned as punishment for flaws in the way he has been created. Unlike Adam – but like Grimes's foundling apprentices – he is nameless: something that prevents him having the rights of a community member. A literal *sans-culotte*, he is a reminder of the French *sans-culottes* whose Revolution Shelley and her family supported:

> I felt cold also, and half-frightened as it were instinctively, finding myself so desolate. Before I had quitted your apartment, on a sensation of cold, I had covered myself with some clothes, but these were insufficient to secure me from the dews of night.

But as I retrace my steps along the seafront Crag Path, I also find myself thinking how aptly Frankenstein and his creature serve as portraits of the artist as outsider; figures on whom society projects and magnifies its fear of the exceptional individual. Shelley's story is also a parable about the evils of creation.

Look back towards Aldeburgh from the Thorpeness road

and a familiar silhouette rises from the shimmering shingle: the pink-washed foreground mass, outlined in brick, of Crag House and – closer, yet stepped back further from the beach – the stooped, intelligent-seeming form of the seat of justice, the mediaeval brick and timber Moot Hall. Britten's *Peter Grimes* also reveals a deep ambivalence about the dialectic between the unusual individual – who might like, say, its librettist and its composer, be an artist – and society.

As I walk up to North Warren, I reflect how Mary Shelley, like her mother and husband, understood her own Romanticism as something radical, and expected to live somewhat outside society – even in exile. Yet both George Crabbe, who left Aldeburgh for the London literary life, and Benjamin Britten, who returned here from the capital, attempted to solve the problem of the artist's role in society by travelling in the opposite direction, towards success within their own community. Each defined that success differently, but Britten's working life was a peculiarly strenuous rehearsal of the public role of the artist. By the end of his life he was Baron Britten, a Companion of Honour and member of the Order of Merit; he was also the composer whose *Young Person's Guide to the Orchestra* Op. 34 had provided the rudiments of musical education in classrooms for three decades. He was internationally renowned; and yet at the same time he lived, accessible and accountable, beside the golf course in this little Suffolk town.

As I turn back that way, towards the Red House, I pass the four-metre-high shell, cupped and seeming to listen, that stands on Aldeburgh beach as a memorial to Britten. Its artist, Maggie Hambling, is another artist who chooses to live in Suffolk although she has become a national figure; and she was a personal friend of the composer. The words she picked to incise around his monument's steel rim come from the libretto of *Peter Grimes*: 'I hear those voices that will not be drowned.' I can't help noticing how the sculpture's scallop form resembles an old-fashioned hand mirror with a deckled edge. It's as if it holds up a mirror to the Borough.

Walk 7: The Red House, Aldeburgh, via North Warren to Aldeburgh Marshes. From: The Red House, Golf Ln, Aldeburgh IP15 5PZ, OS Grid ref TM 454578.

Eighth Walk

Feeling

Painting is but another word for feeling.

JOHN CONSTABLE, letter to John Fisher, 1821

Tucked in my copy of *The Marriage Diaries of Robert and Clara Schumann* is a slip of paper with '24 April' pencilled in my father's immaculate italic hand. My dad's slips of paper are as characteristic as his handwriting: recycled sheets torn into six and bulldog-clipped, or bound together with an elastic band, to make a provisional notepad from which pages could be removed as they were sketched or written on, and to which blanks could always be added. When he died, we found these packs of neatly torn slips in the pockets of all his jackets, in his wallet, on his desk. I think of them as little pieces of hoarded life. My dad delighted in all small free things that came his way: service station biros, the postman's elastic bands, discarded stationery. But he was also hoarding an inner world.

Since he was writing for himself, these notes tend to the

elliptical. A line from a book with the page reference – but nothing to say which book. The name and dates of some nineteenth-century worthy: remembered for what? This one, though, is elliptical even by his standards. It's not an engagement reminder: even in the last year of his life he had a Letts pocket diary, and used it diligently. I find myself wondering whether it's a reference to something within this book itself. If so, it's not going to be easy to identify: the *Diaries*, of course, include more than one 24 April.

In fact there are four. The Schumanns kept a record of their marriage for a little under four years, from the day after their wedding in September 1840 to their return home, in May 1844, from a concert tour of Russia. I page through the years looking for my dad's date and find Robert concluding his record of the week ending 24 April 1841:

> With Clara's health things go on as they can, and much better than in the first weeks of our marriage. In her heart she always feels clear and bright and full of love. That I know. And also in mine; one hears that in my music.

This sounds as though it's been written against the grain of some denial; an unspoken shadow Robert needs to rebut just seven months into what was a much longed-for marriage. 'In her heart she always feels [. . .] full of love. That I know.' As opposed to other things which are, apparently, uncertain – and go unnamed. There's an odd trace of alienation, too, in the implication that Robert can only identify his own feelings by way of his compositions: 'one hears that in my music'. On the other hand, he could be referring to the kind of feelingful thought that reaches past conscious awareness. Either way, music is the body of emotional evidence he admits against himself; and twenty-one-year-old Clara is not only the *Diaries'* confidante and co-author but also the musician most likely to interpret these very works on the international concert stage.

Such a profound overlap of work and feeling seems like the creative ideal. Unless it isn't. After years of pianistic specialisation as both performer and composer, in the year of his marriage Robert, who turned thirty that same summer, decided that purely instrumental keyboard music was 'too narrow to express my thoughts'. 1840 became his *liederjahr*, in the course of which he composed 138 songs. Unlike other forms of chamber music, *lieder* are in a sense made explicit by their lyrics. But Schumann was setting *other* people's words – among them Joseph von Eichendorff's *Liederkreis*, Heinrich Heine's *Dichterliebe*, and poems by J. W. von Goethe, Lord Byron and Robert Burns – so that even in song he expressed himself indirectly. I wonder whether the *liederjahr* sidestep itself constitutes evidence of what the new husband was really feeling. For if we're looking for unspoken shadows and sources of alienation, an obvious pressure point within the Schumanns' marriage was that Clara, though a decade younger – and of course a woman – was much the finer pianist, and far the more famous partner.

By 1841 she was a great performer with an international reputation. Clara was also the household pragmatist: a family woman and at the same time a businesswoman. In 1842, she celebrates 24 April as the day she starts her return journey from Hamburg after a seven-week concert tour, the first she's undertaken without Robert:

I departed by steamboat at 7 o'clock in the morning – Cranz also wanted to take this boat, but oh what fate! He rushed there just as the boat was leaving. I was very happy about this coincidence. I had pleasant company, but only men, which sometimes did become oppressive for me. It took two whole days before we finally arrived.

Cranz, a slanderer of the kind such exceptional women can attract, had been alleging that Robert had left Clara, and that she was highly unpopular. 'Now,' Robert asserts in the *Diaries'* margin a couple of days later, as the Schumanns' domestic routine resumes like a rejoinder to such maleficence, 'there will be better days again.'

He follows this by noting that he and his fourteen-year-old nephew Carl have just bumped into Felix Mendelssohn in Leipzig's expansive Rosental Park, where Mendelssohn gave the youth a flower. I like this moment. The two men are rivals: they must be, born only a year apart and leading similar lives as composer-pianists. Mendelssohn too has married a substantially younger woman: though, unlike the Schumanns', his courtship was both unremarkable and unopposed. Still, here they are, pausing together in the park. Carl, who is an orphaned only child, has arrived this morning from his grandparents' home in Schneeberg, a hundred kilometres to the south; presumably Robert has just gone to meet him. Carl will die at eighteen, and so he remains forever a youth – that figure fetishised as perfection. I suppose I think of this because of the flower. But Mendelssohn's own first-born son, now four years old, is also a Carl: surely that's really what the flower represents? The fragility of childhood, and then the propitiatory hope that his own Carl will fare better than orphaned Carl Schumann? (And, arguably, Carl Mendelssohn Bartholdy did. He became a professor of history at the great universities of Heidelberg and Freiburg – even though he ended by dying in an asylum at fifty-nine.)

A year later, on 24 April 1843, Clara writes in the *Diaries* that:

we were about to hear Sabine Heinefetter in *Fidelio*, but the rest of the mediocre cast and therefore the two-thaler entrée scared us away, and we cautiously went back to our house.

She goes on to the real reason they may not have bothered with Beethoven's opera: 'On the 25th I had a difficult hour, but really only one, until the second little daughter appeared at 9.30.' By 1844, the 'marriage diary' has become the record of a pioneering concert tour of Russia, and is being written for publication: 'On Wednesday 24th Robert completed another poem – this collection of poems shall follow as an appendix to this book.' And so they do. The more than sixty lines of this verse, '*Die Franzosen vor Moskva*', 'The French before Moscow', are divided – after a first brave attempt at quatrains – into irregular stanzas which offer a whistlestop of Napoleon's Russian defeat. It's not perhaps the ideal subject for such summary treatment, and '*Die Franzosen vor Moskva*', like a kind of premature ejaculation of epic material, survives only as a draft clearly written in haste – it's full of corrections – about which the kindest thing one can say is that it perhaps represents William Wordsworth's 'spontaneous overflow of powerful feelings'.

I didn't catch on, as I was trawling through the *Diaries* for a

24 April that might correspond to my dad's note, that today is 25 April. Seven weeks after his death, April is here and now, and spring is starting over. Who knows, maybe this year of lockdown, 2021, has even restored its splendour a little. Climate scientists tell us the air's been cleaned up by the huge reduction in polluting travel. Nitrogen dioxide levels this spring are down 35 per cent on last year's measurements at this time of year (and that's an average. It's better in urban areas: some, like Glasgow and Oxford and Leeds, have seen levels more than halved). There certainly seem to be more birds in the sky than usual. Those of us who have come through the pandemic unscathed so far can't help but feel hope. Surely it won't be as bad again, we think.

In any case April is always an encouraging time to be in the English countryside, as Robert Browning knew. 'Oh to be in England/Now that April's there,' he wrote in 1845 in 'Home Thoughts From Abroad', whose opening stanza has that lovely veering line-length which seems to expand with enthusiasm as one detail adds itself to another:

> And whoever wakes in England
> Sees, some morning, unaware,
> That the lowest boughs and the brushwood sheaf
> Round the elm-tree bole are in tiny leaf,
> While the chaffinch sings on the orchard bough
> In England—now!

'In England—now!' at East Bergholt, on Suffolk's border with Essex, a new estate has sprawled in from the north, shifting the area of settlement. But around the parish church the brick and pargeted houses of the old village stand quietly in the sunshine. In this county of towers, St Mary the Virgin famously lacks a belfry. The parish failed ever quite to hang its mighty peal of (largely) sixteenth-century bells, which remain instead in a kind of slope-roofed stable in the churchyard. Without a tower, the flint-built church seems to cluster around itself. It's all nave, a mighty grasp at height by clear-glassed perpendicular clerestory windows, to which the abbreviated chancel is just a kind of full stop. There is no cross range of transepts. The strange half-ruined west portico and two-storey south porch join the singular movement of the nave to create, in place of the usual cruciform, a structure of high-pitched formality that, without these formal cues, appears almost secular.

There is another way of looking at this church, which is locked today because of the pandemic. From a distance its unresolved, unfinished state creates the illusion that it's still under construction; as if we could revisit that mediaeval experience. You get the same impression from some of the sketches of the building made by John Constable, who was born in East Bergholt in 1776 and spent much of his life here. In one example, a pencil and watercolour of *East Bergholt Church: From the South* executed in 1806, it appears as a series of incomplete curtain walls and entrances. Constable has light flood out through the nave window and porch towards the viewer as from a source *inside* the walls; as if they were still open to the elements. Yet St Mary the Virgin's actual building combines the weight of masonry and the clarity of its glass in a strong statement. About — what? Perhaps the hope that it might serve as an ark, as the food bank in the porch implies. Like the rest of the old settlement, it's built on a shoulder of land above a low-lying flood plain. But it stands on the very edge of this rise, where it can see and be seen from the land below. Directly opposite, Flatford Lane leads downhill and south between curved walls of old brick, out of the village and onto the levels of Dedham Vale.

After exactly a mile, running between birch and hazel trees bright with Browning's 'tiny leaf', the lane arrives at Flatford Mill. It's an easy walk. But I'm unprepared for the force of my emotion when, at its destination, the round-shouldered form of Willy Lott's Cottage slides into view beyond the corner of the Mill's thatched granary. Not that John Constable's 1821 oil painting *The Hay Wain* is among my favourite pictures: rather, I don't really experience it as a *picture* at all. It's just part of my world: part of *me*. When I was a kid it seemed to be repeated wherever I looked: on calendars and mugs and diary covers, in textbooks and on TV programmes, and on my grandparents' tablemats. It had become less image than trope, shorthand for – well, something. Niceness: togetherness: the countryside. Even as a child I understood, without being able to put it into words, that it had shifted from being a painting to becoming a symbol.

Willy Lott's Cottage is the house clustering under trees on the left of Constable's famous painting. Today it doesn't look nearly so cute as it did in 1821. The famous creamy-yellow stucco has been dirtied by mould; the windows are grey with dust and have the dullness of closed-up, unused interiors. No one has been paying attention to the picket-fenced front garden, where sticks of dead and dying plants bend glumly towards the water. The River Stour pools stagnantly in the millpond beside the house, and the thick drifts of waterweed seem half-rotten, half-undone, like the pale bodies of murder victims. The place looks as if it's been exhausted by too much being looked at and yearned over. And yet the familiar, satisfyingly tiny frontage and slightly larger rear wing remain. It's a constellation of forms that would have pleased my dad, though if he ever drew it I've yet to find the sketch.

In his 1955 BBC Reith Lectures on *The Englishness of English Art*, Nikolaus Pevsner brought an outsider's simplifying and clarifying eye to English art history. These seven talks deliver a love letter to the homeland and culture he had adopted upon his arrival as a refugee in 1933. You don't even notice, for the first few sentences of each broadcast, how his native German accent warms the upper-class, clipped diction he's learnt so well. Admittedly, the broad introductory sweep of the first lecture is very much a product of its European time. In it, Pevsner proposes that there's a direct relationship between the notorious British climate and a national aesthetic that has endured through diverse eras. Precisely what exactly this enduring aesthetic is he finds harder to say, but it seems to have to do with an empirical engagement that celebrates action rather than stillness, and that uses line rather than mass to do so.

A mass is a state of affairs; a line travels. For Pevsner, this has to do with keeping moving to keep warm – that climate again! He points out that this principle of keeping moving is also present in the English culture of muddling along – keeping on keeping on – rather than philosophising (or, one might add, resolving a problem). I love the examples he chooses: 'a strictly upheld inefficiency in the little business-things of every day, such as the workman's job in the house, windows that will never close, and heating that will never heat, a certain comfortable wastefulness and sense of a good life.'

Indeed he excels at human observation. The secret of his multivolume county by county survey of *The Buildings of England*, on which he'd already been working for a decade when he gave these lectures, isn't only the profound substratum of architectural science that informs them, but Pevsner's opinionated readings of buildings. His experience of them matters, in the Romantic way; and in the Romantic way, too, it matters all the more because it's a result of his own very particular personhood. The product of a rigorous German education, Pevsner, whose conventional career at home was destroyed by the rise of Nazism, had every reason to want to understand his adopted home.

Tetchy and charming, he ascribes moral values to the achievements of long-dead country patrons and stonemasons. One of the joys of the British countryside is how localism highlights what we could call the 'educated vernacular' of anonymous architects, sculptors and artists, whose names are lost for the same reasons that their work remains: that they were typical. As we move between different counties and parishes, we get to see how art and culture, for all its procession of great international movements, is the work of innumerable particular human beings. John Betjeman (1906–84), whose very different life spanned roughly the same dates as Pevsner's (1902–83), and who was poet laureate for the last twelve years of his life, also understood this matter of 'cherubs in the corner spaces/With wings and English ploughboy faces.' (This couplet, from 'Churchyards', my dad often quoted.)

Though he may have been as much a sentimental popular-iser as a poet, Betjeman too understood the shared human qualities and experiences that inform public structures, from graveyards to railway stations. In their own ways, both he and Pevsner shared in the post-war, New Elizabethan project of democratising culture, in which the new Welfare State – with its care for schoolchildren's nutrition, its public libraries and its free tertiary education – was one powerful partner, and the Reithian BBC of their day another. Having opened his Reith Lectures by trying to identify 'Englishness' Pevsner – after all a refugee from the dangerous essentialisms of Hitler's Germany – changes tack and says this isn't really what he's doing at all. Instead, he's going to talk about paired 'polarities', or opposite approaches to a common object: Hegel would have called this a dialectic; Samuel Taylor Coleridge would probably have called it a '*Tragic Dance*'.

Pevsner identifies one such polarity as uniting these two great Romantic British painters and near contemporaries, J. M. W. Turner and John Constable. Both, he says, are interested in *atmosphere*: a term he seems to use sometimes quite literally, to mean air and moisture, and at other times to mean mood and tone. This is, apparently, very English of them. It's a question of climate again:

England is ill at ease in the world of bodies, self consciously displaying their fleshly presence, and so, when it came to landscape in the Romantic Age, it was England that led Europe away from the landscape arranged with carefully disposed masses and towards the atmospheric landscape.

But while 'Turner's anti-naturalism carried him away into phantasmagoria of nothing but air', Constable's is a 'searching naturalism'. Hence Constable's study of clouds; hence the big skies in his big 'six-footer' paintings, particularly of Dedham Vale.

Sure enough, the walk on from Flatford Mill to Dedham across the valley of the River Stour is all air and sky. A partial lifting of pandemic lockdown means that today, while the coachloads of tourists haven't yet returned, locals are out and about, and we don't need the fingerposts or an OS map to guide us across the water meadows. Other couples and families stroll ahead of us, in the mazey light, toward the tangle of blackthorn and cherry blossom that shelters the village. There's an easy but subdued atmosphere, as if we are all taking part in some mild pilgrimage. Cattle graze the wide, unfenced pasture, where grass already has the slight pallor of drought: that this dry spring is not unusual is apparent in the way it grows in clumps. Bright yellow furze dots the flat valley; pollarded willows line the river.

It could be an eighteenth-century landscape, and it feels as though the walkers ahead and behind us are resuming something left off not just for a few months, but centuries ago. This too is unexpectedly moving. To feel yourself figuring in a landscape you've known all your life (but never visited) is like stepping into the frame of a picture. Below the low horizon, small figures move to and fro. Above, the wide sky is the kind of uncertain blue, halfway between violet and cornflower, that can be so piercingly sweet at this time of year.

And it's marked up with a stuttering of flat-bottomed cumulus that could have come straight out of one of Constable's intensive sequence of cloud studies of 1820–21. These were done in Hampstead, and where their formations do meet the bottom line of a landscape, it's the still-rural Heath. But the sudden opening up of the artist's reputation, and the great 'six-footers' depicting the Stour Valley that he painted as a result (among them *The Hay Wain*), date from the same period and its immediate aftermath, and their racing, vibrant skies are full of the actual formations and movement the artist had studied in London, and rediscovered here. In *The Lock* (1824), for example, a rain shower scurrying across the foreground balances the complacent stasis of summer cumulus above distant Dedham Church. *Look up!* as that anti-contrail graffiti injuncts on the M40 footbridge near Acton. All the same, I've never thought of the scintillations on Constable's trees and grass, water and sky, as physically or meteorologically literal, but as expressions of excitement. Their starry shine reminds me of Samuel Palmer's visionary paintings of the Kent countryside.

Palmer himself described his Shoreham paintings as 'sprinkled and showered with a thousand pretty eyes, and buds . . . and blossoms, gemm'd with dew'. Constable's paintings seem charged with something equally irrepressible. Like the word *scintillate* itself, this shimmer in both Palmer's and Constable's landscapes — the latter Pevsner calls, with too much understatement I think, 'exciting dapple' — is literal, but also symbolic. Exciting and dappled also is the scintillating flint of Constable's home landscape. *Silex Scintillans*: how the alliterative *ss* and *l*s of the Latin strike and slide against each other, like flints striking a flame. Henry Vaughan, seventeenth-century clergyman and poet, gave this title to two volumes of devotional and metaphysical poetry in 1650–55. A neo-Platonist, a medic, and the twin of alchemist Thomas, Vaughan is himself occasionally described as a proto-Romantic. His descriptions of the natural world have a similar quality of inhabited observation – though for him this represented the immanence of God – and his verse about childhood contains pre-echoes of Wordsworth: though his concern is not autobiography but the formation of the Christian soul.

Yet flint itself steals the symbolic and literal thunder of such scintillation. The prehistoric flint mines of Grimes Graves lie just over the county border near Brandon at the other end of Suffolk. This sedimentary cryptocrystalline has since the Neolithic era been the bringer of fire as well as the first blade; both tool and weapon. It's also one of East Anglia's visual signatures. In buildings dotting the countryside, high-lit on a slope or piercing the foliage of sheltering trees, flint flashes to life when the sun catches it. The distinctive flushwork of many of the region's churches, East Bergholt among them, sets walls-full of flint in patterns framed by sandstone or brick quoins.

Split and dressed, knapped flint catches the light particularly well. Belltowers of flint flushwork rise from this shallow rolling countryside like shining paths into the sky – as they were built to do. Among them is the tower of St Mary's Dedham, over the county boundary with Essex that the River Stour draws along its Vale. And here we are, just about to arrive in the village: through a wicket, among a swan's-neck swoon of willow trunks. Primroses. And brush beside the boles, just as Browning remembered it. When the sun flickers behind one of these massy Dedham Vale cumuli, the shine disappears from local towers. Then the dulled flushwork seems to store shadow like a pent-up reversal of light. It's as if the old grey chert walls were charged with all the kilojoules of energy that are stored in matter: that force for which the nuclear reactor at Sizewell, further up the Suffolk coast, stands as metonym.

Constable's oils and watercolours are charged, too. I've always seen them as dense with surfaces on which light can catch and move: clustering leaves, corrugated water. These multiplying surfaces seem to turn both towards and away from us, but most of all they seem to turn towards each other. Every Constable I've ever seen has seemed to me to rustle. It's the opposite of, say, a landscape by the seventeenth-century French Baroque master Claude Lorrain, in which an individual tree lifts its canopy up onto the sky's tabula rasa with the delicate poise of calligraphy.

Yet Claude was one of Constable's earliest inspirations. The Essex-born collector and influential amateur artist Sir George Beaumont, 7th Baronet, who cofounded the British Institution for Promoting the Fine Arts in the United Kingdom in 1805, owned his *Landscape with Hagar and the Angel* of 1646, now in the National Gallery. Visitors to Room 29 can witness that celestial encounter taking place in the foreground of Claude's recognisably Tuscan landscape where, reassuringly, cattle are being watered at a river just as they would have been in Constable's own Stour. And as they still are here today. Beaumont let the young artist copy and learn from this picture when he had access to very little other art; and even in maturity Constable could occasionally resort to Claudean formulae. One example is *Dedham Vale, Morning* (1811), among the most significant works of his early thirties, yet one of the great flops of his career. A dismissive Royal Academy exhibited the picture poorly. But there's also something transitional, as if lacking the courage of the artist's convictions, about the canvas itself. Perhaps that's the trouble with imitation. Despite the opening flourish of the tree silhouetted on far left, which seems lifted straight from Claude, nothing is really *going on* in this composition, where the cattle browsing the middle foreground are neither enough to make a story, nor modest enough to form part of a background.

Generally, though, Constable's foliage is as thick and crunchy as a cabbage. *Salisbury Cathedral from the Bishop's Grounds* (c. 1825) is a brilliant portrait of that building because it captures this same rustling multiplicity of surfaces within Gothic architecture. John Ruskin would define such characteristic excess in Volume 2 of *The Stones of Venice* as:

in the order of their importance: 1. Savageness. 2. Changefulness. 3. Naturalism. 4. Grotesqueness. 5. Rigidity. 6. Redundance. These characters are here expressed as belonging to the building; as belonging to the builder they would be expressed thus: 1. Savageness or Rudeness. 2. Love of Change. 3. Love of Nature 4. Disturbed Imagination. 5. Obstinacy. 6. Generosity.

Unignorably, though it's often ignored, this celebration of density, multiplicity and interaction – both in Gothic sculpture and by Constable's paintings – represents a fundamental feeling for the natural world. Like those anonymous mediaeval artists about whom Ruskin enthusiastically generalises, and whom Pevsner critiques, Constable was a local artist in every good sense of the term. He had been born the son of a prosperous corn merchant at East Bergholt in 1776, and the village would remain his preferred residence for much of his life – although there were also interludes when he lived away. For example, he went to school in Lavenham and studied art at the Royal Academy Schools in London. In adulthood he fell into the pattern of wintering in London but returning for the summers; it was only when his wife contracted tuberculosis that they began summering in Brighton for the healthy sea air.

It's possible to read this creative loyalty to East Bergholt and to Flatford Mill – the setting of some of his most famous paintings was also a family possession, and one source of the relative prosperity that had allowed him to develop his talent in the first place – as simply a matter of personal taste. But Constable, a highly culturally literate professional artist, was also working at a time when rural subjects were newly fashionable. In September 1816 Lord Byron, fresh from his summer at Villa Diodati with John William Polidori and the Shelleys, went on a tour of the Bernese Alps. On 18 September, as he recorded in the 'Alpine Journal' he was keeping for his soulmate and sometime lover Augusta Leigh, he revisited the Chateau de Chillon, at the far end of Lake Geneva, travelling:

> through Scenery worthy of I know not whom – [. . .] on our return met an English party in a carriage – a lady in it fast asleep! – fast asleep in the most anti-narcotic spot in the world – excellent –

Which put him in mind of the sentimental transgressions of other Englishwomen abroad:

I remember at Chamouni – in the very eyes of Mont Blanc – hearing another woman – English also – exclaim to her party – 'did you ever see anything more rural' – as if it were Highgate or Hampstead – or Brompton – or Hayes. – 'Rural' quotha! – Rocks – pines – torrents – Glaciers – Clouds – and Summits of eternal snow far above them – and 'Rural'! I did not know the thus exclaiming fair one – but she was a – very good kind of a woman.

This is as fun to read as it must have been to write. Yet in 1816 the European landscape was not to be taken lightly. It was only four years, after all, since Napoleon's retreat from Moscow. As Robert Schumann's '*Die Franzosen vor Moskva*', that poem collected in the *Marriage Diary* on 24 April 1844, puts it:

And when in the far distance
He saw a small bright dot –
He said, that is no star.
And when he looked once more,
The small dot was a small spark,
He said, 'I don't like to see that.'

This is funny, too. But, unlike the Byron, it doesn't mean to be. And we shouldn't blame the translator – the doggerel is original. Schumann is dabbling in a form which is notoriously more difficult to achieve than hobbyists realise. But isn't there, both in the lack of judgement within the writing itself, and in choosing to publish this stuff, something more seriously out of kilter here: a foreshadowing of the composer's coming madness? By the time he wrote it he had already sunk into depression in reaction to his wife's success. Soon, these depressive symptoms would effloresce into phobias, shivering fits and auditory hallucinations.

Schumann did at least recognise he was no Lord Byron. In 1849 he would pay homage to the English poet. His *Manfred: A Dramatic Poem with Music in Three Parts* Op. 115 is dramatic incidental music that – like its original, Byron's 1817 closet drama *Manfred* – was specifically written not to be fully staged. Schumann's *Manfred* isn't an opera, even though it includes an overture (which has since enjoyed an independent life as a concert staple), and various numbers, some instrumental and others scored for chorus, nine soloists and a narrator, that are divided into three acts. Instead it works rather like a secular oratorio. Not that Schumann was resistant to the operatic form: on the contrary, in 1842 he had written, 'Do you know my prayer as an artist, night and morning? It is called "German Opera". Here is a real field for enterprise . . . something simple, profound, German.' When his only opera *Genoveva*, Op. 81, was premiered in spring 1850, less than two years after he completed *Manfred*, it was the culmination of years of mulling over such possibilities.

His reasons for avoiding an operatic *Manfred* had more to do with the character of the original. On 9 March 1817 Byron sent his publisher, John Murray, a cover note about *Manfred: A Dramatic Poem*:

> The thing I have sent you will see at a glimpse – could never be attempted or thought of for the stage [. . .] I composed it actually with a horror of the stage – with a view to render even the thought of it impracticable, knowing the zeal of my

friends, that I should try that for which I have an invincible repugnance – viz. – a representation.

'Representation' of *Manfred* was 'repugnant' to its author because the work is, in Byron's words, a 'metaphysical drama'. It explores the protagonist's battles with supernatural forces as he attempts to come to terms with guilt over his dead beloved, Astarte. Manfred is a nobleman who lives in the Bernese Alps that Byron was exploring, and recording in his intimate 'Journal', in September 1816. That was also when he composed the bulk of this *'Dramatic Poem'*: timing which suggests we could position it alongside *Frankenstein* and Polidori's *The Vampyre* as another legacy of the famous ghost story writing challenge he had issued that summer at Villa Diodati. Byron's Manfred summons seven supernatural beings to help him forget his mysteriously unspecified guilt – in vain. Fate refuses to allow him to kill himself; and it's only by accepting a natural death in place of both that final act of control and Faustian bargains for supernatural remedies that he is released. In other words this is psychodrama, to be played out in the intimate theatre of the mind.

On 19 September 1816, Byron broke off from work on *Manfred* to note in his 'Alpine Journal' that, 'I have lately repeopled my mind with Nature':

The music of the Cows' bells [. . .] in the pastures [. . .] and the Shepherds' shouting to us from crag to crag & playing on their reeds where the steeps appeared almost inaccessible, with the surrounding scenery – realised all that I have ever heard or imagined of a pastoral existence – much more so than Greece or Asia Minor –

'A pastoral existence . . . Greece or Asia Minor': Byron was enough a product of his classical education for the pastoral, that classical cultural invention, to spring to his mind even when he was in the middle of the actual countryside. But then pastoral, with its golden-era light and shades of nostalgia, *is* seductive. Yesterday my cousin Paul sent me some old photographs taken outside our grandparents' house on Romney Marsh. Their combination of dark background and vivid sunlight is exactly how I remember that garden, which I loved in part because it meant *holidays*. A high hedge secluded it from the lane. The chalet bungalow was rickety if lovely, perhaps rather old-fashioned, but it stood – perfectly – at the edge of woodland. The garden borders were vivid with dahlias and roses in bright blocky colours: the lawn a dazzling opening to the sun that astonished me, a child from rainy Wales.

Paul has cleaned up the images so the people in them are once again as brightly dressed as they must have been on the day my grandfather snapped them. The pictures show my dad's family grouped stiffly for the camera: his mother, his brother and sister-in-law and their sons Paul himself and Julian, and my mum. The boys stand in front, steadied by parental hands on shoulders. Their tousled blond hair says they're ready to shoot off the moment the photos are done. I'm there too: in one a frocked doll on my mother's arm; in another the baby my dad holds as he looks directly through the camera lens at his own father – the only one in the group to do so. He still has the side parting and slightly puckish expression that make him seem like a schoolboy. I'm ever so slightly out of focus, laughing and grasping the finger my grandmother's holding out. Touchingly, my dad carries me with his whole body slightly stooped, as if caught between concern and confidence.

I can't resist looking up this visit in his diary. It turns out to be Sunday 2 August, and I am ten months old:

In the afternoon the Lyminge family came for tea and photos: F behaved very well. We noticed what a charming boy Julian has become . . .

Desmond has acquired a fresh camera, and we were given the old Hunter camera which Father had bought for that Holland holiday of 7 years ago. Anyway we are grateful that we haven't to buy a camera ourselves now.

This is the first visit after my grandfather's retirement and move and, 'We found the house more roomy than expected – partly because the conservatory gave an extra sitting space.' More importantly still, the day before at Canterbury against Hampshire:

Kent batted well: Richardson & Wilson (it was his benefit) made centuries, and Cowdrey 99. Final score 388 for 5 dec. Hants batted losing Marshall and Barnard before bad light stopped play at 6.20.

By the time P and I arrive in Dedham's comfortably handsome main street, it's about five o'clock. In the cricket field behind the flint-built church we come across a village match rambling to its conclusion. We sit down on a bench among table tombs and young meadowsweet to watch a couple of overs. The bowler is one of the worst I've ever seen. His wrist, arm and leg action go severally to pot every time he releases the ball. Yet what a pleasure it is to sit following this game in which we have no stake at all.

The seven beings Byron's Manfred summons for help are 'spirits of earth and air', and when his protagonist invokes them, near the beginning of Act One, he uses a language not of pantheism but of animism. The classical literature of the poet's education was filled to the point of cliché by nymphs, dryads, founts of muses and metamorphosing major and minor gods, and *Manfred* portrays not a world charged up by a single unifying divinity, but one creeping and milling with numerous individuated deities:

> Ye spirits of the unbounded Universe!
> Whom I have sought in darkness and in light—
> Ye, who do compass earth about, and dwell
> In subtler essence—ye, to whom the tops
> Of mountains inaccessible are haunts,
> And earth's and ocean's caves familiar things—
> I call upon ye by the written charm
> Which gives me power upon you—Rise! appear!

Manfred may not summon his helpers quite as memorably as Prospero summons Ariel, or Oberon calls upon Puck, but he shares what is recognisably their occult vocabulary. Perhaps Diodati grafted elements of the German Romantic *Schauerroman* tradition onto Byron's dramatic poem; possibly this too was part of its appeal to Schumann, whose narrative work includes both the *Fantasiestücke*, or *Fantasy Pieces*, Op. 73, composed in the same year as his *Manfred,* and the early

Kriesleriana, Op. 16, based on the fantastical and hypersensitive character of Johannes Kreisler from E. T. A. Hoffman's tales.

As they answer the call, Manfred's spirits declare where they've come from, and offer a roll of dramatic Romantic tastes: sunset, Mont Blanc, the ocean depths, volcanoes, storm-wind, night, even a guiding star. The electric impulses of the supernatural that Byron ascribes to these spots scintillate like the 'jewels' in a painting by Palmer or Cotman. Indeed the origins of Manfred's occult power are:

> in a star condemn'd,
> The burning wreck of a demolish'd world,
> A wandering hell in the eternal space.

This sense of a natural world starred with intensities glitters in the imagination. As we walk back onto the water meadows by way of Dedham Mill, I see how the stripped-back twigs of the willows, not yet in leaf, haze the field boundaries with yellowish green. Their colour seems to be not a constant part of the landscape but something almost illusory, shifting as we shift and changing with the movement of the clouds.

Would it matter, I wonder as we squeeze through the kissing gate, if Palmer added his metaphysical starbursts after he had completed a scene? Must Constable's glitter appear early in the picture-making process to count as an organic part of his vision? I don't feel so. I don't believe there's anything wrong with taking a second look, with taking time to let things change under your gaze. Besides, when I think back to Byron's catty comments about the correct response to an Alpine landscape, what they suggest to me is that his sensibility, too, was — at least when it came to the countryside – conscious to the point of being rehearsed.

Moreover his sheer intelligence, racing ahead as humour and self-knowledge, seems altogether more spontaneous. In the last days of his Alpine tour, he found himself in Brienz, where:

> below stairs I hear the notes of a Fiddle which bode no good for my night's rest.—The Lord help us!—I shall go down and see the dancing.—

Which, he reports the next day, was:

> excellent Waltzing—none but peasants—the dancing much better than in England—the English can't Waltz—never could—nor ever will.—One man with his pipe in his mouth— but danced as well as the others—

This is the kind of glittering detail – the insouciant local who kept his pipe in his mouth as he danced – that makes for great storytelling. But I also love that other glitter, irony: 'bode no good for my night's rest—The Lord help us!' That might be a perfectly innocent comment about insomnia in a hotel bedroom above a noisy bar – but it's being made by a man who knows very well his own inability to resist a party.

Flatford is a scatter of houses along the ridge which East Bergholt's parish church commands, and the path back to our starting point rises over more meadowland, almost a common, on the north side of the Stour. As we climb away from the river, the sun is at our backs. We've left the afternoon walkers behind at Dedham. When we pause at the last stile it's to look back over a scene in which only a lone dog walker serves as eyecatcher, like the single, punctuating figure in a Constable painting. The afternoon light is just beginning to thicken, the way it does against cottage walls in his oils, and the mist of coming foliage is on the trees right across the Vale. There's no traffic noise, just the dense, arrhythmic chorus of birdsong, among which I pick out the piercing *peeeeeeeeee-wit!* of lapwings down by the river and, nearer at hand, a quacking of blackbird alarm calls from the hedge.

Constable records individual experience, within a similarly emptied landscape. The shepherd boy in *The Cornfield* (1826) drinks from a stream alone. He has only his dog for company, though there are reapers in the sunny field at the end of the lane. In *Boat-Building near Flatford Mill* (1815), a man labours alone beside a new hull that towers over him. Watched from the craft moored safely to the other shore, a boatman struggles singlehandedly to calm his tow horse as it hurdles a riverside fence in *The Leaping Horse* (1825). These aren't sylvan figures out of pastoral, mere imaginary tokens whose role is only to provide onlookers a perspective. They are real people immersed in their quotidian reality, the landscape and its obligations.

In 1795, the nineteen-year-old Constable had made a trip to London to explore what his future as an artist might hold. According to his friend and fellow-artist C. R. Leslie, in *Memoirs of the Life of John Constable, RA,* he met the engraver John Thomas 'Antiquity' Smith, who told him, 'Do not set about inventing figures for a landscape taken from Nature; for you cannot remain an hour in any spot, however solitary, without the appearance of some living thing that will, in all probability, accord better with the scene and time of day than will any invention of your own.' Leslie notes that the advice landed: 'Often has Constable, in our walks together, taken occasion to point out, from what we saw, the good sense of Smith's advice.'

Constable's 'living' figures are the little people of society, powerless to change the environment they live and work in. The countryside surrounding them is empty because it was being depopulated, as he painted, by enclosure. They are in a sense the antithesis of their gentry masters whose portraits Thomas Gainsborough painted, large in the foreground of a landscape they dominated both visually and in life. Though Gainsborough continued working until his death in 1788, he was no Romantic but a firmly eighteenth-century servant of the landowning classes. His vigour and sparkle is all in the silky fabrics of his subjects' costly dress, and in their fabulous hair. The landscapes he paints are shaped to these figures – literally composed to set them off – just as in life they were shaped by their fiat. It was Gainsborough's close contemporary and rival Sir Joshua Reynolds (1723–92) who, articulating the imperatives of the genre, remarked that 'The only subjects a painter can paint are milord's horse, house, wife, dog and face.'

Constable, nailed less exactly to the social scale, paints a spaciousness that seems to resist such hierarchies of ownership. Yet it was Reynolds himself who had first identified for Constable the idea of Nature as 'the fountain's head, the source from whence all originally must spring,' as the younger artist put it in a letter of May 1802 to his former mentor John Dunthorne. Or as Reynolds himself said in his 1776 lecture at the Royal Academy, which became the sixth of his *Discourses on Art* and which Constable seems to have attended, 'Nature is the fountain which alone is inexhaustible; and from which excellencies must flow.' Reynolds would come to commend Constable's 'rising ability to translate these earliest images of his boyhood imagination into . . . permanent forms'. He meant more than the simple fact that the younger man remained so deeply in touch with where he had grown up. Constable himself noted that 'so deep-rooted are early impressions' that they can produce both 'over-weening affection' and 'melancholy'; and he painted not just what he could see, but what the surroundings of his birthplace meant to him.

'Painting is but another word for feeling,' he would write, while in his artistic prime, to his friend John Fisher, who was by then Bishop of Salisbury. It's Fisher who strolls with his wife in the famous foreground of *Salisbury Cathedral from the Bishop's Grounds* (1823), gesticulating with his cane towards the light susurrating on the cathedral's south front. To the right, cattle drink from the River Avon much as they drank from the river in Claude's *Hagar and the Angel*, while skinny elms frame and echo the height of the cathedral spire with Claude-like squiggles. Pictures like this, in which there are cattle to graze in the summer heat or walk down into a river to drink, create a feeling that all shall be well; a sense of the biblical 'They shall not hurt nor destroy in all my holy mountain,' from Isaiah 1:19. Here such benison knits the whole painting together because, though Fisher had commissioned it, he died while Constable was completing the work, which has the tenderness of elegy.

It feels strange being able to go walking again on these late April days, after the loosening of a pandemic lockdown. But once again, after a long time, there's a scintillating brightness, fleeting but glimpsed, to being alive. I still don't know which 24 April my dad's note referred to, nor what the date could have meant to him. But this evening I have a brimming sense that I could step back into a world of meadow-sweet and old churches and fireweed and lanes where moss grows between the tyre tracks. Which of course was the real reason for my dad's provisional notepads, always with him. To preserve times and places that seem full of the promise that all shall be well, by drawing them.

Walk 8: East Bergholt-Dedham via Flatford Mill and Dedham Vale. From: St Mary the Virgin, The Street, East Bergholt, Colchester CO7 6TA, OS Grid Ref TM 07003472.

The Cathedral from Danesgate.

Ninth Walk

Transforming

> Nothing, in fact, can equal the beauty of the north-
> ern summer's evening and night; if night it may be
> called that wants only the glare of day [. . .] I con-
> templated all nature at rest; the rocks, even grown
> darker in their appearance, looked as if they partook
> of the general repose, and reclined more heavily on
> their foundation.
>
> MARY WOLLSTONECRAFT, *Travels in Sweden*

Possibly it's the very incompleteness of twilight, the transitional time, that makes it so suggestive. Coming home
from school. Evening buses. A last drink under summer trees,
as pipistrelles whisk past. 'Starlight wood', that phrase from
Percy Bysshe Shelley's 'Hymn to Intellectual Beauty', gives me
a pleasurable frisson every time my eyes run across the little
grove of its ascenders, or snags on the *o*'s that open between
them like starlight.

But it's Shelley's late lyric, 'Song', written around four years after 'Hymn', that most simply evokes the rare sense of possibility and openness that comes with unpremeditated happiness. Its well-known opening, 'Rarely, rarely, comest thou / Spirit of delight!' is already simultaneously melancholic and delighted. 'Song' associates the spontaneity of 'delight' with an 'untainted' natural world:

> I love all that thou lovest,
>   Spirit of Delight!
> The fresh Earth in new leaves dress'd,
>   And the starry night;
> Autumn evening, and the morn
> When the golden mists are born.
>
> I love snow, and all the forms
>   Of the radiant frost;
> I love waves, and winds, and storms,
>   Everything almost
> Which is Nature's, and may be
> Untainted by man's misery.

And with its fleetingness. What unites these phenomena, drawn from across the visual scale and through the seasons, is that each is as changeable as the poet's self:

> Between thee and me
> What difference? But thou dost possess
> The things I seek

It's a moment which glancingly recognises the possibility of what Ruskin had yet to name 'pathetic fallacy', a kind of transferred epithet he would characterise as 'Very beautiful and yet very untrue.' Just for a moment, as Shelley's poem questions the 'difference' between speaker and environment, it acknowledges that an assumption is being made, and that the natural world around the poem's speaker may not actually *feel* as he does. Coming late on, in the seventh of the poem's eight stanzas, this near insight serves as a bridge passage from which Shelley turns back to delight itself. His poem ends with a vocative 'Oh come' that echoes the opening's 'comest thou':

> Thou art Love and Life! Oh come
> Make once more my heart thy home.

I especially like the valiant way this tongue-twisting chime *my/ thy* keeps the alignment of self and surroundings in the poem's mind to the very end.

In summertime on the Kintyre peninsula, that famously long reach of land into the North Channel, I feel like Mary Wollstonecraft during the trip she records in her *Short Residence in Sweden, Norway, and Denmark*:

> Nothing, in fact, can equal the beauty of the northern summer's evening and night; if night it may be called that wants only the glare of day, the full light, which frequently seems impertinent, for I could write at midnight very well without a candle. I contemplated all nature at rest; the rocks, even grown darker in their appearance, looked as if they partook of the general repose, and reclined more heavily on their

foundation. – What, I exclaimed, is this active principle which keeps me still awake?

When I last visited Kintyre I was a new graduate, full of fresh-minted zeal, on a quest to search out Neolithic cup- and ring-marked stones all down the peninsula. Those Cnocs and Cruachs lay around in wet pasture like debris no one could be bothered to move. I swished through long soaking grass, stumbled over hummocks and burrows. In those days I couldn't afford walking boots; my feet stayed wet all week. Sometimes I'd kick off my clinging socks and drive barefoot. As the summer evenings came slowly on, the menhirs and boulders I visited 'grew darker in their appearance' like Wollstonecraft's Scandinavian geology, seeming to 'recline more heavily upon their foundations' among brambles and molehills. When darkness finally fell I would retreat to a guesthouse, where I'd prop my shoes against the bedroom radiator, if there was one, or else turn a hairdryer on the shoe linings. I remember a scent of scorch and wet leaves.

The technology that created the cup marks, those carved dimples, and their concentric rings, fascinated me. No perfect circle gets drawn freehand; they must have been marked out using some early, swinging form of a drawing compass. Satisfying small-scale magic, by which an interval turns into a circle. I remember being astonished by this in primary school. How pleasing it was to swing the pencil arm of the compass around its spike (avoiding your thumb). In the rock art of west-coast Scotland, some ring marks include a radial line passing to their centre-point, almost like the entry passage to the labyrinth, that other form repeatedly carved or laid out in stones during the last millennium BCE, in sites across the north from Ireland to Scandinavia to the White Sea coast.

Summer nights up here, these long twilights that never properly close down into night, are little labyrinths too. They set up an exploratory restlessness: you find yourself invited to step out, or in, to the half-visible, half-occluded outdoor world. P and I are travelling the peninsula with Mary Wollstonecraft in the glovebox. She's a joyful traveller. Yet her actual 'short residence' in Scandinavia lasted only for just over three months, during the summer of 1795, and was undertaken in an attempt to win back her lover Gilbert Imlay. Since Imlay, an American profiteer exploiting the French Revolution, was also the father of her daughter Fanny, the stakes for her were high. But not for him. He strung her along in a way that her last great love William Godwin would later anatomise, with all the feeling of a new widower, in his *Memoirs of the Author of a Vindication of the Rights of Woman*:

> The agonies of such a separation, or rather desertion, great as Mary would have found them upon every supposition, were vastly increased, by the lingering method in which it was effected, and the ambiguity that, for a long time, hung upon it. This produced the effect of holding her mind, by force, as it were, to the most painful of all subjects.

Trapped in the maze of unreciprocated love, from which Imlay did not have the moral courage to release her, in April 1795 Wollstonecraft followed the American from France to London, where the following month she attempted suicide — only to be prevented at the last minute by the man himself.

At the time, as Godwin puts it in his *Memoirs*, 'Mr Imlay was involved in a question of considerable difficulty, respecting a mercantile adventure in Norway.' A crew he'd hired there had gone to ground with an entire smuggled cargo of precious metals. Possibly because she was parasuicidal, even though she was already the distinguished author of, among other works, *A Vindication of the Rights of Men* and *A Vindication of the Rights of Woman* – and a mother – Wollstonecraft seems to have decided that what she now needed was to take on additional responsibilities. That summer she set out for Scandinavia to retrieve the small fortune lost by her philandering ex.

Despite the difficulties and dangers, she clearly enjoyed much of the journey:

> June and July are the months to make a tour through Norway; for then the evenings and nights are the finest I have ever seen; but [. . .] summer disappears almost before it has ripened the fruit of autumn—even, as it were, slips from your embraces, whilst the satisfied senses seem to rest in enjoyment.

'Slips from your embraces': a sense of the fleetingness of natural phenomena, and of delight itself, are already part of the Romantic sensibility a whole generation before Shelley. The description comes from 'Letter Fourteen' of the twenty-five Wollstonecraft sent Imlay during her journey, and which she would subsequently publish as *A Short Residence*. But they are much more than simply a contribution to the development of travel writing: they pack in an entire emotional world, encoded as observation about place. This passage continues:

You will ask, perhaps, why I wished to go further north-ward. Why? Not only because the country, from all I can gather, is most romantic, abounding in forests and lakes, and the air pure, but I have heard much of the intelligence of the inhabitants [. . .] The description I received of them carried me back to the fables of the golden age: independence and virtue; affluence without vice; cultivation of mind, without depravity of heart; with 'ever smiling liberty', the nymph of the mountain.—I want faith! My imagination hurries me forward to seek an asylum in such a retreat from all the disappointments I am threatened with; but reason drags me back, whispering that the world is still the world, and man still the same compound of weakness and folly, who must occasionally excite love and disgust, admiration and contempt.

That reflection on an unnamed universal 'man' also, of course, fits Imlay in particular. In the letters she sent home Wollstonecraft tried every tool in her armoury to seduce him: high literary style, astute and absorbing observation, wit, and deeply emotional appeals. But nothing worked. The last letter is cut short 'as I was hurried on board', when he failed to join her for the voyage home from Hamburg, as he had promised:

I do not feel inclined to ramble any further this year; nay, I am weary of changing the scene, and quitting people and places the moment they begin to interest me.—This also is vanity! [. . .] Adieu! My spirit of observation seems to be fled—

Back in London, finding herself deserted, the thirty-six-year-old made a second suicide attempt. But despite the bitterness of this aftertaste to her adventure, *A Short Residence*, published the following January, would be her most successful book during her lifetime. In it, Wollstonecraft portrays travel itself as a kind of filmic flow: a recurring verb is 'glide'. Even as she waits in vain for Imlay to join her in Altona, on the outskirts of Hamburg, she observes how:

> The moving picture, consisting of large vessels and small-craft, which are continually changing their position with the tide, renders this noble river [Elbe], the vital stream of Hamburg, very interesting; and the windings have sometimes a very fine effect.

A little over two decades later, her daughter would evoke an altogether harsher version of travelling north in her own most successful book. All three protagonists of *Frankenstein* – the sea captain in search of the North-West Passage, the eponymous inventor, and his creature – seem addicted to this journeying. In a sense the whole novel interrupts Frankenstein and his creature in pursuit of each other across the Arctic ice. Our first sight of the doctor, and our last of the creature, are as figures in this unsurvivable environment, which Captain Walton describes in a letter to his sister,

> I am surrounded by mountains of ice, which admit of no escape, and threaten every moment to crush my vessel. [. . .] There is something terribly appalling in our situation, yet my courage and hope do not desert me.

In fact, travel is just one form of the addictive behaviour that is in a sense Mary Shelley's subject. She shows how obsession can build on itself so that what starts out as exceptional enterprise on behalf of humanity – exploration, invention – can reverse into egotistical acting-out with no regard for others. Frankenstein clings to his belief in the idealism of endeavour until the end, scolding the mutinous crew who don't wish to be sacrificed on the ice by Walton:

> You were hereafter to be hailed as benefactors of your species; your names adored, as belonging to the brave men who encountered death for honour, and the benefit of mankind.

But perhaps for him there *is* no alternative to death. Four days later, he has been killed by his own creation.

Here, on the other hand, we are, a little further north than Hamburg and very much alive, if rather tired from travelling. We've arrived at Skipness on the Kintyre peninsula after a long drive, and a series of last ferries caught in the dusk that travelled west with us. There's something dreamlike about our disorientation, as we try to make sense of the dim shapes around us: roof-ridge, trees. In a moment we'll release the dogs, find the keys, switch on a light. But just for a moment, we pause. The engine ticks and cools. There's a crowded stillness in the early summer night around us. It seems almost to crackle with the alertness of dozens of creatures; both the nocturnal and the diurnal. That bird crashing in the beech may not be an owl; it could be a raven, a buzzard, even a heron choosing a high roost. P switches on his phone-torch and catches the shining eyes of small rodents – here, and here, in the grass.

They vanish as abruptly as if they've been switched off when we raise the car boot and release the dogs, who are as over-excited as kids on a sugar rush. Charging round us in circles, they're barely able to concentrate long enough to pee. Perhaps they too sense how this twilight vivid with animal odours presses in on the short summer night, as if to fray it shorter still. P and I are aware how, a month before midsummer, dusk doesn't fall here till after 10.30, and dawn will start to creak open the sky shortly after four. And that we're standing in civil twilight, this strange margin of almost an hour before sunrise and after sunset. I'm torn between enchantment and bracing myself, as a lifelong insomniac, for the 'white' nautical twilight that won't end till midnight and will dawn again at 2.30am, and for the couple of hours in between that will leave us not in soporific darkness, but in the suspended animation that is astronomical twilight.

While we unpack the car I remember how, as a kid, I naively believed these different terms for how far the sun lies below the horizon registered the relative sophistication of occupations. Of course, they're merely measures of practice. When the sun is between six and twelve degrees below the horizon, sailors can see stars clearly enough with the naked eye to navigate. Astronomers come into their own when it's from twelve and eighteen degrees below: though they need full darkness to see fainter objects. I like picturing the lines drawn by these angles to the horizon as levers for light: the steeper the angle, the smaller the amount of light that gets levered up. It reminds me of the light lever in William Blake's *I want! I want!*; how, in that 1793 engraving, desire is a ladder to the moon, and wishing set like a lever against seeing.

The little naked self who steps onto Blake's sky ladder is doing so in the moonlit time between civil twilight and full darkness, since seven stars gleam brightly in the cross-hatched gloaming. Nautical twilight, perhaps. But of course, Blake never saw the white nights of Scotland. At the time he engraved *I want! I want!* he was living at 13 Hercules Buildings, Hercules Road in North Lambeth. Two years earlier he had illustrated the second edition of *Original Stories from Real Life*, a collection of moral tales for children written by Mary Wollstonecraft, an acquaintance with whom he shared a publisher, and who was living just a mile to the east in Southwark. In 1791, when they were cooperating on this conduct book, Wollstonecraft had not yet either met Imlay in France, or travelled to Scandinavia. But even in south London's 'chart'd streets' it would then still have been possible to see the stars on a clear night in May, and to enjoy the long summer twilight that Blake's engraving is, after all, portraying: it's dated 17 May.

Perhaps, too, it's a representation of mercy. What lightens the darkness around Blake's stars isn't a failure of technique — engraving can easily manage inky blacks — but the success of hope. Although Blake eschewed the prevailing national culture of Anglicanism, into which he had been baptised, he would have known the old Evensong collect, 'Lighten our darkness, we beseech thee O Lord,' even though he rejected it — and how it continues: 'And by thy great mercy defend us from all perils and dangers of this night.'

There's been no full darkness on Kintyre since 3 May, and won't be again till 8 August, either. The night after our arrival, we find ourselves walking to Skipness village. As we turn into the lane I half-sense, half-see the verges marking dark, smudgy parallels against the pallor of tarmac; they meet much closer than infinity. We've entered a kind of perspective of gloaming where everything blurs. Our footfalls can't actually be muffled by the twilight, but it feels that way. We come downhill through a copse of small oak and ash that, as so often on the rocky west coast of Britain, seem to be keeping their heads down in the face of the Atlantic. Even at this hour they let through a little light; their leaves appear almost to fan it into brightness. Wollstonecraft has a description of this effect — in daytime — too. In a Norwegian beech grove on the road between Tønsberg and Larvik, on the eastern shore of the Outer Oslo Fjord:

> The airy lightness of their foliage admitted a degree of sunshine, which, giving a transparency to the leaves, exhibited an appearance of freshness and elegance that I had never before remarked.

We cross a bridge over a peat burn, and pass the castellated folly that must in the nineteenth century have been the gatehouse to Skipness Castle. It's uninhabited now, its glassless windows giving onto graffiti and the odours of pee, paraffin and damp.

Behind us, the B8001 makes a long dead end, its paved laneway disappearing into a track between rhododendrons and culminating in the heathland viewpoint of Culindrach. Between this viewpoint and the village lie a patchwork of cattle pastures. As we passed through them just now, we heard the breathing of beasts standing close by hedges and gates, dark masses in the darkness, and it felt wrong somehow to break the membrane of the summer night with talk. So we round the corner onto the strand in silence. And there before us is Arran, crisp against the milky light of the sky and sea. Small wonder, I think, that the art of silhouette was a sensation of the Romantic era: the island in outline is utterly the island itself.

Silhouettes took their name from an unpopularly economising French Treasury Chief, Étienne de Silhouette (1709–67), and gained traction in eighteenth-century Europe primarily as a cheap form of portraiture. But they trick the brain into supplying three-dimensional detail. Just as contemporaries could reconstruct face and personality from an outline like, say, Joseph Neesen's 1786 portrait of Ludwig von Beethoven at fifteen – head tilted back confidently, pigtail tied neatly behind – so at twilight the human eye rebuilds an environment from the outlines of trees, buildings and hills.

Now, in profile, Arran convinces me of its monumental reality. As we walk the lane that skirts the strand, it seems to shift in step with us. One by one, dim promontories and declivities appear to surface from the dark mass and proffer themselves. Rotating slowly, keeping pace with our progress, the island raises and lowers the ridge of its high ground while, beside us, the Kilbrannan Sound shifts almost inaudibly, dribbling a line of phosphorescence on the sand. Skipness is nothing more, really, than this beach, this seaboard lane and the line of crofts standing low beside it. A locked church, a former school, a village noticeboard beside a corrugated tin shed: on this summer night, it's like the start of a story.

Four impressive woodwind chords in chromatic progression announce 'Once upon a time' at the start of Felix Mendelssohn's *A Midsummer Night's Dream* Op. 21, before the concert overture opens into a high seething of pianissimo violins. It's a sound full of the mystery and promise of summer twilight: of everything at once concealed and possible. A rustling of leaves, and creatures both real and imagined hurrying among them.

The seventeen-year-old Mendelssohn completed *Ein Sommernachtstraum* on 6 August 1826. He had recently read Shakespeare's play in a translation by the great German poet and critic August Schlegel – who was also his uncle by marriage. Even in its German home, Romantic expression was not purely spontaneous but was created through a network of relationships and influences. But who cares, when the results are so fantastical and evocative? Mendelssohn's violins are divided to play four parts instead of the usual two, so they sound not dense and symphonic but full of air. Their tumbling lines are spattered with staccato dots that indicate the lightest of touches – as does the pizzicato with which, as the violas join, the lower strings roll in. And it's all in uncanny E minor, that tonally jingling key, whose relationship to the piece's ostensible home key of E major is disconcertingly cavalier. Tingling unison Es drive this point home, as they hold the shifting lines of the music within a shimmer of unison sound.

Even in Berlin, where the precocious composer lived with his family, June nights are never completely dark, and the adolescent Mendelsohn must have known what it was to open a window onto a warm half-light. It would have been a large, handsome window, too. The Mendelssohns lived at Leipziger Strasse 3, a grand property that had previously been both a palace – Palais Groeben – and a silk mill. Its long, porticoed façade was pierced by multiple windows. The year in which the teenager wrote *A Midsummer Night's Dream* was the year that the first of the gas streetlights for which Berlin would become famous were installed. But before that his summer evenings would have meant twilight, snatches of voices from open windows, lamplit rooms glimpsed through the shifting leaves of linden trees: the whole mysterious, story-telling world his overture evokes.

Sixteen years later, in 1842, when Mendelssohn went on to write his incidental music for *A Midsummer Night's Dream,* Op. 61, he incorporated this youthful overture into the new work of his maturity. I hope he did so with pleasure, revisiting his younger self with affection. By then, the trip he'd made to Scotland when he was twenty must have seemed equally ancient history. In summer 1829 he tacked a hectic three-week tour of the country, from Edinburgh to the Hebrides, onto the end of a successful London concert season.

He was travelling with his friend Karl Klingemann, a sometime poet and a career diplomat who had been posted to the Hanover Legation in London for the last two years. The two had met when Klingemann was based at the Hanoverian Legation in Berlin, which occupied the *bel étage* at Leipziger Strasse 3, and it's from Klingemann that we get a description of the summer boat trip to see Fingal's Cave, in the island of Staffa, which produced Mendelssohn's other famous concert overture, which he called *The Hebrides,* Op. 26:

A greener rush of waves surely never rushed into a stranger cavern — its many pillars making it look like the inside of an immense organ, black and resounding, absolutely without purpose, and quite alone, the wide grey sea within and without.

With its mixture of awe and gothic chill, there could hardly be a more Romantic description of the spectacular, black basalt cave that the naturalist and explorer Sir Joseph Banks had 'discovered', for the world beyond its traditional owners, in 1772. Banks may simply have been trying to steal some of the thunder from Captain Cook's second trip to the Antipodes, from which he'd just been excluded. But the fame he'd acquired from his work collecting flora on Cook's first Pacific expedition, the *HMS Endeavour* voyage of 1768–71, guaranteed these fresh discoveries wide attention too.

Klingemann's description, taken from a letter he wrote home on 10 August 1829, makes easy use of Romantic terms that were by now mainstream currency, and he produces an odd echo, in that 'absolutely without purpose, and quite alone, the wide grey sea within and without', of Percy Bysshe Shelley's 'Ozymandias'. The sonnet published in 1818, pulls back to the horizon to evoke existential meaninglessness in a similar way:

> Round the decay
> Of that colossal wreck, boundless and bare
> The lone and level sands stretch far away.

In draft, Shelley crossed out almost every line of this poem to achieve the final zero of his imagined horizon. The manuscript is all horizontals, with its words almost invisible under, or crowded around, the run of deletion lines. (Below them is doodled what looks *mutatis mutandis* like a geometric vulva.) But mutability isn't the same as entropy, change doesn't have to mean loss, and Klingemann's story reveals him to have been far from melancholic, both a family man and a convivial salonist. He seems to have had the good life his good humour deserved, marrying and becoming a father in his late forties, and dying – presumably still in post, since was he buried in London – not till he was in his sixties. This mixture of sociability and steadiness must have made him an attractive travelling companion for a musician more than a decade his junior. He is, though, particularly funny about the twenty-year-old Mendelssohn's showing on the boat trip to Staffa:

> The Atlantic [. . .] stretched its thousand feelers more and more roughly, twirling us about like anything [. . .] Ladies as a rule fell down like flies, and one or the other gentlemen followed their example; I only wish my travelling fellow-sufferer had not been among them, but he is on better terms with the sea as a musician than as an individual or a stomach.

The composer's own journal notes of this trip simply, 'Horrible seasickness, Staffa.' In the event, it didn't matter. He had composition in mind before he even boarded the boat to the island, which lies in the Inner Hebrides some eighty kilometres to the north of Skipness. In a letter to his sister Fanny he had already noted down the distinctive figure that in his overture would become the motion of the sea surging through the orchestra's lower strings. Writing into the summer night at Tobermory on the island of Mull on 7 August, the eve of the trip, he sent her twenty-one bars of keyboard reduction with the famous rolling figure already marked for viola and cello, 'In order to make clear what a strange mood has come over me in the Hebrides,' as he explained.

FIONA SAMPSON

A week earlier, while visiting Edinburgh en route from England, twilight in the ruins of Holyrood had inspired another theme, which would eventually become the slow movement of his third and final symphony, 'The Scottish', Op. 56. As he wrote home 'late at night' on another summer evening, 30 July 1829:

The windows are open, for the weather is beautiful and the sky full of stars [. . .]

In the evening twilight we went today to the palace where Queen Mary lived and loved; a little room is shown there with a winding staircase leading up to the door: up this way they came and found Rizzio in that dark corner, where they pulled him out, and three rooms off there is a dark corner, where they murdered him. The chapel close to it is now roofless, grass and ivy grow there, and at that broken altar Mary was crowned Queen of Scotland. Everything round is broken and mouldering and the bright sky shines in. I believe I have found today in that old chapel the beginning of my *Scottish* Symphony.

In fact, Mendelssohn had been in a state of compositional anticipation ever since the spring when he planned the trip, writing on 26 March from Germany to invite Klingemann that:

Next August I am going to Scotland with a rake for folk-songs, an ear for the lovely, fragrant countryside, and a heart for the bare legs of the natives.

Which is a lovely admission of Romantic intention. Not coincidentally, Mendelssohn's mother was among the many readers whom the auspiciously named Sir Walter Scott had convinced of the historical glamour and beauty of Scotland. Before he even set out for Britain, the young man's ideas had been coloured by this popular European reception of Scott's Hiberno-mediaevalism: so he arrived in Scotland looking forward to meeting the great man. In the event, the trip to Scott's Borders home near Melrose, on 31 July, was a disappointment, as a letter home glumly summarised: 'We found Sir Walter in the act of leaving Abbotsford, stared at him like fools, drove eighty miles and lost a day for the sake of at best one half-hour of superficial conversation.'

But by the time the friends followed Scott – and a procession of Romantic artists and writers from England and Europe, including John Keats – in enduring the boat trip to Staffa, the composer had already seen more than enough to fall for the country himself. From Tobermory's pretty harbourfront the interleaved headlands of Lochaber and Ardnamurchan tempt the eye onward, and in 1829 the Isle of Mull's remoteness must have felt satisfyingly 'Once upon a time'. Mendelssohn's Scottish concert overture starts, like its predecessor, with an announcement by sustained woodwind and upper string chords that, as in the earlier piece, works as a musical incipit. But unlike in the *Dream*, where the chromatic opening lifts the listener somewhere new and strange, here the progression, waxing and waning between a rumbling B minor and the relative D major keys, arcs back on itself like the extended soughing of a wind. Once the theme is restated with roiling semiquaver accompaniment, between the periodic breakers of full orchestral chords, it's evident that this seascape texture is richly descriptive. Though it has a countermelody that's a perfect formal fit, the piece is, unlike *Dream*, not written in the conventional sonata form of the era, but comes much closer to an early tone poem, evoking atmosphere and location even though it doesn't quite resolve into fully narrative programme music.

Tone poems can be bearers of cultural ideas all the same. Decades later, Richard Wagner would dismiss Mendelssohn as 'a landscape-painter of the first order' in his notorious antisemitic article, and then book, *Das Judentum in der Musik* (1850, 1869). Wagner's fantasy that music belonged to a kind of authentic *Volk* lifeworld was muddled as well as bone-headed. Still, the 'folk' tradition to which Mendelssohn now found himself contributing was neither authentic nor German but Scottish, and to some extent confected. In the months after his Scottish tour, the composer found himself working not on his Scottish symphony, as he'd intended, but on the piece he'd started to compose on Mull, which he called his *Hebrideanlegend*. When he finished it at the end of 1830, he gave it the title *The Lonely Isle*; by its first performance, he was calling it *The Hebrides*. But it only began to enjoy real success in 1832, admittedly after some compositional tinkering but also when publishers left his note, 'Fingal's Cave', on the printed first edition of the full score and this became the name by which the overture is popularly known.

'Fingal', more properly Fionn mac Cumhaill, was the hero of epic poems said to have been composed by the ancient singer Ossian, in a Scotland every bit as mythic and far away as Shakespeare's Athens on a midsummer night. A gift for a composer: but it wasn't Mendelssohn who had given the name Fingal's Cave to the great columnar black basalt opening that pierces Staffa's 'Lonely Isle'. The coinage was Joseph Banks's own: an early instance of the European passion for folklore that would both lead to and arise from Romantic nationalism. It was also ironically misdirected. In naming the cave for a literary figure in order to create an atmosphere of antique tradition, the explorer disavowed its actual traditional owners, Clan MacQuarrie.

It's further back again, to the German philosopher and poet Johann Gottfried Herder (1744–1803) that the origins of such forms of Romantic nationalism can be traced. Herder's own practice of collecting folk material, and his interest in translation, together led to the highly influential volumes of *Volkslieder*, translations of folk songs from around the world, which he published in 1774 and 1778–79. He now began to develop a proto-anthropological sense of history as the multiple histories of multiple cultures. This sounds immensely benign and modern, but Wagner's idea of the German *Volk* hadn't come from nowhere. Herder argued for an essential difference between different peoples, who are 'nationalities wonderfully separated not only by woods and mountains, seas and waste-lands, rivers and weather, but more particularly by languages, tastes and character'. The result was a movement that both co-opted local myth and tradition to thicken up the sense of national identity, and created a European taste for folklore as the way to encounter that identity.

All of which meant that Scots, at least imagined the way Mendelssohn pictured them, as 'noble savages' striding across picturesque mountains and islands with their 'bare legs' and their authentic traditions, became fashionable across Europe. The Ossian poems were an international cultural sensation and did much to confirm Scotland's Romantic reputation. Widely translated, they were set by Franz Schubert in Vienna as *lieder*, and in Paris as a hugely successful 1804 opera, *Ossian, or the bards*, by Jean-François Le Sueur. The stories appeared in dozens of lavish paintings, including oils by Jean-August-Dominique Ingres and a pair of flamboyantly hallucinatory canvasses on the theme which Napoleon commissioned for the reception hall of his Chateau Malmaison. Allusions even appear in J. W. von Goethe's 1774 epistolary novel *The Sorrows of Young Werther*.

We now know no such indigenous epic ever existed; though Fionn mac Cumhaill evidently did. The antiquarian James Macpherson, who was also a genuine collector of folk material, had faked it up, first in his *Fingal: An epic poem* (1761), and then in subsequent books, *Temora* (1763) and *The Works of Ossian* (1765). (He seems to have faked up my own name while he was at it.) Part a somewhat free 'reconstruction' of fragmentary traditional sources – like Elias Lönnrot's 1835 re/construction of the Finnish *Kalevala* epic from Karelian folk material – but in part brazen literary fraud, Macpherson's work gave the world 'Fingal', a third-century king he imagined ruling this westerly region of Scotland, together with Fingal's son Ossian, the blind bard supposed to have authored the epic, and Ossian's dead son Oscar and living daughter-in-law Malvina. Contemporaries seem not to have worried that early Celts went by such Hispanic names.

Not every piece of folklore rediscovered during the Romantic era was fake, or even a reconstruction. The cultural momentum

Herder initiated would help set in motion not only the shift in nineteenth-century Europe towards national self-determination and away from Austro-Hungarian and Ottoman imperial rule, especially in the revolutions of 1848, but – as that century ended – the emergence of the milder cultural manifestations of Jugendstil. During the century that followed, it would allow smaller nations from Slovenia to Wales to rediscover a digni-fied sense of identity, often centred in a national language, and in some cases to establish a degree of self-determination. Irish Romanticism and the era's tragic culmination there in the Irish Potato Famine of 1845–52 are a crucible of struggle for modern identity. But cultural nationalism would also reveal a darker side. Not long after Jugendstil had established itself as a charm-ing cultural style in much of Europe, Nazism was recruiting the German *Volk* to massacre 'rootless cosmopolitans', including some of the Mendelssohns' descendents, in the Holocaust. In the 1990s, traditional epic poems and turbo-folk music would be used by local politicians and warlords to fuel the wars that broke apart the former Yugoslavia.

Yet if the geopolitical world that is partly its legacy would be sometimes quite forcibly redrawn, the moment of Romantic 'enthusiasm' itself was altogether more innocent. The inter-national success of Mendelssohn's '*Fingal's Cave*' overture, and the way it helped build the reputation of the cave on Staffa, had a wide and benign reach. In the years following the compos-er's 1829 visit, the island became a must-see, and the bumpy voyage to Staffa a regular part of the picturesque itinerary. J. M. W. Turner visited in 1831 in order to illustrate Scott's *The Lord of the Isles*, a poetry collection set on the island. William Wordsworth's 1833 visit resulted in the twilit 'Cave of Staffa':

> Ye shadowy Beings, that have rights and claims
> In every cell of Fingal's mystic grot,
> Where are ye?

The poem manages to combine Gothic sensibility with his by-then customary inveighing against popular tourism:

> We saw, but surely, in the motley crowd,
> Not one of us has felt the far-famed sight;
> How could we feel it? each the other's blight,
> Hurried and hurrying, volatile and loud.

Jules Verne, who visited in 1839, would exploit the island's Gothic potential to the full in his science fiction, not only using it as a setting in his 1882 novel *The Green Ray*, but also alluding to it in *Journey to the Centre of the Earth* and *The Mysterious Island*. Staffa's fame continued throughout the nineteenth century. The Hibernophile Queen Victoria visited in 1847, and Robert Louis Stevenson in 1870. In 1901, August Strindberg set part of *A Dream Play* in 'Fingal's Grotta'.

And here we are, on this not quite midsummer night nearly two centuries after Mendelssohn's expedition, the latest in the long line of tourists following in those nineteenth-century footsteps as we walk the shore road beyond Skipness to the Claonaig ferry. This is recognisably the coast that the composer visited. From the Mull of Kintyre on a clear day you can see, less than fifteen miles across the Straits of Moyle on the Antrim Coast, the dolerite columns of the Fair Head cliffs which match those at Fingal's Cave. Even in this twilight I can make out, among the new bracken, the lichened boulders characteristic of the region, and mattresses of heather and bilberry bushes growing invitingly beside the road as they have for centuries. The dogs, who have never quite accepted the sea as a good thing and are glad we've left the beach itself behind, fossick earnestly among them for rabbits.

But we change the world we move through. Skipness, rapt on a summer's night, is not just at the mercy of the sea now breathing calmly alongside us. Kintyre is being changed by the Glaswegian middle classes who buy up crofts as week-end cottages which, however much they're loved, stand empty through the long winters. Holidaymakers crowd in to admire Skipness Castle – that Romantic ruin – and climb its thirteenth-century keep-cum-tower-house, from whose pitched roof a flag still flies. They look down on the curtain walls massy with rubble and 'Cooee!' to friends who linger below. At picnic tables set out next door on the lawn of the Seafood Cabin, families eat the fresh Loch Fyne seafood, mussels and salmon, patés and smoked fish: all of them once quotidian, but now luxurious. Today we ate the best scallops of our lives there, squinting into the salty light of the Sound – from which they had just come.

A layby, a bus shelter, and the short concrete landing stage where the Claonaig–Arran ferry docks lie just ahead. Deserted at this time of night, of course, as water slaps lightly against the piers. It's hard to say exactly what the changes of recent years here add up to. But it feels like a hollowing out of something. We pause in the dimness. The water shines peaceably. A heron crakes somewhere further along the shore. A curlew calls in its inimitable way. The heron crakes again and then, as if completing the thought, rises into view and skims away left, slowly flapping its double-jointed wings. The night seems to wait, uncanny and spacious, posing its question: what next?

Each of the trio of Romantics and their works that I've brought with me on this walk has made me think about the 'what next?' of change that is continually at our feet. I think of it like the advancing and retreating sheet of shallow waves. Felix Mendelssohn's early concert overtures, *A Midsummer Night's Dream* and *The Hebrides,* helped shift what were then the classical formal tendencies of contemporary music towards something more programmatic, expressive and often playful. The Romanticism of, for example, Ludwig van Beethoven's music is often political, even intellectual. It comes to us in the title of the *Eroica* Symphony Op. 55, in the plotline about individual political heroism from his opera *Fidelio* Op. 72, or in the stormy striving of the late great quartets, from Op. 127 onwards, which he was producing as the adolescent Mendelssohn composed his first *A Midsummer Night's Dream.* Beethoven's is the often-overwhelming Burkean territory of the sublime and the beautiful. But Mendelssohn contributed to a second shift, into a musical Romanticism of distinctive textures – it *sounded* different, lighter and more feelingful – whose affinities with the tumbling, subjective picturesque would make it particularly, charmingly accessible.

Percy Bysshe Shelley's apprehension, in 'Song', that we're always changing like the natural world of which we're part, and that our pleasures are mutable, seems so very much his personal fingerprint that I imagine it to have been both a conscious and an unquestioned thought: the kind he might have called an 'intuition'. It makes me think of his entire life as a single restless grasp away from the present and after the next thing. (The dogs' impatience as they tug at their leashes suddenly seems a comic echo.) I remember the schoolboy scientific experiments – the novel romantic and sexual arrangements – and how frequent travel must have scratched an itch for change.

Frankenstein holds up a tragic mirror to this kind of perpetual motion. A gull flaps hugely, silently overhead. Inhaling the salty night air, I wonder: did Mary Shelley hope her husband would catch sight of himself reflected there? By late 1817, when she completed the novel, the Romantic intensity of his search – for what? For meaning? – had already turned from the early, political idealism of his period as William Godwin's disciple into a bruising solipsism. Mary must have realised that her dream of a deeply committed soulmate had become simply that.

Out in the sea channel, water shifts in the glassy light of this summer night. It makes a conversational sound, like discreet throat-clearing, as if to remind us of the tragic culmination of Percy Bysshe's restlessness in the Gulf of Poets. But it was his wife's mother who truly cared about social and political change. Mary Wollstonecraft witnessed Romanticism's violent worst in the years from 1792 to 1795, when she lived in France surrounded by the Revolutionary Terror. Yet her educational work and political philosophy make clear her belief in the movement's redemptive value, and in the importance of individual development as much as societal change. As a young teacher in London and Ireland, in her writing on education (*Thoughts on the Education of Daughters* appeared in 1787), and later as a parent, she adopted the radically child-centred approach Jean-Jacques Rousseau had influentially expounded in *Emile, or On Education* (1762), a work whose gendered flaws she ignored. But her commitment to change seems to have been balanced by an understanding of its costs. As she wrote in 1795, concluding what would become her *Letters Written in Sweden, Norway, and Denmark*, 'I am weary of changing the scene, and quitting people and places the moment they begin to interest me.'

I stand on the dock and watch the shadowy wavelets shift to and fro. In both Mendelssohn's concert overtures, *A Midsummer Night's Dream* and *The Hebrides*, we share what is very much a young man's vision not merely of changing musical forms but, more fundamentally and excitingly, of the transformative power of particular times and spaces. The young composer's name was Felix, after all; and he probably he did feel lucky in that first flush of success and good health, though he never outlived it. At the age of thirty-eight he would die at home in Leipzig after a series of strokes – apparently caused by inherited disease. But those opening chords still rise out of the summer night, summoning us once again to enchantment: Once upon a time . . .

Walk 9: Skipness Castle to Claonaig ferry via B8001 OS Grid reference NR908575.

A Farm Near
War Eagle   4·IV·44

Tenth Walk

Paying Attention

Sylvan historian . . .

JOHN KEATS, 'Ode on a Grecian Urn'

Every story finishes somewhere. Elizabeth Barrett Browning's last words were 'Beautiful . . . beautiful . . . ': at least, according to her widower. When she died in Robert Browning's arms, on 29 June 1861, one coda to the Romantic era was complete. Barrett Browning and Alfred, Lord Tennyson had, in a kind of unspoken tandem, driven British poetry forward from Romanticism into the Victorian era of mass readerships, with its new, mainstream tastes for narrative verse full of colourful descriptions of populated settings, and couched in a language that was as easy on the tongue as it was on the intellect. Yet she had retained even into the later, Italian phase of her life an admiration for the great British Romantic poets, John Keats, Lord Byron and Percy Bysshe Shelley, who preceded her there. And, in becoming deeply caught up in the

Risorgimento, she played a part in the great Romantic movement towards democratic revolution that swept Europe during
1848, that Year of Revolutions, and beyond.

Robert has his wife kissing her hands towards him as she
utters her last words:

> She put her arms round me 'God bless you' repeatedly —
> kissing me with such vehemence that when I laid her down
> she continued to kiss the air with her lips, and several times
> raised her own hands and kissed them: I said 'Are you com-
> fortable?' 'Beautiful.'

I can never forget, when I read this touching scene from the
letter he wrote home next day to his sister Sarianna, the
domestic frame of Elizabeth's death. She died at home in the
Oltrarno district of her beloved Florence, in the *piano nobile*
rooms, opposite the church of San Felice and near the Boboli
Gardens, that the couple had made their own. Elizabeth had
taken great pride in occupying this section of the old Palazzo
Guidi, with its:

> rooms [. . .] very much larger than any room in Wimpole
> Street, & [. . .] eight windows which are very large, opening
> from ceiling to floor, open on a sort of balcony-terrace . . .
> not quite a terrace, yet no ordinary balcony neither . . .
> which is built out from the house, giving it an antique &
> picturesque appearance to the exterior — [. . .] Opposite is
> the grey wall of a church, San Felice, and we walk on the
> balcony listening to the organ & choir —.

As letters to her sisters Arabella and Henrietta record, she particularly delighted in refurbishing what on their arrival was:

> furnished & overfurnished [with] marble consoles, carved & gilt arm chairs, all in crimson & white satin, noble mirrors,

Renamed Casa Guidi, the apartment had been the Brownings' main residence during their fifteen-year marriage. In its drawing room they had entertained many of the leading artists and writers of their late Romantic day, from Thomas Carlyle and Hans Christian Andersen to John Ruskin.

The domesticity of this death scene also seems peculiarly Victorian: fittingly so, given the trajectory of Elizabeth's own work. It fits the clichés of the era's sentimental fiction and verse, which pulls between those twin poles of family values and obsession with mortality. Yet I also hear gritty certainty within what's come down to us, mistakenly I think, as a wandering exclamation: 'Beautiful . . . ' Robert mentioned in letters home, to both to his own family and – writing to his brother-in-law George Barrett a couple of days later – Elizabeth's, that he had noticed her intermittently withdraw from life in her final days. At moments she had seemed to hallucinate; but he had overridden his 'instinct' to worry, telling himself, 'a little wandering, after a week's absolute refusal of solid food, and a (prescribed) slight addition to the morphine dose, what was in that?' In Elizabeth's own 'Beautiful . . . ', though, I hear the equivalent of a camera pulling back to take a wider view. It seems to me that she was kissing goodbye not only to her husband but to the whole of a life: one Robert represented and more than represented, since it was built around him. As if she were looking back at life itself, and kissing her hands not only to the man beside her, but to the entire beautiful world.

Glimpse, smudge, flash. The corner of the eye notes what the visible world would smuggle past: *Motacilla alba*, the pied wagtail. On the bank below the blackthorn, tight green buds are an early promise of celandine. With a time-lapse blur of wings, a thrush leaps from the lane into the hedge; but not before I glimpse his breast, printed with the cock bird's prisoner uniform of dark arrows.

The dogs are pulling uphill so hard that Zed is choking herself in her collar. She rasps and coughs, straining straddle-legged along the lane ahead of us. Two steps to one of mine, and then a pause; how authoritative the little dog makes me feel. But in this dampish winter valley, walking locates me as just one embodied creature among many, seen and unseen: the December moth, *Poecilocampa populi*, shabby among the old leaves on a birch twig; rooks bundling in and out of nests; stickleback down on the riverbed.

Chronic ill-health meant walking was often difficult for Elizabeth Barrett Browning; her delight when she managed it is touching. On 11 May 1846, during her courtship with Robert, she writes to him with triumphant amazement about taking her first steps in Regent's Park:

Arabel & Flush & I were in the carriage – & the sun was shining with that green light through the trees [. . .] & I wished so much to walk through a half open gate along a shaded path, that we stopped the carriage & got out & walked, & I put both my feet on the grass . . . which was the strangest feeling! [. . .] I never enjoyed any of my excursions as I did today's – the standing under the trees & on the grass, was so delightful [. . .] And all those strange people moving about like phantoms of life –

In the 'green light' through today's roadside hedges, streamers of bramble instruct, *Pay attention*. They catch in Dee's long lurcher coat when she trots too close. She startles, yaps in protest, shakes herself free, then guilelessly back she draws again, led by the odours of field mice and voles in the hedge bottom.

We've been drawn back willy-nilly ourselves. We've come back to visit Herefordshire, where Barrett Browning grew up, and where this book opened. In part that's because I picture these ten walks as describing a labyrinth's circular form, with its parallel ingress and exit. It's also because I still love this county – though my father didn't. Its clustering hills and green lanes seemed to him to lie too deep in shadow; I suspect his feeling had less to do with meteorology than with a certain material, cultural intractability about the region. History is close at hand in these districts in part because it's never moved on. Yet at the same time and for the same reason it's here, where the environment is least degraded, that I feel I can get closest to my dad's original passion for old buildings in an old landscape.

The Tenth Walk in Jean-Jacques Rousseau's *Reveries of a Solitary Walker* is a return to favourite territory, too. At the end of the book – and of his life – he turns back to the memory of his great love, 'Madame de Warens', with whom (*'J'avois désiré la campagne: je l'avois obtenue,'* he summarises) he first enjoyed the country life:

An isolated house, leaning over a valley, became our asylum, and it's there that, in the space of four or five years, I rejoiced in an epoch of life, in a pure and complete happiness, which covers with its charm of its remembrance every horror of my present fate.

Françoise-Louise, baroness de Warens, born Louise-Éléanore de la Tour de Pil, met Rousseau in 1728, not in that rural idyll but in the city of Annecy where, in order to secure royal protection, she seems to have been spying for the King of Savoy as well as persuading Protestants to convert, like herself, to Catholicism. A somewhat exposed figure, she had left her husband and had a number of failed businesses behind her. Rousseau, equally rackety, was one of her converts: a sixteen-year-old runaway from his birthplace, Geneva, and from an apprenticeship as an engraver. Four years later, when he had presumably grown up a little, this intellectual and entrepreneurial woman installed him as her lover, even though he was twelve years her junior and called her, somewhat unsexily, 'Maman'.

The emotional logic of this transaction, for him at least, is clear: his own mother had died within days of his birth. And it worked, at least for a while. In 1736, the lovers moved into de Warens's country house near Chambéry. The stone villa of Les Charmettes, now a museum dedicated to Rousseau's life and work, is situated just as he describes it in *Rêveries*. It stands high on the side of a gently sloping, wooded valley that forms part of the northern rim of the massif de la Chartreuse in the Alpine region – after the Revolutionary reorganisation of 1790 it would become a *département* – of Haute-Savoie. The views from the terraced gardens are still stunning, though Les Charmettes is no longer an 'isolated' spot. Rousseau summons up the spaciousness of the country life he and his mistress lived there:

> The taste for solitude and contemplation was born in my heart, with the expansive and tender feelings made to nourish it. Tumult and din contract and suffocate them; calm and peace reanimate and lift them up.

His final Walk portrays such isolated, rural 'calm and peace' as neither personal solipsism nor a rejection of society. On the contrary, he argues, the country life enables affection:

> all my time was filled with paying loving attentions, or with bucolic activities. I wanted nothing but the continuation of such a sweet state of affairs.

This is markedly different from a portrait of the solitary walker as embittered obsessive that mars many of the *Reveries'* preceding chapters. 'Paying loving attentions . . . ' threads a seam of tenderness and pleasure through the rural experience, and it's on this note that what was to be the author's final book breaks off:

> From then on I dreamt of giving myself at the same time alternatives to anxiety, and the resources to prevent its effects. I thought that the attainment of talents was the most secure insurance against misery, and I resolved to employ my free time to put myself in the position, if possible, one

day to return to the best of women the help I'd received from her . . .

In fact, Rousseau's 'best of women' had died in poverty while he was in unhappy exile in England. His misery at this period was only underlined by a gratuitous trick played on him by Hugh Walpole, that Gothic novelist, advocate of Gothick architecture, and all-round British man of influence. It seems that community was not, after all, an automatic function of Romanticism. For some, the movement was more a matter of style, and Walpole faked a mocking letter from Frederick the Great, which tumbled Rousseau from fashionable favour, and saw him once again hurrying into rural retreat.

My own tenth walk, like Rousseau's, tracks a thinly populated, wide valley, whose wooded higher slopes lead down into pasture. The morning's dullness has lifted into a sky patched with cloud and blue. What light there is catches the bare crowns of the trees along each ridge, staining them the faintest shades of orange and purple. We've returned not to the Wye but to the Lugg, a tributary which joins the river some forty miles downstream from here. Just east of Hereford, a handsome fourteenth-century bridge brackets the confluence in a loop of water meadows between the satellite villages of Hampton Bishop and Mordiford. But, like the Wye, the Lugg rises in the mountains of mid-Wales. Also like the Wye, it enjoys public rights of navigation for its entire course and remains, despite environmental degradation, a fishing destination.

Its source lies west of the Radnorshire village of Llangynllo, about fifteen miles west-north-west of here as the crow flies though, of course, rivers don't flow straight. The modest Lugg, which runs to only sixty-three miles, is at least straighter than the expansively meandering Wye. It floods with vigour, partly because it springs in the eastern foothills of the rainy Cambrian massif, and partly because of its fall. Rising in Radnor Forest near the 490-metre mark, it descends precipitately to the little town of Presteigne, and by the time it arrives here, another seven miles downstream, it's just 114 metres above sea-level.

We've parked today at Lyepole Bridge, where the river is at its most picturesque, describing elegant curves through the west Herefordshire meadows. It narrows under this little stone bridge, with its slightly humped back and neat nineteenth-century parapets, and between banks that have been fenced for private fishing. According to the *Concise Oxford Dictionary of Placenames*, 'Lugg' comes from *llug*, and this is Welsh for light – although surely the lexicographers were thinking of the Latin *luce* and its cognates? Most Welsh light today is *golau*, which needs some robust metathesis to get near *llug*, and in modern south Welsh, *llug* has the brightness of *rage*. Still, there's clarity in the water racing over its peaty bed, on the surface brightened by reflections this winter afternoon and, overhead, in the pale twigs starred with paler lichen. The entire length of the Lugg is a Site of Special Scientific Interest. This section at Upper Lye, today as fast-moving and as mineral blue as some melt-water Alpine stream, is fed by Lime Brook: the cleanest of all its own, yet smaller, tributaries and in 2019 the only one to score a 'Good' for its ecological status from the Environment Agency. Not coincidentally, the bridge is a fixture with birders. Recently, for example, the internet has lit up with several recorded sightings of the handsomely and onomatopoeically named *Nycticorax nycticorax*, the black-crowned night heron.

Rousseau started to write his Tenth Walk on Palm Sunday, 1778, the fiftieth anniversary of his first meeting with baroness de Warens – or so he claims; though he was not, famously, an especially reliable narrator. Easter came early that year, so Palm Sunday fell almost at the equinox, on 23 March. On the other hand the writer's death, a little over four months later on 2 July, is incontrovertible. Our walk today also marks an anniversary. In the logic of this book, we should have arrived at midsummer by now. Instead we're marking the opposite solstice. There is, you could say, a problem with continuity. But these walks are no more, or less, a work of testimony than Rousseau's embroidered 'factions'. In this pandemic year I've walked when I could. Today is 19 December, almost the year's shortest day and its darkest time, and it's the first posthumous anniversary of my dad's birthday. The walk P and I are taking to mark it follows the Lugg upstream to Kinsham Court.

In late 1812, Lord Byron moved in to this modest brick mansion almost at the Welsh border in order to pursue a relationship with the married Countess of Oxford, Jane Elizabeth Harley, whose country seat was Eywood, near Titley, six miles to the south-west. On 6 November 1812 Byron wrote to his confidante Lady Melbourne, 'I believe I mentioned in my last that I have taken Kinsham Court in this vicinity.' 'Take' seems financially somewhat vague, especially given that the property was a dower house belonging to the Harleys, who had been Marches aristocracy for centuries. Monarchists in the Civil War, when their castle at nearby Brampton Bryan was torched, before that they had been Lancastrians in the Wars of the Roses when this area was a rallying ground for both sides in the conflict.

Pay attention, such connections warn. Cultural moments seed places; movements such as Romanticism run through a landscape like mycelia. Byron's affair took place in what was by his standards an interlude, between the end of his liaison with Lady Caroline Lamb and the apparent rekindling of his incestuous relationship with his half-sister Augusta Leigh in summer 1813, as well as during a pause in his more strategic courtship of Annabella Milbanke, whom he would marry in January 1815. It's hard to tell how much time the peer actually spent by the Lugg, since he shuttled back and forth from London in the fashionable manner of his day. Indeed he also spent time in the spa town of Cheltenham which, while perhaps now counterintuitive as a Byronic destination, was then a newly fashionable resort as well as more or less en route between this north-western corner of Herefordshire and the capital.

Unlike Rousseau at Les Charmettes, Byron did not find that '*occupations champêtres*', 'bucolic activities', filled his time at Kinsham. Later in his 6 November letter to Lady Melbourne, he borrows a phrase from Shakespeare's Falstaff in *Henry IV Part One* Act V Sc iv l. 146 to mock-grumble:

> Not being aware of any amusement which can possibly last four & twenty hours by 'Shrewsbury clock' sans intermission I suppose one may look at a Roman encampment now & then & yet be exceedingly occupied nevertheless with more serious entertainments.

Still, he did manage to share with his Genevan predecessor those 'more serious entertainments', which Rousseau called 'loving attentions' ('*soins affectueux*'). Both men, after all, billeted themselves on their married, titled lovers.

October had seen Byron's publisher, John Murray, selling out a second edition of the first two Cantos of *Childe Harold's Pilgrimage,* his verse epic about a young man who, in a quest to find himself, takes a route not dissimilar to that of Byron's own Grand Tour. The poet was riding high: it's perhaps not surprising if time on the Welsh borders seemed to drag. On the other hand, Lady Oxford was evidently a bit of a sexual catch. Fourteen years his senior she was, though beautiful, so notoriously promiscuous that her children were known as the 'Harleian miscellany', a nice pun on a mid-eighteenth-century anthology of works from the Oxford family library as well as on questions of paternity. She had remained intellectually and emotionally close for years to another of her lovers, the Reform politician Sir Francis Burdett. In 1813 she miscarried a child by Byron himself. Born in 1774, she was a model first-generation Romantic, full of idealism and activity, and a believer in French revolutionary principles, the British Reform movement – and free love. And not just a believer: she was Byron's 'tutelar genius', a 'woman, who, amid all her fascination, always urged a man to usefulness or glory'.

All this meant that she paid a high price in social disapprobation. It also allowed Byron to feel she was not in the first flush of youth. He would later reminisce to Lady Blessington, with what he presumably thought was gallantry, that:

Even now the autumnal charms of Lady____ are remembered by me with more than admiration [. . .] A woman is only grateful for her *first* and *last* conquest. The *first* of poor dear Lady ____'s was achieved before I entered this world of care; but the *last*, I do flatter myself, was reserved for me, and a *bonne bouche* it was.

Which if true would imply Lady Oxford had lost her virginity at thirteen. Or again, with less lip-smacking but still exaggerating the age difference, to Percy Bysshe Shelley's second cousin, the writer Thomas Medwin:

There was a lady at that time double my own age [. . .] with whom I had formed a liaison which continued without interruption for eight months. The autumn of a beauty like hers is preferable to the spring in others. She told me she was never in love till she was thirty; and I thought myself so with her when I was forty. I never felt a stronger passion [. . .] I [. . .] once was on the point of going abroad with her, and narrowly escaped this folly.

Yet there seems to have been a sweetness to this bed-hopping too. When Jane Elizabeth Harley died, at fifty, Sir Uvedale Price wrote to the fashionable poet Samuel Rogers, a friend of Byron's:

Poor Lady Oxford! [. . .] I had, as you know, lived a great deal with her from the time she came into this country, immediately after her marriage. [. . .] There could not, in all respects, be a more ill-matched pair than herself and

Lord Oxford [. . .] It has been said that she was, in some measure, forced into the match. Had she been united to a man whom she had loved, esteemed, and respected, she herself might have been generally respected and esteemed, as well as loved; but in her situation, to keep clear of all misconduct required a strong mind or a cold heart; perhaps both, and she had neither. [. . .] There was something about her, in spite of her errors, remarkably attaching, and that something was not merely her beauty.

In short, her marriage appears to have been more dynastic than loving. But the 'autumnal charms' of her affair with Byron may have been ended in the cruellest of ways by his interest in her own second daughter, Charlotte, who turned eleven in December 1812. He called the child 'Ianthe' and in 1814 would dedicate the seventh and subsequent editions of *Childe Harolde* to her with a set of extravagant verses: 'Young Peri of the West! – tis well for me/My years already doubly number thine.' This sounds like nothing so much as the mumbling of an ageing roué; and must have been excruciatingly unpleasant for the girl herself.

Still Kinsham Court itself was a Romantic contrivance in more than one sense. A stout work of Herefordshire Georgian brick, its thunder has since been stolen by the mid-nineteenth-century addition of some unusually hefty coved eaves. Nevertheless, it stands among trees thirty metres above a sheer drop to the Lugg, where the river winds through pretty Kinsham Dingle, in which nature seems to have been helped along by picturesque planting. In 1812 the house had its own thirteenth-century church close by, like a very superior landscape folly – even perhaps a toy hermitage. Victorian sincerity has since put paid to that, however: in the 1880s Henry Curzon modernised the little structure with heavy and undistinguished hand.

This picturesque frame should come as no surprise. Lady Harley had become a good friend not only of Sir Uvedale, that influential author of *An Essay on the Picturesque* (1794), whose property at Foxley lies just a dozen miles south of here, but of his close friend Richard Payne Knight. Knight's own Romantic fantasy castle on a crag, Downton, stands only a dozen miles to the north west. Knight too had become a leading advocate of the picturesque in British landscape gardens, not least with his didactic poem *The Landscape*, which also appeared in 1794 –the year of Lady Harley's marriage. When she arrived in Herefordshire shortly after, both men, each a quarter century her senior, were eager to share their expertise with this charming new neighbour whose cultural sympathies were so expressly Romantic.

Hart's-tongue (*Asplenium scolopendrium*), bracken (*Pteridium aquilinum*), ground elder (*Aegopodium podagraria*) on the banks along the lane. If Byron worked on any poetry at Kinsham, it would most likely have been *The Giaour*. He drafted the poem between September 1812 and March 1813 and, after originally toying with adding it to later editions of the first *Childe Harold* cantos, published a short first edition of some seven hundred lines in June 1813. *The Giaour* later grew to one thousand three hundred lines and is the first of the four 'Turkish Tales' in verse, including the buccaneering *The Corsair,* which was published the following year. It's in every sense the original of the quartet, the one whose success encouraged Byron to compose the other three. It also develops a more radically wrought structure than its successors. Instead of a single linear narrative, *The Giaour* tells its fatal story of adultery, punishment, retribution and regret from the viewpoint of each of its three protagonists: the Turk Hassan; Leila who, imprisoned in his harem, cheats on him with an infidel, or 'giaour' and is drowned as punishment; and the infidel himself, who murders the Sultan before retiring to a monastery, that nineteenth-century code for stepping out of life.

Orientalism was an easy win for such stories of risk and lust, in which guilt could be conveniently projected onto the foreign 'other', and sexuality salaciously explored. The innocence of Edward Lear's picturesque views 'taken' on travels abroad is left behind. Byron was evidently fully engaged by his own sexuality at the time he wrote *The Giaour*, though he had not yet become a figure of scandal. The poem's setting afforded him the same kind of fig-leaf of respectable impunity that historical or mythic themes – such as the rape of the Sabine women by the Romans – have traditionally afforded painters since Peter Paul Rubens to cover canvasses in nudes and (literally) graphic portrayals of sexual violence.

Yet some elements of this poem's melodrama may have been the result of personal conviction. By the time he wrote it in 1812, Byron had visited Ottoman-held territories in the Balkans; and like other British men of his generation who had received a Classical education, his cultural reflex was to side with Greece in its struggle for independence. His writing was helping to shift British popular sympathies further in this direction, and away from the Ottoman Empire. *The Siege of Corinth* (1816), for example, would tell the story of an historic

Ottoman massacre of the Venetian garrison at the acropolis of Ancient Corinth which took place exactly a century earlier. (Nor in fact would the circumstances of his own death at Missalonghi in 1824 hurt the cause.)

It's rather disconcerting to think of world affairs funnelling through this quiet stretch of the Lugg valley. Byron, too, seems to have found it difficult to sustain a sense of himself as simultaneously a famous literary figure, an actor on the world stage and a local resident. Had he paid attention, though, he would have realised he was living in a landscape long formed by violent conflict. The 'Roman encampment' he complained of is actually not Roman but Norman, a motte-and-bailey castle built by Hugh Mortimer in the mid-eleventh century. It stands among the trees of Camp Wood on a steep bluff close to Lyepole Bridge, where we could see it from the car. Gone half back to nature now, its sloping oval outer bailey seems almost like a portion of the hill that has slipped loose from itself.

If a spot's worth defending, it's worth defending. This point where two valleys meet is of obvious strategic importance. As we climbed the lane leading to Upper Lye, we found ourselves ascending through the doughnut rings of what's evidently a Neolithic hill fort. Although they're overgrown with scrub, blackthorn and oak, we glimpsed its concentric terraces through the pencil-scribble winter branches. Four muntjac deer startled away among the bushes. They bounced uphill, moving not hurriedly but smartly through the levels, their pretty heads held high as if balancing something, like a girl wearing pendant earrings for the first time. We held the dogs tight on short leads as we watched them go; seeing quite clearly the tender grey coats, the wide bleached scuts, and the yellow speckling their bellies and rising up their flanks – markings that made them look both expensive and rare.

At Upper Lye there's a junction where a ruinous farm, its barns lined up along the lane, faces down a smart nineteenth-century house perched on high foundations, which looks as though it may have been the local shop, or perhaps a school-master's house. One road runs east to Lower Lye. But turn west, as we did, and you pass the fifteenth-century hall house that – on the map of Herefordshire from his great national survey commissioned by Lord Burghley, Elizabeth I's Lord Chancellor – Christopher Saxton represents with his char-acteristic icon of pitched roof and pinnacled gables. Saxton records 'Kynsham', too, as a recognisably Elizabethan manor with twin towers. A blob of red indicates its landowning status.

The sweep of contour where we descend from the lane to the riverside bridleway is generous, as valleys worn in sedi-mentary rock so often are. This is a region of early Wenlock Silurian limestone. Those fortifications we climbed at Camp Wood mark the junction of the Lugg with the dry valley of Covenhope: together these frame the rising back of Shobdon Hill Wood, of which we now have an uninterrupted view. Trees cram this slope beyond the river, scrub along the bottom of the sky. Out of sight beyond are the parklands of Shobdon, an estate both celebrated and notorious for its eighteenth-century landscaping by Sir John, second Viscount Bateman.

The Viscount was advised by his uncle the Hon. Richard Bateman, a personal friend of that high master of Gothic fash-ion, Hugh Walpole, and a member of Walpole's 'Committee of Taste'. The decade from 1746 saw the Batemans misappropriate the ideal of the picturesque to knock down one of the country's finest Romanesque churches, leaving only a folly, confected from some of its unique twelfth-century sculpture, which became known as the Arches. On the site where the original St John the Evangelist had stood they placed the icing-sugar vulgarity of their successor church, built in Strawberry Hill Gothick style. Its painted pews are out of every Hollywood wedding scene, and the whole interior, where plasterwork has run riot, seems to protest too much that it must add up, architecturally, to more than the simple galleried meeting hall that is its underlying structure. Meanwhile on the crest of a ridge some three hundred metres away, where they can be sure to catch the very worst of the prevailing weather, the Arches continue even today to blur under the erosion from which they remain unprotected.

Shobdon poses a question about what happens when innovative ideas begin to spread. This is just what they're designed to do, yet it's exactly when their original radicalism seems most at risk of becoming reduced to mere style. The phenomenon of Byron's *Childe Harold* asks the same question in a slightly different form. Its huge literary success, a kind of early superstardom, seems a world away from ideas of rights and revolution, even though the poem itself explores what makes the sovereign self. By 1812 Romanticism had become popular. As the nineteenth century wore on, it would increasingly slip away from its principal actors to take its place in mainstream culture. Byron's cultural reputation by the time he lived beside the Lugg looks very different from, say, the impoverished but recognisably literary life Mary Wollstonecraft had eked out a generation earlier: the disparity holds true even if we ignore differences of gender and of family wealth.

As we enter shadowy, green Kinsham Dingle, the Covenhope valley drops out of sight behind us. But I have in mind how it leads directly from Lyepole Bridge to Mortimer's Cross, a couple of miles away. Today a hamlet at a crossroads, on 2 February 1461, Mortimer's Cross was the site of a major, and temporarily decisive, battle in the Wars of the Roses. Wales, which is just five miles away, played an important part in these wars of succession. The Lancastrian Tudors were Welsh; their uneasy border location had developed the Marcher Lords' authority and military strength. At Mortimer's Cross the Yorkist Earl of March, later King Edward IV, defeated the Lancastrians loyal to Henry VI, who were led by the Earl of Pembroke. (One result was the beheading the following year, on Tower Hill, of one of Lady Harley's precursors, the 12th Earl of Oxford – not yet a Harley, but a de Vere – together with his eldest son.) These fifteenth-century struggles for the throne, which concluded in 1487, would only be fully resolved by dynastic marriage between Edward IV's heir, Elizabeth of York, and the Lancastrian Henry VII, who in 1485 defeated Richard III (Yorkist and celebrated baddie) at the Battle of Bosworth Field. These victorious forces were commanded by another of Lady Harley's precursors, the 13th Earl of Oxford.

History seeds the landscape. So does its reception. In the eighteenth century, when Romantic nationalism was stirring up interest in traditional myths, Tudor histories helped Wales acquire a picturesque reputation that paralleled Scotland's, if on a smaller scale. The Welsh, too, were portrayed as attractively rugged: warriors, druids and bards. In Herefordshire, this created space for a little local Orientalism – or, more literally, Occidentalism:

From royal ancestry of ancient line
Of noble daring *Owen Glendower* sprung,
And round Cambria's mountains, years lang syne,
The tuneful bard his great achievements sung;
But when from the mountain tops, his injuries rang,
His despoliations, by cruel injustice, plann'd,
Harsh and discordant did the wild harp clang
And rous'd revenge, arm'd his indignant hand.

This passage comes from Thomas Horton's *The Battle of Mortimer's Cross: An Historical Poem in Two Cantos*, published in 1830. Horton's high-energy verse goes bounding down the page, and his book's closing leaves list a couple of hundred subscribers amassed to crowdfund the volume, which was printed in nearby Ludlow by Edward Hodson of Broad Street.

I imagine both Horton and Hodson as enterprising young men on the make. Hodson would move to Birmingham around a decade later, but the stationer's business he established there failed and he was bankrupted in 1844. Horton, whose Dedication for *The Battle of Mortimer's Cross* is dated Christmas Eve 1829, and establishes that he's already in Birmingham, had previously published a verse play rejoicing in the title(s) *Nell Gwynne, The City of the Wye, or the Red Lands of Herefordshire: an historical play*, on 1 January 1828. He had dedicated that work to a local 'gentleman', E. T. Foley of Stoke Edith Park and, on its title page, styled himself 'comedian'. Whatever his successes or otherwise as an actor, he seems to have been a persuasive entrepreneur; someone with a feel for cultural fashion. Though no Batemans or Harleys appear in the subscriber's list for *Mortimer's Cross*, E. T. Foley ordered five copies of the book, as did its dedicatee, 'Sir Harford Jones Brydges, Bart, of Presteigne.' The names of its subscribers are arranged in etiquette order, down to plain 'Mr', and there are titles – and clergy – aplenty.

The result of this enterprise is a gloriously vernacular Romanticism. I think of it as the textual equivalent of those 'cherubs . . ./With wings and English ploughboy faces' in John Betjeman's chuchyard: carrying on, in good faith though without sophistication, what was being more crisply and radically developed elsewhere. The pages of *Mortimer's Cross* are crammed with juxtaposed quotations, most but not all from Shakespeare's *Henry IV*; the slim volume is topped and tailed with a summary narrative of the historical events themselves, presumably in case the verse itself does not make them clear – as it does not. Aping scholarship (Shakespeare was writing dramatic fiction, after all, not historical fact), Horton's apparatus reminds me, perhaps unkindly, of the explanatory 'notes' the Mechanicals in *Midsummer Night's Dream* give as they perform their 'tedious brief scene of young Pyramus/And his love Thisbe; very tragical mirth' to the Athenian court.

Horton had some problems with narrative detail, and with differentiating his battle's various engagements. But he has a great, rollocking, oral style:

> Now sinewy arms, the clanging bow-string drew,
> Now flights of arrows suck in human blood
> And frowning fate, as o'er the field she flew,
> Beheld earth delug'd in a crimson flood.
> [. . .]

> The daemon *Carnage*, in her blood-stain'd car,
> With crimson goading lash drove madly round,
> And the destructive storm of horrid war,
> Blew wildly o'er the hot ensanguined ground.

Even though my poet's ear blinks at '*Carnage*/car', I can't help but enjoy the sheer declamatory relish of this writing by someone who clearly has an excellent ear, IF little eye for punctuation. He is no Byron: but then he'd received none of Byron's education. An actor in nineteenth-century England would likely have been educated at best at grammar school, like Shakespeare himself, rather than following Byron to Oxbridge.

Yet Horton understands the Romantic formulae. His opens with an invocation:

> All Hail! majestic oak! the forest's pride,
> Let me beneath your spreading arms implore,
> Screen'd from the sun beneath your branches wide,
> Fain would I mediate on days of yore.
> Here would my muse in solemn silence stray,
> Here would she seek some silver-bearded sage:
> Some white-clad *Druid* of the olden day.
> [. . .]
> Come sacred *Druid*, ope thy hidden store,
> [. . .]
> Give me a ray of information's light
> Forth from thy burning altar's vivid flame,
> To guide my muse's inexperienc'd flight,
> Who ardent seeks "'mong sons of song," a name.

This manages simultaneously to tick the boxes of Romantic nationalism (those '*Druid*'s), the picturesque, and an expanding contemporary interest in local history. In 1830 archaeology was one of those emergent gentleman's hobbies, like botany, astronomy, or even chemistry, that saw those who had the means to do so exploring the world around them with less acceptance, and more curiosity, than had marked the pre-Romantic, church-centred world. In 1799 even the local village of Kingsland, a couple of miles the other side of Mortimer's Cross, had muscled in for its share of the Tudors, taking up a subscription to commemorate the battle of 1461 and erecting what Horton calls a 'neat Tuscan Pedestal' where the village street meets the main road from Hereford. Its inscription is lengthy and emphatic – 'an obstinate, bloody, and decisive battle fought near this Spot [. . .] This was the decisive battle which fixed *Edward* the *Fourth* on the Throne of England' – and Horton, who reproduces it in his book, shares this conclusion so emphatically that I half wonder whether it was his chief source on the subject. Both texts clearly owe much to *The Leominster Guide: containing and Historical and Topographical View of the Ancient and Present State of Leominster* published and, one assumes, anonymously compiled by F. J. Burlton, self-styled 'bookseller, in the High-Street,' whose 'correct and minute information' Horton commends.

The 'burning altar's vivid flame' being tended in *The Battle of Mortimer's Cross* by a 'white-clad *Druid* of the olden day' reminds me of an altogether greater, and much shorter, poem first published ten years earlier:

Who are these coming to the sacrifice?

> To what green altar, O mysterious priest,
>   Lead'st thou that heifer lowing at the skies
>   And all her silken flanks with garland drest?

After Horton's clotted provincialism this is a breath of fresh air. Yet the poet who wrote it hadn't been formed by the great public schools of England, or an Oxbridge education, either. Instead, orphaned at fourteen, he had been apprenticed to an apothecary at fifteen. When John Keats wrote 'Ode on a Grecian Urn' in Hampstead in the spring of 1819 he was twenty-three, and had just left a poorly paid, frustrating job as an assistant surgeon at Guy's Hospital to devote himself to poetry, even though he couldn't really afford to do so. That year would prove both a vindicating poetic *annus mirabilis* for the young man, and the one in which he was destroyed as a poet by hostile critical reception – or so both Byron and Shelley came to believe.

It's hard to write briefly about tragedy, which always feels as though it deserves respectful breathing room, but the milestones of John Keats's tragic progress are well known. How he nursed his brother Tom, who succumbed to tuberculosis in December 1818, and in doing so probably caught the illness that would kill him too; his love for Fanny Brawne; his hopeless grasp at life in the warmer, drier and cleaner air of Rome; his death on 23 February 1821 in an apartment overlooking the city's Spanish Steps, tended by Joseph Severn in the little room whose coffered ceiling is still starred with pale roses. All of this story is packed around the five Odes Keats wrote in spring 1819, and the sixth – 'To Autumn' – with which a few months later he completed his great experiment in a new, refreshed and open form of odal hymn. It was a moment of possibility, for poetry in English and for Keats himself: his long poem *Endymion* – which also opens on a rustic scene from antiquity – had been recently published. But this spring was to be brief. In April *Endymion* was influentially rubbished by John Wilson Croker in the *Quarterly Review* while, writing in *Blackwood's*, John Lockhart coined the term 'Cockney School' for Keats and William Hazlitt, and sneered:

> It is a better and a wiser thing to be a starved apothecary than a starved poet; so back to the shop Mr John, back to plasters, pills, and ointment boxes.

In the Dingle the footpath runs level with the water, and it's slick with mud. There's a continual busy lapping, as water works industriously around small rocks and between the branches of a willow that has sagged into the river. The dogs pause to drink. Dee tries a quick paddle, and Zed follows her into the river – then swiftly out again. A kingfisher spins brightly between branches of oak and ash: blue star. We catch glimpses of the brick-built bay of Kinsham Court above us. Its windows, occluded by reflections of the sky, still seem to overlook our progress. From the safe heights of his own popular success, Byron would remark rather snarkily that John Keats had been 'snuffed out by a review'. But Shelley, slightly closer to the Londoner both in age and in the degree of his own success, had published alongside Keats and took him seriously as both a man and a poet, urging him to Italy for his health and, once he'd arrived there, corresponding with him. Seven weeks after Keats's death, he composed 'Adonais' in elegy for him.

'Ode on a Grecian Urn' is like a still point before this bitter free-fall into tragedy. That's also how Keats describes the urn itself, in the poem's much quoted opening: 'Thou still unravished bride of quietness, / Thou foster-child of Silence and slow Time,' and its ending:

> Thou, silent form! dost tease us out of thought
> As does eternity. Cold Pastoral!
> When old age shall this generation waste
> Thou shalt remain, in mist of other woe
> Than ours, a friend to man, to whom though sayst,
> 'Beauty is truth, truth beauty, – that is all
> Ye know on earth, and all ye need to know.'

This famous final stanza is a great statement of attentive acceptance. It concludes a poem that is concerned throughout with paying attention. The Ode tries to trace the stories portrayed on an artefact from a time and place so different that they can't be decoded, but only questioned:

> What men or gods are these? What maidens loth?
> What mad pursuit? What struggle to escape?
> What pipes and timbrels? What wild ecstasy?

We have questions, too. Is this urn funerary or merely domestic? Is it made of marble or alabaster and covered in monochrome carving, or is it a ceramic in whose glaze the characteristically fine drawn terracotta forms move on a black background? This matters to me because I'm in thrall to the visual; though it's not the point of the poem, which spins past such material questions to evoke — and freeze — Time itself.

The urn belongs simultaneously in an over-there, some-where back where it was made, a Classical past so distant as to seem hardly real — 'deities or mortals, or of both,/In Tempe or the dales of Arcady?' — and right where the poet approaches it with humility in 1818, and again in us as we read the poem today. But Keats offers no facts or definitions, only questions. (He remains, in fact, 'in uncertainties, mysteries, doubts, without any irritable reaching after fact and reason,' in those famous words from a letter he had written to his brothers George and Thomas on 22 December 1817.) This radical open-ness to cultural unfamiliarity is the opposite of orientalism, which imposes its own local, western viewpoint on whatever it encounters. He does, though, slyly follow tradition in using antiquity as a licence to portray both the rape of 'maidens loth', and sexual consent:

> More happy love! More happy, happy love!
>   For ever warm and still to be enjoyed,
>   For ever panting and for ever young;

And, as if to hold the reimagined lovers forever on the brink of orgasm before its fall, the poem takes upon itself the obligation to hold all times together in the idea of eternity, symbolised by the perfect O of the urn, which 'doth tease us out of thought/ As does eternity.'

'Cockney' John Keats was neither wholly a Londoner, nor as uneducated as Lockhart's slanderous dismissal implied. He came from an aspirational family who owned the Swan and Hoop Inn at 199 Moorgate, and who had hoped to send him to one of the great public schools, but could not afford to do so. When he was eight he was sent to school outside London in what was then the Middlesex village of Enfield; soon after, however, his father died and John and his three younger siblings joined their grandmother in nearby Edmonton. From 1817 until he left Britain for good in September 1820, the poet lived on Hampstead Heath, first at Well Walk and then at Wentworth Place. The Heath was then still a fully rural stretch of land, as the cloud studies John Constable was making there at the time – and Keats's own 'Ode to a Nightingale', and the famous encounter with a bird that preceded it – remind us. But in his short life Keats did not particularly advocate or reinvent notions of rural life. Instead, he turned the steady intelligence of his gaze on whatever was at hand. I wonder whether, in the patience and circumscribed range of that gaze, he doesn't ultimately offer the Romantic countryside's most useful lesson. *Pay attention*, his poems seem to say, '– that is all / Ye know on earth, and all ye need to know.'

Shadows fill spaces between the trees. The December dusk is rallying round us; blackbird alarms ricochet down the valley. Near the rim of the little gorge, a buzzard shakes out the untidy bundle of its wings and slides sideways from its branch into the air. We stumble among tussocky reeds clogged with the debris of eighteen months of floods: we're walking, it seems, in the changing climate's muddy footprints. Ahead, blue construction-site clay betrays where Lower Kinsham Weir is being rebuilt to try and manage the new violence with which these water levels are changing. Flash floods, their accumulated vehemence born of several high-rising tributaries, are to be contained here: the onward stream managed and measured out as if the movement of water in a landscape could be rendered rational.

Still, perhaps it is possible to negotiate with irrationality. The traditional water-meadows we've just walked are a sequence framed by hedges and trees. Low-intensity grazing keeps their grass healthy, binding the friable clay and preventing erosion when the river leaks across the pasture, as it does every year. The fields themselves act as a system of locks, storing water until it can move away downstream; they emerge fertilised and replenished, just like the deltas of the Fertile Crescent we were taught about in school geography lessons. As for the sheep that wandered away from us this afternoon, slowed as their pregnancies began to tell, their wool is up to 50 per cent carbon. They sequester it like trees: apparently, 1 kg of cleaned wool equals 1.8 kg of carbon dioxide. Astonishing fact, I reflect, thinking of the sheep we keep in the top paddock at home: the cumbersome way they trot to greet us, their ridiculous habit of getting the feed bucket stuck over their ears. Such unlikely instruments of environmental technology.

Not all farmers are agribusiness monsters. Water-meadows, like other local forms of environmental cohabitation, have emerged over centuries of patient practice. Surely they require patience in the observer, too. *Pay attention*: Romanticism isn't locked up in famous lines of poetry or images reproduced so many times that they've become part of the cultural commons, nor in museums or stately homes, however handsome. Bothersome and active, it's at work today: in rail travel and high-spec scientific instruments; in the rise of nationalism but also of legal rights to self-determination; as child-centred education, vegetarianism, non-traditional social and sexual relationships; in atheism and in clinical practice, in heavy industry and scientific soil management; as questions about the nature of existence. Above all, it's alive in the insight that the countryside opens a threshold to radical action.

Every story finishes somewhere, and I think this one must end where the bridle path emerges from under the trees onto the lane at Lower Kinsham. Ends with the gate standing ajar and the path beyond it leading on through the fields. When my dad was hospitalised, not far from here, it was his first admission in ninety-four years of life. I'm certain he hated it. He was the brainy, subtle man he'd always been. He was also profoundly deaf and nearly blind, and he had been taken away into a lockdown within lockdown. Because of the pandemic he was allowed no visitors; and in those anonymising wards, where I was unable to visit and so he had no one to advocate for him, those superficial disabilities shut him away from any communication with his inattentive carers.

In that last fortnight of his life, as he lived it out alone, he was allowed just one video call. While the occupational therapists who were supposed to enable it chatted away to each other, paying no attention, he gazed at me. He couldn't hear a word I was saying but, 'Beautiful . . . beautiful . . . ' he exclaimed, using that upward inflection of pleasure and astonishment with which he had always encouraged the good things in the world to come towards him. He didn't mean me, of course. (I am not beautiful.) He simply meant the world of his own life, which in these brief moments opened up for him again.

Pay attention. The visual was my dad's vocabulary for everything that gave his life meaning: roofs angling together to form a village. A church standing among trees on the flat horizon of a marsh. The way shadows fall from a gate at the far end of a field, something falling into place, *decus et tutamen*. 'Beautiful . . . beautiful . . . ' like Elizabeth Barrett Browning. It was the last thing he said to us.

Walk 10: Lyepole Bridge to Kinsham Court via Kinsham Dingle. OS Grid ref SO3964.

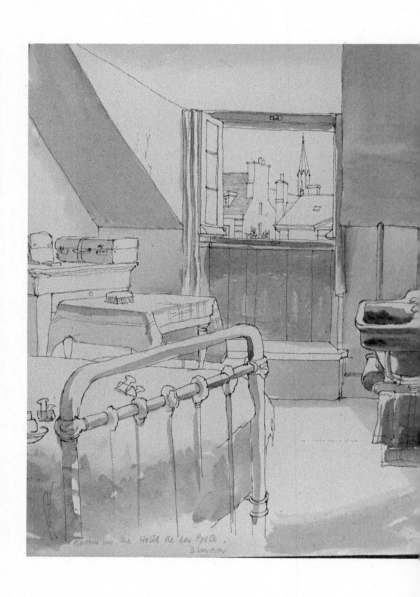

Room in the Hotel de la Poste,
Dinan

Acknowledgements

For her faith in commissioning this book, I am enormously grateful to Sarah Castleton. I'm also very grateful to the rest of the Corsair team, especially Caroline Knight. My particular thanks go to Sarah Chalfant and Jessica Bullock, at the Wylie Agency, whose unending and proactive support never ceases to amaze me. Thank you so much. I'm most grateful, also, to Sarah Bardwell Britten Pears Arts for a creative residency at The Red House, Aldeburgh which allowed me to take my Seventh Walk: it was as inspiring as ever to be with you. I'd like to thank Alison Grant, Ella McCreath and the Wigtown Book Festival for enabling my trip to Skipness. Alison, the invitation to Wigtown which came out of our work together, and your loan of the family cabin on Loch Fyne — made an unwieldy project practicable and fun. I'm deeply indebted to Julian and Beryl, and Paul and Carey, Sampson for all their family knowledge and friendship. They know that Folkingham and the Dilke have been left out of this story. I would like to thank the Dilke Memorial Hospital, Cinderford, for treating my father with care and dignity in the last few hours of his life; I could wish he had been transferred to you earlier. Finally, but in so many ways first of all, I want to thank 'P', Peter Salmon: for his consummate editing, for his patience with this book and its author, and for his walking companionship. For all of it.

Notes

3   **choice un-advocated** George Richmond, in ed. A. M. W. Stirling, *The Richmond Papers* (London: Heinemann, 1926) p. 18.

6   <u>**£23 a year, taxes included!!**</u> Samuel Taylor Coleridge to Robert Southey 17 July 1797, in ed. E. L. Griggs, *The Collected Letters of Samuel Taylor Coleridge* (Oxford: Oxford University Press 1956–71) Vol. 1, pp. 334–36.

7   **British research chemist Joseph Priestley** S. T. Coleridge, 'Religious Musings: A Desultory Poem, Written on the Christmas Even of 1794' L. 371, in *Poems on Various Subjects* (London: C. G. and J. Robinsons, and J. Cottle, Bookseller, Bristol, 1796), p. 163. https://books.google.co.uk/books?id=U4qSQAAACAAJ&printsec=front-cover&source=gbs_ge_summary_r&cad=0#v=onepage&q&f=false [retrieved 29/7/2021].

8   **follow a century later** Though of course Morris and Gill both experimented with models of family life.

11   **wash one's hands of the contemporary world** Ch. XIII (World's Classics p. 119).

12   **graceful taste of the inmate** Mary Shelley, *The Last Man* (Ware, Hertfordshire: Wordsworth Editions, 2004), Vol. 1, ch. 4, pp. 31–32.

12   **for worlds give up that** Mary Godwin to Percy Bysshe Shelley, 5 December 1816 and 27 July 1815, in ed. Betty T. Bennett *The Letters of Mary Wollstonecraft Shelley Vol. 1: 'A part of the Elect'* (Baltimore and London: The Johns Hopkins University Press, 1980), pp. 22, 15.

13   **without subjects [...] like music** In 1824. Charles Rosen and Henri Zerner, *Romanticism and Realism: The Mythology of Nineteenth Century Art* (London: Faber, 1984), p. 34.

17   **'valley of vision'** ed. A. H. Palmer *The Life and Letters of Samuel Palmer* (London: Seeley & Co,1892), p. 17.

18   **Martin Heidegger's walking paths** Something strikingly apparent in his titles from the 1950s, the period of his post-war disgrace, like *Holzwege* (*Wooded Paths*), and *Unterwegs zur Sprache* (*On the Way to Language*).

28   **continuing his route** Mary Shelley *Journal*, July 23 & July 24, 1816.

35   **Schelling christened this** Aphorism eleven.

36   **Schelling, his target here** Nietzsche published his first book, *The Will to Tragedy*, in 1872; madness ended his publishing career in the year Robert Browning died.

37   **early *Journal* records** Mary Shelley *Journal*, 6 November 1814.

40   **arose fresh and strong** Mary Shelley, *Rambles in Germany and Italy, in 1840, 1842 and 1843* (London: Edward Moxon, 1844), Letter v, pp. 62, 60 and 61.

41   **waterfall in a dell** Dorothy Wordsworth to Mary Hutchinson, 4 July 1797, ed. Ernest de Selincourt and Chester L. Shaver, *Letters of William and Dorothy Wordsworth, Vol 1: The Early Years: 1787–1805,* Second edn, (Oxford: Oxford University Press, 1967) (*LWDW* 1), p. 189.

41   **Mary six weeks later** Dorothy Wordsworth to Mary Hutchinson, 14 August 1797, *LWDW* 1, p. 190.

41   **to me memorable evening** In the *Fenwick Notes* he dictated in 1843.

44   **covers at a time** Rousseau was run over by a carriage accompanied by a large dog.
https://www.histoires-de-paris.fr/barriere-menilmontant/ [retrieved 27/7/20].

45   **must have known** Were they flowering? Rousseau says, '*Plusieurs autres plantes que je voyais encore en fleurs.*' (italics mine). https://ebooks-bnr.com/ebooks/pdf4/ rousseau_reveries_promeneur_solitaire.pdf p. 13. [retrieved 27/7/20].

45   **having read this work** *The Confessions* was also published posthumously, in 1782. p. 1.

46   **cause of all he feels** *Reveries*, p. 50.

47   **subject of falsehood** *Reveries*, Fourth Walk.

47   **that beautiful place** *Reveries*, p. 90.

48   **Derrida's *Carte Postale*** MS Ashmole 304, 31v. Michael Camille, 'The Dissenting Image: a Postcard from Matthew Paris' in ed. Rita Copeland, *Criticism and Dissent in the Middle Ages*, (Cambridge: Cambridge University Press, 1996), pp. 115–150. http://cplong.org/2014/04/cover-art-pariss-plato-and-socrates/#easy-footnote-bottom-1-8116 [retrieved 28/7/20].

49   **token of such things** Mary Shelley, 'Introduction' to 1831 edition of *Frankenstein* (Oxford: Oxford University Press, 1980), pp. 8–9.

49   **among the Angelic/Orders** Even as he moved away from lyric subjectivity towards expressionism, Rilke prolonged the Romantic era in European poetry into something more contemporary with musical Romanticism.

49   **won by spirituality** Hölderlin, 'denn, was auch Dichtende sinnen/Oder singen, es gilt mesitens den Engelm und ihm.' 'Heimkunft' #3; 'Engel des Hauses, kommt!' in 'Heimkunft' #6. English p. 255. Rilke, 'Wer, wenn ich schriee, hörte mich denn aus der Engel/ Ordnungen?' *Duineser Elegien* #1, Ll. 1–2.

Hölderlin, 'Überzeugung':

> Als wie der Tag die Menschen hell umscheinet,
> Und mit dem Lichte, das den Höhn entspringet,
> Die dämmernden Erscheinungen vereinet,
> Ist Wissen, welches tief der Geistigkeit gelinget.

50   **in Coleridge's discourse** Ed. Christopher Wordsworth, *Memoirs of William Wordsworth* (London: Edward Moxon, 1851), Vol. 2, p. 443.
https://www.frontporchrepublic.com/2019/03/why-heidegger-stayed-in-the-provinces-and-why-it-is-not-time-for-the-robert-penn-warren-option/ [retrieved 19/02/21].

50   **gleaming white** The valley used to be thickly planted with abbots. The seventh-century *Llandaff Charters* list them: at Ballingham, Dewchurch, Foy and Sellack (where Saint Tysilio was still alive), downstream at Doward, west at Llandogo, Moccas, Garway and Welsh Bicknor.

50   **live in silence** Friedrich Hölderlin ed. Michael Hamburger, 'Der Main' in *Selected Verse* (London and Dover: Anvil Press, 1986) p. 33–5.

54   **view there is none** Edward Lear, *Journals of a Landscape Painter in Greece and Albania* (1851), from ed. Herbert van Thal, *Edward Lear's Journals: a selection* (London: Arthur Baker, 1952), pp. 17–18.

56   **between the banks** William Martin Leake, *Travels in Northern Greece* Volume 3 (London: J. Rodwell, 1835), pp. 258–9.

57   **interest and novelty** Edward Lear, *Journal of a Landscape Painter in Corsica* (1868), from ed. van Thal, p. 146.

57   **published their experiences** Edward Lear, *Journal of a Landscape Painter in Southern Calabria*, from ed. van Thal, p. 70.

62   **Mouldering quarries and mines** R. S. Thomas,
        Collected Poems 1945–1990 (London: Phoenix,
        1993), p. 37.

63   **a romantic thrill** Claude-Henri Watelet, trans. Samuel
        Danon, *Essay on Gardens: A Chapter in the French Picturesque*
        (Philadelphia: University of Pennsylvannia Press,
        2003), pp. 44–5.

65   **Summer of the Year 1770** William Gilpin, *An Essay on
        the Picturesque* (London: J. Robson, 1794). Gilpin first artic-
        ulated the idea in 1768 in his at the time anonymous *Essay
        on Prints.* His identity was revealed in the third edition:
        William Gilpin, *An Essay on Prints* (London: R. Blamire,
        1781). See also Réné Girardin, *An Essay on Landscape*
        (London: J. Dodsley, 1783).

69   **his home near Dunfermline** Elizabeth Barrett
        Browning to George Goodin Moulton-Barrett 1 April
        1846, #2285.

74   **is it acquired?** *Letters from Percy Bysshe Shelley to Elizabeth
        Hitchener in Two Volumes,* (London: Privately printed 1890)
        Vol. I, Letter VI, July 26 1811, p. 38.

75   **craggy hillside beyond** http://history.powys.org.uk/
        history/rhayader/nantgwyllt.html [retrieved 26/8/20].

76   **itself of felicity** Percy Bysshe Shelley to William Godwin
        25 April 1812 *Letters* 1, 287 q. in Priscilla P. St. George,
        'Cwm Elan and Nantgwillt: Two Vanished Sites' in
        Keats-Shelley Journal Vol. 17 (1968), pp. 7–9 (5 pages) Keats-
        Shelley Association of America https://www.jstor.org/
        stable/30210591 [retrieved 26/8/20].

76   **mountains than for houses** Mary Wollstonecraft
        Godwin to Percy Bysshe Shelley 3 November 1814 in ed.
        Betty T. Bennett, *The Letters of Mary Wollstonecraft Shelley
        Vol. 1* p. 4.

77   **without paiyng of mony** John Leland, ed. and tran-
      scribed Lucy Toulmin Smith, *The Itinerary in Wales* (London:
      George Bell and Sons, 1906) #122.
      http://www.tpwilliams.co.uk/leland/leland_2010.pdf
      [retrieved 18/11/21].

79   **counterfeit neglect** Richard Payne Knight, *The Landscape:
      a Didactic Poem in three books Addressed to Uvedale Price Esq.*
      (London: W. Bulmer & Co, 1794) Bk. 1 p. 1, Ll 1–7.

80   **deserted and bare** W. Linnard, *Ceredigion*, v. 309.

80   **put the artist's way** Thomas Johnes to George
      Cumberland 21 January 1796: 'A good sale might be made
      of your work at the Devil's Bridge where *crowds still increas-
      ing* come every year.' 'Last summer there were 40 in one
      day; some for the place, but more, I believe for the wine.'
      George Cumberland, *An Attempt to Describe Hafod, and the
      Neighbouring Scenes about the Bridge Over the Funack, Commonly
      Called the Devil's Bridge, in the County of Cardigan. An Ancient
      Seat Belonging to Thomas Johnes, Esq. Member for the County of
      Radnor* (London: W. Wilson, 1796).

80   **Hafod Arms Hotel** *Aberystwyth Observer* 18/09/1858,
      http://pint-of-history.wales/explore.php?func=showim-
      age&id=891 [retrieved 18/11/21].

82   **pupil of [Richard] Wilson** William Gilpin to William
      Mason, 23 April 1787, Bodleian Library, ms. Eng. Misc d
      571, ff 7, 23; Carl Paul Barbier, *William Gilpin: his drawings,
      teachings and theory of the Picturesque* (Oxford: Clarendon
      Press, 1963), pp. 71–72, fn. 3. Mason was a landscape gar-
      dener and author of *The English Garden: A Poem in Four Books*
      (York: A. Ward, 1783).

82   **for Johnes in 1814** Uvedale Price to Lord Aberdeen,
      29 June 1810, ed. Charles Watkins, Charles and Ben
      Cowell, *Letters of Uvedale Price* (Cambridge, MA:
      Produced for the Walpole Society by Maney Publishing,
      2006), p. 199.

84   **let in the fresh air** *A Pedestrian Tour through North Wales: in a series of Letters* (London: J. Debrett and J. Edwards, 1795), pp. 122–23.

85   **continued to be welcomed** https://www.history-ofparliamentonline.org/volume/1790-1820/member/johnes-thomas-1748-1816 [retrieved 23/9/20].

85   **striking and almost ludicrous** *Murray's Handbook for Travellers in South Wales and its borders, including the River Wye* (London: John Murray, 1860), pp. 116-117; 1868 edition, pp. 152–53.

86   **decay is overpowering** John Piper, 'Decrepit Glory' in *Buildings and Prospects* (London: Architectural Press, 1948), p. 38.

93   **startled parents before expiring** Rosalind C. Love, <u>St Rumwold of Buckingham and</u> VITA SANCTI RVMWOLDI (Oxford: Oxford Mediaeval Texts, 1996), pp. cxl–clxxxix.

95   **calamity such nakedness recorded** William Wordsworth, *The Excursion,* Book One, Ll. 30–31.

96   **call itself hauntology** The term was coined by Jacques Derrida in *Spectres of Marx* (*Spectres de Marx: l'état de la dette, le travail du deuil et la nouvelle Internationale* (Paris: Éditions Galileé, 1993)), more specifically for the way Marxism was still widely used by other forms of thought as a conceptual 'over-there'.

99   **the Romantic era** 'Thomas Ingoldsby' makes the claim in the Introduction to the first collected edition, in 1840, but also in 'The Leech of Folkestone', one of the collections' earliest stories, which was published in July 1837 in *Bentley's Miscellany* Vol. 2 pp. 91–108. https://upload.wikimedia.org/wikipedia/commons/9/95/Bentley%27s_Miscellany_1837-07-_Vol_2_%28IA_sim_bentleys-miscellany_1837-07_2%29.pdf [retrieved 3/4/21].

100   **their valves of gold** William Blake, *Milton: A poem in Two Books* (1804–10), plate 28, Ll. 4–24.

100   **infinitely slow motion** https://www.youtube.com/watch?v=1AkicOwc-uU [retrieved 19/4/21].

110   **exertions of those powers** Humphry Davy, 'A Discourse Introductory to a Course of Lectures on Chemistry, Delivered in the Theatre of the Royal Institution, on the 21st of January, 1802' in ed. John Davy, *The Collected Works of Sir Humphry Davy* (London: Smith, Elder and Co., 1839) II, [307]-26: pp. 311–2. http://knarf.english.upenn.edu/Davy/davy2dis.html [retrieved 10/6/21]

117   **as Robert put it** Robert Browning to Euphrasia Fanny Haworth, 29 June 1847, #2683. https://en.wikipedia.org/wiki/Gran_Caff%C3%A9_Doney [retrieved 15/04/21].

118   **He was so thin** Elizabeth Barrett Browning to Arabella Moulton-Barrett, 22–25 June 1847, #2681.

120   **beyond the grave** The event on 12 December 1890 was written up by H. R. Haweis.

120   **'transcriptions', in 1948** Mary Stephenson Barnes, *Encore Browning* (New York: Frederick-William Press, 1948).

121   **lost from the record** 'Ten horses, eight enormous dogs, three monkeys, five cats, an eagle, a crow, and a falcon.' When the poet Shelley visited the count a few months later, he was met on the staircase by 'five peacocks, two guinea hens and an Egyptian crane'. In 1819 Byron wrote happily to his friend Francis Hodgson, 'I have got two monkeys and a fox – and two new mastiffs – Mutz is still in high old age. The monkeys are charming.' http://www.praxxis.co.uk/credebyron/menagerie.htm [retrieved 16/06/21].

126   **somewhat worked up** Charlotte Gordon, *Romantic Outlaws: The Extraordinary Lives of Mary Shelley and Mary Wollstonecraft (London: Hutchinson, 2015), p. 191; Ed. William*

Michael Rossetti, *The Diary of Dr John William Polidori 1816*
(London: Elkin Matthews, 1911), p. 128.

126   **all coming down** Mary Shelley to Maria Gisborne, 15
August 1822.

126   **found the prices** *enormous* Elizabeth Barrett Browning
to Arabella Moulton-Barrett, 23–25 June 1849, #2797.

129   **without a sixth sense?** Marina Tsvetaeva trans. Elaine
Feinstein, *Selected Poems* (Oxford: Oxford University Press,
1993), pp. 90–91.

142   **'cottages' and 'Timber'** Edward Moulton-Barrett to
Elizabeth Barrett Browning, 5 September 1809, #1.

143   **the eggs at breakfast** Elizabeth Barrett Browning to
Julia Martin, 5 November 1846, #2627.

147   **part of the earth** Mary Shelley, *History of a Six Weeks' Tour*
(London: T Hookham, Jun, 1817), p. 44.

149   **after our two oclock' dinner** Elizabeth Barrett
Browning to Mary Russell Mitford, 19 December
1846, #2642.

157   **almost overcame me** Elizabeth Barrett Browning
to Robert Browning 13 June 1846, #2414. *Browning
Correspondence* footnote: 'The new and enlarged engine built
by Daniel Gooch, and operated by the Great Western Line.
Elizabeth Barrett Browning and Kenyon saw the locomotive
come in prior to its "experimental trip," which, according
to *The Times* of 15th June was made on the 13th of June in
the presence of the company chairman and officers. The
train was "driven by the chief engineer, Mr. Brunel".'

163   **the constituting dialectic** *Herrschaft und Knechtschaft*
is ultimately a struggle to the death. Since even a master
requires an other – not a slave – freely to recognize him, he
destroys his own defining dialectic if he 'wins'.

170   **all traffic system** The Lake District National Park
Authority, *Smarter Travel: A vision for sustainable visitor
travel in the Lake District National Park, 2018–2040*, https://

www.lakedistrict.gov.uk/caringfor/smarter-travel [retrieved 8/9/21].

173   **sent the prime minister** https://www.jstor.org/stable/j. ctv11qdtt1 [retrieved 17/10/21].

175   **closest, all-concealing tunic** Percy Bysshe Shelley, *Peter Bell the Third*, Lls 313–7; 683–4, 688–92; and 703–7.

180   **its heirs, particularly Turner** John Ruskin, *Modern Painters* Vol. III, part IV, ch. XVI (London: J.Wiley, 1856).

180   **the onshore light** He gave the southern range extra heft a couple of decades later, adding a storey to accommodate his artist housemate and cousin-in-law Arthur Severn, and Severn's growing family.

183   **Weep at a Tale of Distress** The Philological Society of London, *The European Magazine and London Review, Vol XI January 1787* (London: J. Sewell, 1787), p. 202.

186   **propensities of man** Both quotes are from William Godwin, *An Enquiry Concerning Political Justice* (1793) Book 8 ch. 6 pp. 849–50.

187   **Wednesday Morning** Repository Amherst College Archives & Special Collections, Shelf Location Box 1 Folder 2. https://acdc.amherst.edu/view/asc:85384 [retrieved 9/12/21].

191   **Their place of convocation** https://h2g2.com/ approved_entry/A87793988 [retrieved 18/1/22].

193   **dewy shadows yesterday** Elizabeth Barrett Browning to Sarianna Browning, 28 August 1856, #3849.

193   **the Brownings visited** Though it's possible the name Ventnor, which dates from c. 1617, came from le Vyntener, (vintners), which seems to have been a local family name. University of Nottingham, *Key to English Place-Names,* http://kepn.nottingham.ac.uk/map/place/Isle%20of%20 Wight/Ventnor [retrieved 12/3/22].

194   **& be at rest** Elizabeth Barrett Browning to Anne Jameson 12 September 1856, #3860.

195   **chairs & telescopes** Elizabeth Barrett Browning to
Arabella Moulton-Barrett, 7 September 1856, #3855.

202   **change of place** Jeremy Bentham, *Proposal for a new and
less expensive mode of employing and reforming convicts* 1796,
'Printed in the Appendix to the Parliamentary Report of
the Committee, on the laws relating to penitentiary houses:
May, 1811', p. 3.

205   **at liberty, at last** John Gwilliam, *Rambles in the Isle of
Wight: With Miscellaneous Additions* (London: Simpkin,
Marshall & Co, 1844), pp. 185–92.

206   **his influential** *Essays* 'An. Christi 1571 aet. 38, pridie cal.
mart., die suo natali, Mich. Montanus, . . . dum se integer . . .
recessit sinus, ubi quietus et omnium securus . . . istas sedes et
dulces latebras, avitasque, libertati suae, tranquillitatique, et otio
consecravit.'

211   **himself in 1795 or 6** ed. Seamus Perry, *Coleridge's
Notebooks: A Selection* (Oxford: Oxford University Press,
1984), #20 p. 2.

215   **the two – *Tragic Dance*** ed. Perry, #547 p. 130.

216   **on the hunt, track me** *The Notebooks of Samuel Taylor
Coleridge*, ed. Kathleen Coburn and Merton Christensen, 5
vols. (Princeton: Princeton University Press, 1957–2002)
Vol. 2, 2375.

216   **process of creating it** Samuel Taylor Coleridge,
Marginalia, ed. George Whalley and H. J. Jackson, 6 vols.
(Princeton: Princeton University Press, 1980–2001)
Vol. 2, 990.

217   **Plastic Arts to Nature** Samuel Taylor Coleridge,
Biographia Literaria, ed. James Engell and W. Jackson Bate
(Princeton: Princeton University Press/Bollingen, 1983),
Vol I, ch. 13, pp. 296–7.

218   **rise up before you** ed. Perry #481 p. 110.

219   **named Thibault** In a letter to his childhood friend Laura
LeBeau, quoted in Scott Horton, 'Nerval: A Man and His
Lobster', *Harper's*, 12 October 2008.

219   **dogs howling on the shore** Richard Holmes, *Footsteps*
(London: Hodder & Stoughton, 1985), p. 236.

220   **where I belonged** BBC Radio broadcast, 11 August 1965.

222   **such narrative verse** Crabbe was still alive in 1830, when
the twenty-one-year-old Alfred Tennyson published *Poems
Chiefly Lyrical*, which despite its title includes the mini-
narratives 'Mariana' and 'Claribel'.

223   **influence went underground** Perhaps the closest of his successors is Edgar Lee Masters, whose *Spoon
River Anthology* appeared a century later, in 1915. Robert
Lowell's 1959 collection *Life Studies* is a kind of family
album in verse.

226   **vicious the individual** 'Opera's New Face', *Time*, 16
February 1948.

240   **hears that in my music** ed. Gerd Nauhaus, trans. and
intro. Peter Ostwald, *The Marriage Diaries of Robert and Clara
Schumann* (London: Robson Books, 1994), p. 75.

242   **the youth a flower** *Ibid.* p. 149.

244   **levels more than halved** Valentine Quinio and
Kathrin Enenkel, *How have the Covid pandemic and lockdown
affected air quality in cities?* (London: Centre for Cities,
2020), pp. 3–5.

245   **curtain walls and entrances** John Constable, 'East
Bergholt Church: From the South', reproduced in Lowell
Libson and Jonny Yarker, *'The Art of Seeing Nature': Ten
Drawings by John Constable* (London: Lowell Libson and
Jonny Yarker Ltd, 2018), p. 25.

251   **blossoms, gemm'd with dew** Pevsner's Sixth Reith
Lecture BBC transcript, p. 4.

254   **5. Obstinacy. 6. Generosity** John Ruskin, 'The Nature
of Gothic' in *The Stones of Venice. Volume the Second. The Sea-
stories* (London: Smith, Elder & Co, 1853).

256   **I don't like to see that** ed. Nauhaus, *The Marriage Diaries*
pp. 333–5.

257   **simple, profound, German** Pref. J. G. Jansen, trans.
May Herbert, *The Life of Robert Schumann told in his Letters*
(London: R. Bentley and Son, 1890).

258   **viz. – a representation** ed. Peter Cochran, *Byron's
Correspondence with John Murray, 2: 1816–1819 [work in progress]*
p. 37. Though Cochrane footnotes this, 'B. is writing the
opposite of the truth. Manfred's scenic demands are tai-
lored for Drury Lane.'
https://petercochran.files.wordpress.com/2011/01/byron-
and-murray-1816-18192.pdf [retrieved 29/4/21].

260   **bad light stopped play at 6.20** http://static.espn-
cricinfo.com/db/ARCHIVE/1960S/1964/ENG_LOCAL/
CC/KENT_HANTS_CC_01-04AUG1964.html
[retrieved 5/4/22].

265   **sense of Smith's advice** C. R. Leslie, *Memoirs of the Life of
John Constable* (London: J. M. Dent, 1843) p. 6.

267   **between the tyre tracks** 'Psychoanalytic ethnography,
like clinical investigation, shows that feelings and selves
are both given and created, naturally, culturally, and
individually, and that projective and introjective recast-
ings [. . .] are found wherever meanings are accorded to
people and situations.' Nancy J. Chodorow, *The Power of
Feelings* (New Haven and London: Yale University Press,
1999), p. 215.

270   **with unpremeditated happiness** Likely in May 1820,
though later attributed to 1821. https://www.taylorfrancis.
com/chapters/mono/10.4324/9781315847863-109/song-
percy-bysshe-shelley [retrieved 16/7/20].

272   **keeps me still awake** Mary Wollstonecraft, *A Short Residence in Sweden* in Mary Wollstonecraft and William Godwin ed. Richard Holmes, *A Short Residence in Sweden and Memoirs of the Author of 'The Rights of Woman'* (Harmondsworth: Penguin 1987, p. 69.

273   **painful of all subjects** Godwin in ed. Holmes 1987, pp. 244–5.

275   **admiration and contempt** Wollstonecraft in ed. Holmes 1987, pp. 148–9.

275   **seems to be fled** Wollstonecraft in ed. Holmes 1987, p. 197.

276   **sometimes a very fine effect** Wollstonecraft in ed. Holmes 1987, p.194.

280   **never before remarked** Wollstonecraft in ed. Holmes 1987, p. 123.

281   **trees, buildings and hills** 'Beethoven at the age of 15', reproduction of the lithograph by the Becker brothers after the silhouette by Joseph Neesen, Beethoven-Haus, Bonn, B. 322.

285   **an individual or a stomach** Karl Klingemann letter home, 10 August 1829. Ed. Sebastian Hensel, trans. Carl Klingemann et al., *The Mendelssohn Family (1729–1847) from Letters and Journals* (New York: Harper & brothers, 1882) Vol. I, p. 204.

285   **Hebrides,' as he explained** Initial sketch in Felix Mendelssohn to Fanny Mendelssohn, 7 August 1829, Music Division, New York Public Library.
David R. Glerum, Orlando Philharmonic Orchestra Program Notes 30 September 2006, pp. 4–5. Archived from the original on 2007-09-27. http://orlandophil.org/downloads/program-notes/2006-07/opo-prog-notes-pac1.pdf [retrieved 2006/11/08].

286   **my *Scottish Symphony*** https://www.sfsymphony.org/Data/Event-Data/Program-Notes/M/

Mendelssohn-Symphony-No-3-in-A-minor-Opus-56,-Sco [retrieved 26/5/21].

286 **legs of the natives** https://petermedhurst.com/tours/ mendelssohn-scotland-2-8-may-2018/ [retrieved 26/5/21].

288 **overture is popularly known** Mendelssohn himself conducted the Berlin premiere on 10 January 1833.

291 **set on the island** https://interactive.britishart. yale.edu/critique-of-reason/360/staffa-fingals-cave [retrieved 2/5/21].

295 **gendered flaws she ignored** *Émile,* like *The Social Contract*, is ultimately a programme for producing a citizen who can live true to his own nature but also to the 'nature' of society. Women were not then citizens in any full economic or electoral sense anywhere in the world, and Sophie, the little girl Rousseau imagines, serves despite her name only to complement Emile, whom she 'ought not to resemble in mind any more than in looks'.

300 **'Are you comfortable?' 'Beautiful.'** Robert Browning to Sarianna Browning 30 July 1861, British Library 61108-00.

301 **Arabella and Henrietta record** Elizabeth Barrett Browning Arabella Moulton-Barrett 26 July 1847, #2686.

301 **what was in that** Robert Browning to George Goodin Barrett, 2 July 1861, The Morgan Library and Museum, 61113-00.

303 **like phantoms of life** Elizabeth Barrett Browning to Robert Browning 11 May 1846, #2355.

304 **horror of my present fate** Translations are mine.

310 **child by Byron himself** Adam McCune, 'The name "Ianthe" and a pregnancy by Byron in a letter of Lady Oxford's' in *The Byron Journal* (2019), 47 (1), 43–54.

311 **narrowly escaped this folly** Thomas Medwin, *Journal of the Conversations of Lord Byron* (London: Henry Colburn, 1824), pp. 255, 93–4.

312 **not merely her beauty** Peter William Clayden, *Rogers and his Contemporaries* (London: Smith, Elder & Company, 1889), Vol. 1, pp. 397–8.

319 **bankrupted in 1844** Cf. *The London Gazette* 1844, p. 1666. https://books.google.co.uk/books?id=JxhKAQA-AMAAJ&pg=PA2161&lpg=PA2161&dq=edward+hodson+broad+street+ludlow&source=bl&ots=gSYHnHvR-5W&sig=ACfU3U2CqdJBdwQsRDTOF68fP1eDjGSzgA&hl=en&sa=X&ved=2ahUKEwi7tJqSo4b1AhVJVsAKHUyT-DKUQ6AF6BAgSEAM#v=onepage&q=edward%20hodson%20broad%20street%20ludlow&f=false [retrieved 28/12/21].

322 **minute information' Horton commends** *The Leominster Guide: containing an Historical and Topographical View of the Ancient and Present State of Leominster* (Leominster: F. J. Burlton, 1808), p. 181.

328 **1.8 kg of carbon dioxide** Paul Swan, 'Wool as a carbon sink: a comparative analysis. Dec 2009', cited in *Complementary Role of Sheep in Less Favoured Areas*, National Sheep Association, 2013.